INTERNATIONAL BESTSELLER JEAN SASSON

DAUGHTERS OF ARABIA

'Women with everything but freedom . . . "Sultana" has
described her family life to American writer Jean Sasson
– and if it didn't come from within palace walls, no
one would believe it . . . *gripping*'
Daily Mail

'Brutality hidden behind the veil . . . more
horrific stories'
Sunday Express

'The first book [was] instrumental in bringing to the
attention of the western world a situation in Saudi
Arabia which is a continuing violation of the
fundamental principles of human rights . . . The
stories of oppression and brutality are horrific'
Australian Bookseller & Publisher

PRINCESS

'Unforgettable in content, fascinating in detail . . . a
book to move you to tears'
Fay Weldon

'The startling truth behind the veiled lives of Saudi
Arabia's women . . . frank and vivid revelations'
Sunday Express

'Mind-boggling . . . absolutely riveting'
People magazine

'Anyone with the slightest interest in human rights will
find this book heart-wrenching. It is a well-written,
personal story about the violation of human rights
in Saudi Arabia . . . It had to come from a
native woman to be believable'
Betty Mahmoody, bestselling author of
Not Without My Daughter

www.booksattransworld.co.uk

Also by Jean Sasson

THE RAPE OF KUWAIT
PRINCESS
DESERT ROYAL
ESTER'S CHILD
MAYADA: DAUGHTER OF IRAQ

To learn more about Jean Sasson and
her books, please visit her website
www.jeansasson.com

DAUGHTERS OF ARABIA

Jean Sasson

BANTAM BOOKS

LONDON · TORONTO · SYDNEY · AUCKLAND · JOHANNESBURG

DAUGHTERS OF ARABIA
A BANTAM BOOK : 0 553 81693 4

Originally published in Great Britain by Doubleday,
a division of Transworld Publishers

PRINTING HISTORY
Doubleday edition published 1994
Bantam Books edition published 1994

17 19 20 18 16

Set in 10½/12pt Sabon by
Kestrel Data, Exeter, Devon

Bantam Books are published by Transworld Publishers,
61–63 Uxbridge Road, London W5 5SA,
a division of The Random House Group Ltd,
in Australia by Random House Australia (Pty) Ltd,
20 Alfred Street, Milsons Point, Sydney, NSW 2061, Australia,
in New Zealand by Random House New Zealand Ltd,
18 Poland Road, Glenfield, Auckland 10, New Zealand
and in South Africa by Random House (Pty) Ltd,
Endulini, 5a Jubilee Road, Parktown 2193, South Africa.

Printed and bound in Great Britain by
Cox & Wyman Ltd, Reading, Berkshire.

Papers used by Transworld Publishers are natural, recyclable
products made from wood grown in sustainable forests.
The manufacturing processes conform to the environmental
regulations of the country of origin.

This is a true story. Names have been changed and various events slightly altered to protect the well-being of recognizable individuals.

In telling this true story it is not the intention of the author or of the Princess to demean the Islamic faith.

To Mom and Dad

Contents

SAUDI ARABIA

THE REGIONS OF ARABIA

RULERS OF THE KINGDOM OF SAUDI ARABIA

THE FIRST FIVE KINGS

ABDUL AZIZ, 'IBN SA'UD'
1876 – 1953
FIRST KING

SA'UD
1902 – 1969
SECOND KING

FAISAL
1904 – 1975
THIRD KING

KHALID
1912 – 1982
FOURTH KING

FAHD
1922 –
PRESENT AND
FIFTH KING

Author's Note

Since *Princess* was first published, much has happened to Princess Sultana, her friends and family, and she has requested that I share some of this information with readers of *Daughters of Arabia*.

When the first Gulf War of 1991 ended, there was a universal desire for peace in the Middle East. Many proposals from leaders of many nations were presented through the United Nations in the hope that the violence so common to the Middle East would finally end. Sadly, that was not to be. Violence continued to erupt across the area.

Along with a desire for peace, the world yearned for change in the ancient traditions that bind the women of the Middle East. Most of these traditions are not based on religion, but the men of the religion claim otherwise, determined to keep their women in bondage. Although Princess Sultana was hopeful that the events bringing Western media attention to her land would serve to improve the lot of women, that did not happen. Where Princess Sultana and other like-minded women saw hope for social change, men felt the danger of *any* progress or change in a society that keeps half their population intimidated, with some women even locked away in their homes.

Husbands, fathers, and sons were unwilling to challenge radical religious forces for women's rights. Actually, it was the men of Princess Sultana's own family, the rulers of the country, who allowed the religious authorities to assume even greater power over the lives of Saudi women. When this happened, the cause of freedom for women in Arabia withered in a backlash from religious extremists.

Princess Sultana watched and mourned, for she knew that any daughters born to her and Kareem would be forced to veil, not allowed to drive, banned from careers not deemed suitable for women, and kept separated from all that is normal in modern Western life. But a determined Sultana kept fighting in her own way.

Princess Sultana received her master's degree in philosophy several years ago. She has not used her degree professionally, but says the knowledge she acquired has provided her with an inner peace and feeling of oneness with the world. In her studies, she discovered that many peoples have survived grave injustices. She has found that human progress is indeed slow, but there are many others who continue to push forward, seeking change, and Princess Sultana is proud to be one of those people.

Princess Sultana also wants readers to know that Kareem has once again become the kindly man she first met. Their bonds of love have been restored. They are now the parents of three healthy children, two of whom are daughters, beautiful girls you will meet for the first time in this book. Despite her fierce love for her daughters, Princess Sultana says that the saddest aspect of her life is watching the black forms of her two young daughters, now wrapped in cloaks and veils, that, after all the years of rebellion, still cling to a new generation of young women in Saudi Arabia. Sultana declares that, as always, primitive customs determine women's roles in Saudi society.

Sultana's father is still alive, but his temperament has not improved. As allowed by the Muslim religion, he maintains four wives in four palaces. He has many young children from his youthful wives. Sadly, his relationship with Sultana has not improved. While he takes great pride in his sons and grandsons, he rarely visits his daughters or granddaughters.

Sultana's brother Ali has not changed for the better. If anything, Ali has become even more cruel. Unfortunately, his streaks of cruelty are reserved for his female children, whom he treats as he saw his own father treat his sisters. Following in his footsteps, Ali is also the husband of four wives. He divorces frequently, marrying females as young as fourteen years. Ali keeps numerous mistresses, in and out of the kingdom and spends millions of dollars a year on the most frivolous expenses. His unrestrained behaviour knows no bounds. Ali is the kind of Al Sa'ud prince who causes the people of Saudi Arabia to yearn for a change in government.

Sultana's beloved sister Sara, and her husband Asad, have remained joyful in their marriage and with their family. The happy couple are the parents of five lively children. Who knows if Huda's prediction of six children for Sara will come true? Only Sara, of all Sultana's sisters, knew that Sultana was the princess in the first book I wrote, *Princess*.

Omar, the faithful family servant, was killed in a car accident on the road to Dammam. His wife and children in Egypt are supported by Sultana's father.

Randa's father purchased her a villa in the South of France, where Randa now lives most of the year. She has not remarried after being divorced by Sultana's father. There is a rumour in the family that Randa has a French lover. Sultana hopes the rumour is true, while some of her more conservative sisters are scandalized.

Sultana never again heard from her childhood friend Wafa. Often Sultana imagines her vivacious friend living in a village, beaten and mistreated by her husband, and surrounded by a large number of children, leading the life Wafa so dreaded.

Marci returned to the Philippines and realized her ambition as Sultana knew she would. Then she went to Riyadh and worked for a while as a nurse in one of the main hospitals. The last Sultana heard, Marci was planning to go and work in Kuwait. Sultana hopes that Marci survived the Gulf War, but she has heard nothing further from the young woman.

The loyal servant Huda died and was buried in the sands of Arabia, far from her native land of Sudan.

Saddest of all, Sameera remains locked in the woman's room. Tahani heard several years ago that Sameera had gone mad. The servants reported that she had screeched for days before speaking in a strange gibberish that none could understand. However, the food trays slipped through the door are emptied, so it's clear that Sameera still lives. Sameera's family claims that she will be released when her cruel uncle dies, but he is in fine health even at an old age. In any case, it is thought that freedom would not benefit Sameera now.

After the publication of *Princess*, Princess Sultana

and I took a vow that we would never meet again. Yet, a short while after the first book was published, I received an unexpected telephone call from her. Something very dramatic had occurred, and she wanted me to write a second book about her life, the lives of her children, and the lives of other women she knew. Thus, this second book, *Daughters of Arabia*, came to be.

Like *Princess, Daughters of Arabia* is a true story. While *Princess* set the arena by depicting the life of Princess Sultana from early childhood to the first Gulf War, this book picks up the story from October 1992.

While it is hoped that readers have the time to read *Princess* first, *Daughters of Arabia* is a story in itself.

I'd like readers to remember that while many facts are revealed of a land little understood by the Western world, neither *Princess* nor *Daughters of Arabia* is meant to be a complete history of Saudi Arabia, or to reflect the lives of all women who live in the desert kingdom. These two works are the story of one brave and spirited Saudi princess and her family.

Princess Sultana and I come together to say:

Thanks for caring,

Jean Sasson

July, 2004

Prologue

A great rock is not disturbed by the wind; the mind of a wise man is not disturbed by either honour or abuse.
Buddha

Once I read that any good pen can stab any king. As I study the photograph of my uncle, Fahd Ibn Abdul Aziz, the King of Saudi Arabia, I contemplate the fact that I harbour no desire to stab our king, or even to spark the wrath of a man whom I know to be kindly.

I trace my fingers across his face, recalling the Fahd of my childhood days. The photograph portrays the King in maturity and reveals nothing of the youthful man I remember. The King's stern brow and strong jaw belie the charming man whom I wistfully call to mind. My thoughts wander back in time, remembering the King before he was crowned. Standing tall and broad-shouldered, with his large hand outstretched, he had offered a sweet date to a child in awe. That child had been me. Fahd, like his father before him, was a robust man, and to my young eyes had looked more like the son of a bedouin warrior whom he was, than the states-man he would become. Contrary to my usual boldness, I had reacted timidly, accepting the desert fruit from his fingers reluctantly, then running into my mother's arms. I had heard Fahd laughing fondly as I savoured the sweetness of the date.

As is our Saudi custom, I have not been unveiled in the presence of the King since the age of puberty. Since that time, he has grown into a man of age. The King now appears a sombre figure, and I cannot help but conclude that, while the years of statesmanship have strengthened him, the responsibilities of leader-ship have chastened him. And, though massive and regal, our king cannot be judged handsome. His eyelids droop too heavily over his protruberant eyes, his nose overshadows his upper lip, which tightly frames a delicate mouth. In the picture so familiar to all Saudis and visitors to the kingdom – the official photograph that hangs conspicuously in every business and institution in my country – the King appears to be what I know he is not: forbidding and insensitive.

In spite of his unquestioned power and vast wealth, his position is not to be envied. As absolute sovereign of one of the wealthiest nations on earth, King Fahd's rule over the hot, dreary land of Saudi Arabia is a perpetual struggle between ancient and modern.

While most nations maintain themselves by abandoning or recasting the old ways, growing slowly into newer and better systems that advance civilization, our king has no such options. He, a mere mortal, must unite and keep the peace between four divided and completely distinct groups of citizens: the religious fundamentalists, stern, unyielding men of power who demand a return to the past; the prominent, well-educated middle class that cries out for release from the stifling, old traditions; the bedouin tribes who struggle against enticements to abandon their nomadic way of life and yield to the lure of the cities; and lastly, members of the vast royal family who want nothing more than wealth, wealth, and yet more wealth.

Behind these four factions is the one group of natives who have been forgotten: the women of Saudi Arabia, as diverse in our desires and demands as the individual men who rule our daily lives.

Yet, strangely, I, a woman of great frustrations, have little anger with the King over our plight, for I know that prior to moving against the disciplined men of religion, he must have the loyal backing of ordinary husbands, fathers, and brothers. These clerics claim that they correctly interpret the historic code of laws in allowing men to rule harshly over their women. Too many ordinary men of Saudi Arabia are content with the *status quo*, discovering that it is easier to ignore the complaints of their women, rather than follow their king in negotiating change.

In spite of the difficulties, the bulk of Saudi citizens support King Fahd. It is only the religious fundamentalists who call for his downfall. To the remainder of Saudi citizens, he is known as a man of generosity and good cheer.

And, I remind myself that the women of our family know that the King is well loved by his wives, and who knows a man better than his wives?

While King Fahd rules with a milder hand than

did his father and his three brothers, it does not require the wisdom of a sage to know that *Princess*, the earlier book that tells the story of my life, will be viewed as a slap in the face to the man who rules my country.

That, alone, I regret.

I admonish myself that, under no duress, I made the decision to break the precedent of generations by flinging family secrets to the wind. Now, for the first time, I wonder if I acted with passion rather than wisdom; perhaps my earnestness and enthusiasm led me to overestimate my capacity for intrigue.

In an attempt to assuage my conscience and calm my fears, I vividly recall the intensity of my emotions as I wrote it – my anger that our rulers' world has continued to dominate, oblivious of the fact that we women languish in oppression.

It was my fury at male indifference that led me to revolution.

Chapter One

UNVEILED

Despair weakens our sight and closes our ears. We can see nothing but spectres of doom, and can hear only the beating of our agitated hearts.
Kahlil Gibran

It is October 1992, and I, Sultana Al Sa'ud, the Princess of a revelatory book, follow the days of the calender with a mixture of feverish excitement and morose depression. The book that exposed the life of women behind the veil was released in the United States in September 1992. Since its publication, I carry with me a sombre presentiment of my doom, feeling as though I am precariously suspended in space, for I am aware that no deed great or small, bad or good, can be without effect.

Taking a deep breath, I hopefully remind myself that I am likely to be safe in the anonymity of the extended Al Sa'ud family. Still, my trusty instincts warn me that I have been discovered.

Just as I conquer my conflicting guilt and fear, my husband, Kareem, enters our home in a rush, shouting out that my brother, Ali, has returned early from his trip to Europe and that my father has called an urgent family meeting at his palace. With black eyes glaring, his pale face blotched fiery red, my husband looks madder than a mad dog.

I am struck by a horrifying thought. Kareem has been told of the book!

Imagining suffocating confinement in a subterranean dungeon, deprived of my beloved children, I surrender to my agitation for a moment, and in a thin high voice that bears no resemblance to my own, ask, 'What has happened?'

Kareem shrugs his shoulders, answering, 'Who can know?' His nostrils flare with irritation when he remembers, 'I informed your father that I have an important appointment in Zürich tomorrow, that you and I could see him when I return, but he was adamant that I cancel my plans and escort you to his home this evening.'

Like a figure blown by the wind, Kareem charges into his office exclaiming, 'Three meetings have to be cancelled.'

Weak-kneed, I collapse on the sofa with relief, thinking I had been premature in my conclusions. Kareem's anger has nothing to do with me! My courage flickers hopefully.

Still, the threat of discovery persists, and I have many long hours before the unexpected family meeting.

Feigning gaiety that I do not feel, I smile and chat as Kareem and I walk through the wide entrance hall and over the thick Persian carpets into an enormous and grand sitting-room in my father's newly constructed palace. Father has not yet arrived, but I see that Kareem and I are the last of the family to make an appearance. The other ten living children of my mother, without their spouses, have been summoned to my father's home. I know that three of my sisters had to fly into Riyadh from Jeddah, while two sisters flew in from Taif. Looking around the room, I verify that Kareem is the only outside member of the family present. Even Father's head wife and her children are nowhere to be seen. I surmise that they have been dismissed from the premises.

The urgency of the meeting leads me back to the book, and my chest tightens with fear. My sister Sara and I exchange worried glances. As the only member of my family aware of the book's publication, her thoughts reflect mine. Each of my siblings greets me warmly, except for my only brother, Ali, and I catch a glimpse of his sly eyes following me.

Within moments of our arrival, Father enters the room. His ten daughters stand respectfully to their feet, and each of us expresses our greetings to the man who has given us life without love.

I have not seen my father in some months, and I think to myself that he looks exhausted and prematurely old. When I lean to kiss his cheek, he impatiently turns away, failing to return my greeting. Giving my fears full range, I know at that moment that I have been naïve, thinking that the Al Sa'uds are too busy accumulating wealth to care much for books. My trepidation mounts.

In a stern voice, Father asks us to sit, saying that he has some disturbing news to relay.

Lured by a stare, I see that Ali, with his morbid

interest in the suffering of others, is gloating, regarding me with a pitiless stare. There is little doubt in my mind that Ali is privy to the evening's business.

Father reaches into his large, black briefcase and retrieves a book that none of us can read. It is written in a foreign language. My mind in conflict, I think that I have made a mistake with my earlier fears, wondering what this particular book has to do with our family.

In a voice filled with undisguised rage, Father says that Ali recently purchased the book from Germany, and that the book tells the life of a princess, a stupid and foolish woman who is not aware of the royal obligations that accompany the privileges of royalty. While circling the room he holds the book in his hands. The picture on the cover is plainly that of a Muslim woman, for she is veiled, and is standing against a backdrop of Turkish minarets. I have a wild thought that an aging, exiled princess from Egypt or Turkey has written a revealing book, but quickly realize that such a tale would hold no interest in our land.

When Father steps closer, I read the title: *Ich, Prinzessin aus dem Hause Al Sa'ud.*

It is my story!

As I have not been in touch with the book's author since learning of its sale to a large and respected American publishing house, I am unaware at the time that the book, *Princess*, is a huge success and has been sold to numerous foreign publishers. The book in front of me is quite obviously a German edition of it.

I have a short moment of elation followed by

sheer terror. I feel the blood rush to my face. I am numb and can barely hear my father's voice. He explains that Ali had been curious when he saw the book upon his arrival at Frankfurt Airport. Since my brother was spending two months in Europe, he had taken the time and expense to have the book translated when he saw that our family name was written on the cover.

At the time, Ali had an irritated thought that some obscure, disgruntled princess within the Al Sa'ud family had divulged gossipy secrets of her life story. Once Ali read the book and clearly recognized himself from our childhood dramas, the truth of the book was revealed, and he cancelled the remainder of his holiday and hastily returned to Riyadh in a fury.

Father had copies of the translated version made for the meeting.

He nods at Ali, while giving a small signal with his hand. My brother gropes with a bulky pile of papers at his side and proceeds to hand each person a bundle of them secured with a large rubber band.

Confused, Kareem nudges me, raising his eyebrows and rolling his eyes.

Until the last possible second, I express my denials, returning a face of bewilderment. I shrug my shoulders and stare, unblinking and unseeing, at the papers in my hand.

With mounting voice, Father shouts out my name, 'Sultana!'

I feel my body jump.

Father begins to speak rapidly, spitting out words as I imagine a machine-gun expels bullets, 'Sultana, do you recall the marriage and divorce of your sister, Sara? The wickedness of your childhood friends? The death of your mother? Your trip to Egypt? Your marriage to Kareem? The birth of your son? Sultana?'

I have stopped breathing.

Relentlessly, my father continues to accuse. 'Sultana, if you have difficulty in recalling these momentous events, then I suggest that you read this book!'

Father throws the book at my feet.

Unable to move, I stare mutely at the book on the floor.

My father orders, 'Sultana, pick it up!'

Kareem grabs the book and stares at the cover. He gasps – a deep, ragged breath – and then turns to me. 'What is this, Sultana?'

I am paralysed with fear. My heart stops beating. I sit and listen, longing for the life-giving thump.

Quite out of control, Kareem drops the book to the floor, grabs my shoulders and shakes me like a rag doll.

I again feel the familiar heart beat, though I have a childlike thought – a moment of sorrow that I cannot die on the spot and so burden my husband's conscience with lifelong guilt.

I can hear my neck muscles snapping from the force of Kareem's strength.

My father yells. 'Sultana! Answer your husband!'

Suddenly, the years evaporate. I am a child again, at my father's mercy. How I long for my mother to be alive, for nothing less than maternal fervour can save me from this vicious encounter!

I feel a whimper forming in my throat.

I have told myself many times in the past that there can be no freedom without courage, yet my courage fails me when I need it the most. I had known that if members of my immediate family read the book, that my secret would be discovered, since they are key figures in my life, and in the book. Foolishly, I had felt protected by the fact that, in my family, only Sara reads books. Even if gossip of the book had spread throughout the city, I had assumed that my family would take little note of the event, unless a mention was made of a particular incident that they would recall from our youth.

Now, ironically, my brother, a man who scorns the mention of women's rights, has read the book that focused attention on abuses of women in my land. My demon of a brother, Ali, has foiled my precious anonymity.

Timidly, I look around the room at my father, my sisters and brother. Together, as if they had practised, their looks of surprise and anger are slowly forged into a united, hard stare.

After only one short month, I have been discovered!

Finding my voice, I weakly protest, blaming my deed on the highest authority, saying what all good Muslims say when caught in an act that will bring punishment on their heads. I thump the papers with my hand. 'God willed it. He willed this book!'

Ali is quick to retort, scoffing, 'God? Not so! The devil willed it! He willed it! Not God!' Ali turns to my father and says with perfect seriousness, 'Since the day of her birth, Sultana has had a little devil living inside her. This devil willed the book!'

29

Quite rapidly, my sisters begin to leaf through the pages in their hands, to see for themselves if our family's secrets had been made public.

Only Sara gives me her support. She quietly stands up and slips behind my back, resting her hands on my shoulders, reassuring me with her soft touch.

After his initial outburst, Kareem is quiet. I see that he is reading the translated copy of the book. I lean sideways and see that he has discovered the chapter that tells of our first meeting and consequent marriage. Sitting perfectly still, my husband speaks aloud the words that he is seeing for the first time.

Father's angry shouting arouses Ali's enthusiastic hatred, and my father and brother quite outdo each other in their verbal assaults on my stupidity. Amid the passionate disorder, I hear Ali shout out the accusation that I have committed treason.

Treason? I love my God, country, and King, in that order; and I shout back that 'No! I am not a traitor! Only a haphazard council of mediocre minds can reach a conclusion of treason!'

As my anger builds, my fear is receding.

I think to myself that the men in my family are proof that men and women can remain at peace only when one sex is strong enough to dominate the other completely. Now that we women in Saudi Arabia are becoming educated, and are beginning to think for ourselves, our lives will be filled with additional discord and mayhem. Still, I welcome renewed battle if it means more rights for women, for a false peace does nothing more than further women's subjugation.

Yet, I know that this is not the most opportune moment for refutations.

The hot controversy continues to rage, and I become lost in the details. My initial fright makes me forget why I requested Jean Sasson to write my story in the first place. I stop listening to the accusations, and force myself to remember my friend Nada's death by drowning and Sameera's crushing imprisonment, wondering if their tragic lives have yet touched readers' hearts. Even before the book was published, I had realized that neither tale seemed credible, unless the book's readers acknowledged the barbarities that men inflict upon women. Yet, something was telling me that those with genuine knowledge of my land – its customs and traditions – had recognized the truth of my words.

The memory of my unfortunate friends and their sad fate gives me fresh strength.

With mounting exasperation I think that those who want freedom must be willing to pay for it with their lives. The worst has happened. I have been discovered. Now what?

It is a pivotal moment. Feeling my strength return, I get to my feet and face my foes. I feel the warrior's blood of my Grandfather Abdul Aziz surge through my body. From the time that I was a child, I am most to be feared when I stand in real danger.

My courage gives me a hardened resolve. Thinking back, I remember the face of a kind man that offered a little girl succulent dates. I have a wild idea. Without hesitating, I shout brave words over the din of the confusion, 'Take me to the King!'

The shouting stops. Incredulous, my father repeats my words, 'The King?'

Ali makes an impatient tskking sound with his tongue. 'The King will not see you!'

'Yes. He will! Take me to him. I wish to tell the King the reasons why the book came to be. To tell him of the tragic lives of the women he rules. I will confess, but only to the King.'

My father looks askance at his son, Ali. Their eyes lock in a shocked look. It is as if I can read their minds: 'One must be honourable, but not too much!'

'I insist upon confessing. To the King.' I know this King well. He hates confrontation. Even so, he will punish me for what I have done. I realize I will need someone from outside Saudi Arabia to keep my memory alive. I say, 'But before I go to the King, I must talk to someone on a foreign newspaper to make my identity known. If I am to be punished, I refuse to be forgotten. Let the world know how our country deals with those who unveil the truth.'

I walk toward the telephone that sits on a small table next to the hallway door, thinking that I must notify someone of my plight. I am desperate, trying to recall a telephone number of an international newspaper that I had memorized for such an occasion.

My sisters begin to wail, crying out to our father that he must stop me.

Kareem jumps to his feet, rushing to beat me to the phone. My husband stands tall over me, blocking my path. With a stern face, he holds out his arm and points to my chair as if it were the executioner's block.

Despite the serious moment, something about Kareem's expression amuses me. I laugh aloud. My husband can be a foolish man and still has not learned that to silence me, he must bury me. That, I know, he can never do. My knowledge of Kareem's inability to commit violence has always given me strength.

Neither Kareem nor I move. Keenly feeling the drama of the moment, I shout out, 'When the beast is cornered, the hunter is in danger.' The thought enters my mind to ram his stomach with my head, and I am considering the option just as my oldest sister, Nura, takes centre stage and quietens us all with her calm approach.

'Enough! This is no way to solve a problem.' She pauses, glancing at Father and Ali. 'All this shouting! The servants will hear every word. *Then* we are in a true dilemma.'

Nura is the only female child of my father to gain his love. Father motions for everyone to be quiet.

Kareem leads me by the arm and we return to sit in our chairs.

Father and Ali continue to stand, both quite speechless.

Since the book's publication, I have been weakened by my fear. Now, for the first time in weeks, I feel absolutely fierce, recognizing that the last thing on male minds is to turn me over to the authorities.

The meeting continues much more calmly, with serious talk of how to keep my identity a secret. We understand that there will be much talk and speculation within the kingdom about who the princess in the book is. My family decides that it will be impossible for the common man of Saudi to uncover the truth, for they are outside our family circles. And there is no real danger from male relatives within the extended Al Sa'ud family, for females and their activities are carefully guarded from male view. In Father's mind, there is genuine concern regarding close female relatives, since they sometimes participate in our intimate gatherings.

There is a moment of panic as Tahani remembers that one old auntie who was closely involved in Sara's calamitous marriage and divorce is still living. Nura calms their fears by revealing that our auntie, just a few days ago, has been diagnosed as having a disabling brain disorder that affects the elderly. Nura says that our auntie is rarely, if ever, coherent. If by some remote chance she hears of the book, nothing she says or does would now be taken seriously by her family.

Everyone breathes a sigh of relief.

I, myself, have no fear of the old woman. She is an anomaly in her time. I understand her frisky character better than others. My intimate knowledge has come from past conversations when she whispered in my ear that she supported me in my quest for small female freedoms. This auntie has bragged to me that she was the world's first feminist, long before the European women thought of such matters. She said that on the night of her marriage, she had insisted to her startled husband that she handle the money from the sale of the sheep, since she could figure numbers in her head and he had to use a stick in the sand. Not only that, her husband never even thought of taking another wife, saying often that with my auntie he had women enough.

With a toothless laugh, my auntie had confided in me that the secret to controlling a man was a woman's ability to keep her husband's 'leather stick' rigid and ready. I was a young girl at that time, and had no idea what a 'leather stick' might be. Later, in my adult years, I often smile, thinking of the lusty activities that must have shaken their tent.

After her husband's early death, my auntie confessed that she missed her husband's tender caresses and that it was his memory that kept her from accepting another mate.

Over the years, I have jealously guarded her happy secret, fearing that such a confession would nibble at my auntie's soul.

For several hours, my family pore over the translated pages and satisfy themselves that no-one else alive, or traceable outside our immediate family, is aware of the family dramas and squabbles divulged in the book.

I can see that my family feels a keen sense of relief. In addition, I catch a trace of mild admiration that I had so cleverly altered the pertinent information that would have led the authorities directly to my door.

The evening closes with Father and Ali warning my sisters not to notify their husbands of the night's business. Who knows which husband might feel compelled to confide in a sister or mother? My sisters are instructed to tell their husbands that the meeting involved nothing more than personal female matters that were not worthy of their husbands' attention.

Father sternly orders me not to 'come out' in public and announce my 'crime'. The fact that the book is the story of my life must remain a well-kept secret within our family. My father reminds me that not only would I suffer dire consequences, house arrest, or possibly imprisonment, but that the men of the family, including my own son, Abdullah, would be scorned and shut out by Saudi Arabia's patriarchal society that values nothing more highly than a man's ability to control his women.

As a token of submission, I lower my eyes and promise compliance. My heart is smiling, for on this night I have made a brilliant discovery, that the men of my family are locked to me like a chain, that their dominant role imprisons them as surely as it does me.

As I say goodnight to my father and brother, I think to myself that: complete power poisons the hand of the person who holds it. The men of my family cannot punish me without risk to their own well-being within the kingdom.

Cheated of my blood, Ali is displeased and gruff in our parting. He would like nothing better than to see me placed under house arrest, but he cannot risk the wound to his male pride to be associated by blood with someone like me.

I give him an especially warm farewell, whispering in his ear that: 'Ali, you must remember that not *everyone* in chains can be subdued.'

It is a great triumph!

Kareem is sullen and stubborn as we make our way home. He smokes one cigarette after another, soundly cursing the Filipino driver on three occasions for not driving to suit his master.

I lean my face against the car window, seeing nothing of what we pass on the Riyadh streets. I brace myself for a second battle, for I understand that I cannot escape Kareem's great anger.

Once locked in our bedroom, Kareem grabs the pages of the book. He begins to read aloud the passages that are must insulting to him: 'His façade was wisdom and kindness, his very bowels were cunning and selfish. I was disgusted to discover that he was merely a shell of a man with little to commend him, after all!'

There is a thread of sympathy in my thoughts, for what human would not feel pain and fury at a public statement of their weakest traits. I fight the emotion, forcing myself to recall my husband's activities that led to my own pain and grief so vividly portrayed in the book.

I am in a dilemma, not knowing whether to laugh or cry.

Kareem solves the problem for me with his exaggerated behaviour. My husband waves his arms and stamps his feet. I'm reminded of the Egyptian puppet show that I attended a week ago at my sister Sara's palace, a hilarious event, featuring puppets dressed in full Saudi dress. The closer I look, the more Kareem resembles Goha, a lovable but eccentric imaginary figure in the Arab world. Goha the puppet had been his usual foolish self in the play, prancing across the stage, disentangling himself from complex situations.

My lips quiver with the urge to laugh. At any moment now, I expect my husband to fall to the floor and throw a childish temper tantrum.

'He swore, he blushed with shame; I thought

perhaps he was angered by his inability to control his wife.'

Kareem glares hatefully at me. 'Sultana! Don't you dare smile! I'm truly angry.'

Still battling conflicting emotions, I shrug. 'Do you deny that what you're reading is the truth?'

Ignoring my words, Kareem foolishly continues to seek out the most damning passages concerning his character, reminding his wife of the particular traits of her husband's temperament that had led her to leave him years ago.

Actually shrieking, he reads aloud, 'How I yearned to be wed to a warrior, a man with the hot flame of righteousness to guide his life.'

His rage growing with every word, Kareem holds the book under my nose and points with a finger to the words that he deems most insulting,

Six years ago, Sultana was stricken with a venereal disease; after much distress, Kareem admitted that he participated in a weekly adventure of sex with strangers . . . After the scare of the disease, Kareem promised he would avoid the weekly tryst, but Sultana says she knows that he is weak in the face of such a feast, and that he continues to indulge himself without shame. Their wonderful love has vanished except in memory; Sultana says she will stand with her husband and continue her struggle for the sake of her daughters.

Kareem is so angry at that particular revelation that I fear he will start to cry. My husband accuses me of 'poisoning paradise', claiming that, 'our lives are perfect'.

Admittedly, over the past year, I have regained some of my earlier love and trust for Kareem, but it is in moments such as this that my dismay grows over the cowardice of the men in our family. I realize by his behaviour that Kareem gives not a thought to the reasons I risked my safety and our happiness to make known the events of my life, or to the very real and tragic events ending the lives of young and innocent women in his own land. Kareem's only concern is that of his appearance in the book, and the fact that he has fared poorly in many passages.

I tell my husband that he and other men of the Al Sa'ud family alone hold the power to make change in our country. Slowly, quietly, in their subtle manner, they can pursue and encourage change. When he makes no response to my plea, I understand that the men of the Al Sa'ud family cannot risk their power for their women. They are passionately in love with the crown.

Kareem regains his composure, after I remind him that no-one outside our family, other than the author, knows who he is! And those persons know him well, aware of his good and bad traits, even without this published book.

Kareem sits beside me and lifts my chin with his finger. He looks almost appealing as he ponders, 'You told Jean Sasson about the disease I caught?'

I wiggle in shame as Kareem slowly shakes his head from side to side, visibly disappointed in his wife. 'Is nothing sacred to you, Sultana?'

Many battles end in an outpouring of goodwill. The evening ends with unexpected displays of affection. Strangely, Kareem says that he has never loved me more.

I find myself being courted by my husband and the intensity of my feelings increases. My husband reawakens the desire that I had once deemed lost for ever. I wonder at my own ability to both love and hate the same man.

Later as Kareem sleeps, I lie awake by his side and replay in my mind, moment by moment, the events of the day. I realize that despite the evening's end – the guaranteed protection promised by my family (due solely to their own fears of royal banishment and/or punishment) and the renewal of my marriage – I cannot rest peacefully until genuine social adjustment for the women whose burden I share comes to the land I love. The hard necessities of female lives are pushing me to continue my efforts to gain personal freedom for the women of Arabia.

I question myself: am I not the mother of two daughters? Do I not owe my daughters and their daughters after them every effort to bring transformation?

I smile, once again thinking back to the puppet show that I had watched with Sara's youngest children, and recall the words of the funny but wise puppet Goha. 'Does a faithful saluki[1] stop barking in his master's defence when a single bone is thrown his way?'

I shout, 'No!'

Kareem stirs and I rub the back of his head, whispering sweet words, lulling my husband back to sleep.

I know at that moment that I will not keep a

[1]Desert dog.

pledge that was made under coercion. I will let the world community decide when I should return to silence. Until people choose to close their ears to the plight of women in despair, I will continue to reveal the true happenings behind the secrecy of the black veil. This is to be my destiny.

I make a decision. Contrary to the promises I had made under threat of detention, when I next travel out of the kingdom, I will contact my friend, Jean Sasson. There is more to be accomplished.

When I close my eyes to sleep, I am a more focused but a much sadder woman than the Sultana who awoke this morning, for I know that, once again, I am entering a risky arena, and even though my punishment – and possibly even my death – will be cruel, failure will be more bitter, for failure is everlasting.

Chapter Two

MAHA

*The more prohibitions you have, the less
virtuous people will be.*
Tao Te Ching

Those whom Kareem and I love best have proved
the worst. Abdullah, our son, troubles us; Maha,
our eldest daughter, frightens us; while Amani, our
youngest daughter, puzzles us.

I had no foreboding of doom as our only son
Abdullah smiled with boyish happiness and told us
with relish of his wonderful success on the soccer
field. Kareem and I were entranced, as most parents
would be, upon hearing the successful exploits of
their well-loved child. From a young age, Abdullah
was seldom surpassed in physical games, and this
fact was a particular source of glee for his athletic
father. As we proudly listened, we took no note of
his younger sisters, Maha and Amani, who were
amusing themselves with a video game.

When Amani, our youngest child, began to
scream in alarm, it was with a terrible shock that

Kareem and I saw flames licking at Abdullah's clothing.

Our son was on fire!

Acting on instinct, Kareem quickly threw our son to the floor and extinguished the flames by rolling Abdullah in a Persian carpet.

After we assured ourselves that our son was unharmed, Kareem tried to find the source of the inexplicable fire.

I cried out that the fire was caused by an evil eye, that we were too boastful of our beautiful son!

Fighting back tears, I turned to comfort my daughters. Poor Amani! Her small frame was racked with sobs. While I held my baby, I motioned with my free arm to her older sister, Maha, to come to me. Suddenly, I drew back in horror, for Maha's face was a frightful mask of anger and hate.

After investigating the confusing incident, we learned a terrible truth: Maha had set her brother's *thobe* on fire.

Maha, meaning 'She Gazelle', has not fulfilled the promise of her gentle name. From the age of ten, it was apparent that our eldest daughter was possessed by the demonic energy of her mother. Often I have thought that there must be a battleground of good and evil spirits hovering over Maha, with evil spirits usually overpowering the good. Neither her life amid imperial splendour, nor the unconditional love of a devoted family, has tempered Maha's spirit.

Without justification, she has tormented her brother Abdullah and her youngest sister Amani for as long as they both can remember. Few children have brought so many crises to one family as Maha.

In appearance, Maha is a stunningly attractive

girl, with a frighteningly seductive personality. She has the look of a Spanish dancer, all eyes and hair. Combined with this great beauty is a gifted mind. Ever since her birth, it seemed to me that too many blessings had been bestowed upon my eldest daughter. With so many abilities, Maha is unable to focus on one goal, and lacking a unifying purpose, she has failed to harness her talents in one direction. Over the years, I have watched as a hundred promising projects have been started, but none completed.

Kareem said once that he feared that our daughter was nothing more than a girl of brilliant fragments, and would fail to accomplish one single idea in her lifetime. My greatest concern is that Maha is a revolutionary seeking a cause.

As I too am such a person, I am aware of the turmoil raised by a mutinous character.

In her earlier years, the problem seemed a simple matter. Maha loved her father to distraction. The intensity of her feelings increased with her years.

Whereas Kareem adored his two daughters as he did his one son, and strove to avoid the resentments that I endured as a child, the make-up of our society drew Abdullah more closely into Kareem's life outside our home. This basic fact of our Muslim heritage was the first shock of Maha's young life.

Maha's intense jealousy of her father's affections brought to mind my own unhappy childhood – a young girl who had chafed under the harsh social system into which she was born. For that reason, I failed to comprehend the seriousness of my child's discontent.

After Maha set fire to Abdullah's *thobe*, we knew that her possessiveness of Kareem went far beyond that of normal daughterly affection. Maha was ten years old and Abdullah was twelve. Amani was only seven, but she had watched her sister slip away from their game, fetch her father's gold lighter, setting fire to the edge of Abdullah's *thobe*. Had Amani not cried out a warning, Abdullah could have been seriously burned.

The second shocking incident occurred when Maha was only eleven. It was the hot month of August. Our family had left the sweltering desert city of Riyadh and gathered at my sister Nura's summer palace in the cool mountain city of Taif. It was the first time in years that Father had attended a family gathering of his first wife's children, and his attentions were devoted to his grandsons. While admiring Abdullah's height and figure, my father ignored Maha, who was tugging on his sleeve to show him an ant farm that the children had built and proudly displayed. I saw Father as he brushed her aside and proceeded to squeeze Abdullah's biceps.

Maha was stung by her grandfather's preference for her brother and his indifference to her. My heart plunged for the pain that I knew was in her heart.

Knowing Maha's ability to create a scene, I walked over to comfort my daughter just as she assumed a masculine stance and began cursing my father with fiery invectives of the coarsest indecency, peppered with vile accusations.

From that moment, the family gathering rapidly deteriorated. Though humiliated, I had a quick thought that Maha had expressed to my father his manifest due.

Father, who had never held a high opinion of the

female sex, made no pretence of his feelings. Scornfully, Father ordered, 'Remove this horrible creature from my sight!'

I saw plainly that my daughter had awakened Father's contempt for me. His eyes were penetrating, and his lips were curled in scorn as he looked from his daughter to his granddaughter. I overheard him mutter to no-one in particular, 'A mouse can only give birth to a mouse.'

In the blink of an eye, Kareem snatched Maha from Father's sight and took her squirming and cursing into the villa to wash out her mouth with soap. Her muffled cries could be heard in the garden.

Father left soon after, but not before announcing to the entire family that my daughters were doomed by my blood.

Little Amani, who is too sensitive for such accusations, collapsed into hysterics.

My father has not acknowledged the existence of either daughter since that day.

Maha's belligerence and hostility did not prevent her from occasional bouts of kindness and sensitivity, and her temperament cooled somewhat after the incident in Taif. My daughter's angers ebbed and flowed. In addition, Kareem and I doubled our efforts to assure our daughters that they were as loved and esteemed as our son. While this proved fruitful in our home, Maha could not ignore the fact that she was considered less worthy than her brother in the world outside our walls. It is a distressing habit of all Saudi Arabians, including my own family and Kareem's, that they pour attention and affection on the heads of male children, while ignoring female children.

Maha was a bright girl who was hard to deceive, and the uncompromising facts of Arab life burned into her consciousness. I had strong presentiments that Maha was a volcano that would one day erupt.

Like many a modern parent, I had no clear notion of how to help my most troubled child.

Maha was only fifteen during the Gulf War, a time that no Saudi Arabian is likely to forget. Change was in the air, and no-one was more tempted by the promise of female liberation than my elder daughter. When our veiled plight piqued the curiosity of numerous foreign journalists, many educated women of my land began to plan for the day that they could burn their veils, discard the heavy black *abaayas*, and sit at the steering-wheel of their own cars.

I, myself, was so caught up in the excitement, I failed to notice that my older daughter had become involved with a teenage girl who took her idea of liberation to the extreme.

The first time that I met Aisha I was uncomfortable – not because she was unrelated to the royal family, for I, myself, had cherished friends outside the royal circle. Aisha was from a well-known Saudi Arabian family who had made their fortune importing furniture into the kingdom to sell to the many foreign companies who needed to fit out numerous villas for the swarm of expatriate workers invading Saudi Arabia.

I thought that the girl was too old for her years.

Only seventeen, she looked much more mature, and acted in a tough manner that smelled of trouble.

Aisha and Maha were inseparable, with Aisha spending many hours at our home. Aisha had an unusual amount of freedom for a Saudi girl. Later, I discovered that the girl was virtually ignored by her parents, who seemed not to care about their daughter's whereabouts.

Aisha was the oldest of eleven children, and her mother, the only legal wife of her father, was embroiled in a never-ending domestic dispute with Aisha's father over the fact that her husband took advantage of a little-used Arab custom called *mut'a*, which is a 'marriage of pleasure', or a 'temporary marriage'. Such a marriage can last from one hour to ninety-nine years. When the man indicates to the woman that the temporary arrangement is over, the two involved part company without a divorce ceremony. The Sunni sect of Islam that dominates Saudi Arabia considers such a practice immoral, condemning the arrangement as nothing more than legalized prostitution. Still, no legal authority would deny a man such an arrangement.

As an Arab woman belonging to the Sunni Muslim sect, Aisha's mother protested the intrusion of temporary, one-night or one-week brides that her depraved husband brought into their lives. The husband, disregarding his wife's challenge, claimed validation through a verse in the Koran which says, 'you are permitted to seek out wives with your wealth, indecorous conduct, but not in fornication, but give them a reward for what you have enjoyed of them in keeping with your promise'. While this verse is interpreted by the Shiite sect of the Muslim faith as endorsement of the practice, these temporary unions are not common with Sunni Muslims. Aisha's father was the exception rather than the rule in our land, in embracing the freedom to wed young women for the sole pleasure of sex.

Occupied by the plight of helpless girls and women in my country, I questioned Aisha closely on the indecent practice that I had heard discussed by a Shiite woman from Bahrain, whom Sara had met and befriended in London some years before.

It seemed that Aisha's father did not want the responsibility of supporting four wives and their children on a permanent basis, so he sent his trusted assistant on monthly trips into Shiite regions in and out of Saudi Arabia to negotiate with various impoverished families for the right of temporary marriages with their virgin daughters. Such a deal could easily be struck with a man who had four wives, many daughters, and little money.

Aisha sometimes befriended these young girls who were transported into Riyadh for a few nights of horror. After Aisha's father's passion waned, the young brides were sent away, returned to their families wearing gifts of gold and carrying small bags filled with cash. Aisha said that most of the youthful brides were no more than eleven or twelve years old. They were from poor families and were uneducated. She said that they seemed not to know what exactly was happening to them. All the girls knew was that they were very frightened, and that the man Aisha called father, did very painful things to them. Aisha said that all of the girls cried to be returned to their mothers.

The hard-eyed Aisha wept as she related the story

of Reema, a young girl of thirteen who had been brought to Saudi Arabia from Yemen, a poverty-stricken country that has a large number of Shiite Muslim families. Aisha said that Reema was as beautiful as the deer after which she was named, and as sweet as any girl that she had ever known.

Reema was from a nomadic tribe who roamed the harsh land of Yemen. Her father had only one wife, but twenty-three children, of which seventeen were girls. Even though Reema's mother was now shriv-elled and bent from childbearing and hard work, she had once been a lovely girl and had given birth to seventeen beautiful daughters. Reema proudly said that her family was known as far away as Sana'a, the capital of that country, for the beauty of their women.

The family was very poor, with only three camels and twenty-two sheep. In addition, two of the six sons were handicapped from difficult births. One son's legs were twisted and he could not walk, and the other had strange, jerking spasms and could do no work. For these reasons, Reema's father strove to sell his sought-after daughters to the highest bidder. During the summer months, the family would travel through high mountain passes, along narrow, tortuous roads into the city, and a deal would be struck for the daughter who had reached a marriageable age according to Islam.

The year before, at the age of twelve, Reema had reached puberty. She was her mother's favourite child, and the girl attended to her handicapped brothers. The family had pleaded with her father to let her remain with them for a few more years, but he sadly confessed that he could not allow it. There were two sons after Reema, and the sister closest in age was only nine years old. Reema's younger sister was small and undernourished, and her father feared that the girl might not reach puberty for another three or four years. Reema's family could not exist without the marriage money.

Reema was taken to Sana'a to be wed. While her father scouted the city for a suitable bridegroom, Reema remained in a small mud house with her sisters and brothers. On the third day, her father returned to the hut with a rich man from Saudi Arabia. Reema said that her father was very excited, for the man represented a wealthy man from Saudi Arabia, a man who would pay much gold for a beautiful girl.

The Saudi agent insisted upon seeing Reema before he paid the money, a request generally met with the blade of a Yemeni sword rather than the humble compliance from a Muslim father. The gold in the agent's hands overcame the family's religious convictions. Reema said that she was inspected in the way that her father inspected the camels and sheep at market. Reema confessed that she did not protest the shame, for she had always known she would go to another family, as the purchased property of another man. But she squirmed and pushed when the man insisted upon viewing her teeth.

The agent pronounced Reema satisfactory and paid a portion of the agreed money. The family celebrated by killing a fat sheep, while the agent had Reema's documents prepared to fly to Saudi Arabia. Reema's father happily announced that the family could wait out the four years until Reema's younger sister reached the proper age, for the man from Saudi Arabia had paid a large sum for Reema.

Reema herself forgot her anxieties, even becoming excited, after her father told her that she was the most fortunate of girls. Reema was going to a life of leisure, that she would eat meat every day, have servants at her beck and call, and that her children would be educated and well fed. Reema asked her father if the man might purchase her a doll, one like she had seen in a discarded European magazine that the children had discovered in the rubbish bins in Sana'a.

Her father promised that he would make Reema's request a high priority.

When the man returned a week later, Reema first learned the terrible truth, that the marriage would not be honourable, that it was a marriage of *mut'a*, a temporary union. Her father became angry, for his honour was at stake, his daughter should not be treated in such a lowly manner. He pleaded with the man from Arabia, mentioning that it would be difficult to find another husband for his daughter, who would no longer be considered fresh and clean. He might be forced to provide for Reema for many years while seeking a man who would accept her as a second, less honoured wife.

The man sweetened the deal with a bundle of bills. He said that if Reema's father refused, then he would be forced to insist upon the return of money already paid.

Reluctantly, Reema's father had relented, admitting that he had already spent a portion of that sum. Ashamed, he turned his face to the ground and told Reema that she must go with the man, that it was God's will. Reema's father requested the Saudi man to find Reema a permanent husband in Saudi Arabia, since there were many Yemeni labourers working in that rich country.

The agent had agreed to try; otherwise, he said, Reema could become a servant in his own home.

Reema said goodbye to her family, and left the land of her birth, haunted by the pitiful weeping of her two handicapped brothers.

During the trip, the man had promised a homesick Reema that he would buy her a doll, even though such an item was expressly forbidden by the men of religion.

Like most Arab girls, Reema had full knowledge of a wife's responsibilities. She has slept in the same room with her parents since the day of her birth. Reema understood that a woman must submit to her husband's every wish.

Aisha said it was the girl's calm acceptance of her life of slavery that she found so distressing, recalling that the girl's tears had belied her declaration that she was not displeased with her lot. Reema wept for the six days that she was in Aisha's home, all the while defending the right of Aisha's father to do with her as he pleased.

Aisha told me that her father's employee easily located a Yemeni man who worked as a tea boy in one of their offices, a man who had been willing to accept Reema as his second wife. His first wife was in Yemen, and he admitted that he needed a woman to cook his meals and serve him.

The last day that Aisha had seen Reema, the young girl was clutching a small doll, obediently following one man out of their home, to go and wed another man whom she did not know.

Aisha's mother, a pious Sunni Muslim, had become so distraught over Reema's situation that she had gone to her husband's family to complain. Her desperate act had created quite a furore in the family, but nothing the man's parents could say or do convinced their son to cease the godless act. Their advice had been for Aisha's mother to pray to God for her husband's soul.

I often wondered what became of those children, the *mut'a* brides, for it is quite difficult in the Muslim world to arrange a good marriage for a girl who is no longer a virgin. As dispensable girls in fortuneless families, I suppose they were eventually married off as the third or fourth wife to a man without wealth or influence, much in the same manner as Reema, or of my childhood friend, Wafa, who had been wed to such a one against her will.

Aisha's home life was agony for a thinking girl, and the stress and strain of her father's debauchery pushed Aisha into inevitable teenage decline.

My daughter, Maha, who was imprudent by nature, was captivated by Aisha's antics. Recalling my own rebellious youth, I knew the futility of prohibiting Maha from meeting Aisha.

Forbidden fruit is too tempting for all children, regardless of nationality or sex.

During the height of the Gulf War, our king harnessed the most aggressive of the roving bands of 'morals police', forbidding them to harass Western visitors to our land. Quite sensibly, the men of our family knew that it would not do for journalists from the West to view life as it really is in our country. Happily, the women of Saudi Arabia benefited from this royal order. The absence of sharp-eyed religious police patrolling the cities of Saudi Arabia, searching for uncovered women to strike with their sticks, or spray with red paint, was too good to be true. This policy endured no longer than the war itself, but for a few months we Saudi women enjoyed welcome respite from probing eyes. During this heady period, there was a universal call for the women of Saudi Arabia to take their proper place in society, and we foolishly thought that the favourable situation would continue for ever.

For some of our women, too much freedom given quickly proved disastrous. Our men were disappointed that all women did not behave as saints, without understanding the confusion caused by the contradictions of our lives.

Now I know that Aisha and Maha were two Saudi girls not yet psychologically prepared for unfamiliar and complete freedom.

Due to the unusual times brought about by war, Aisha had managed to have herself appointed a volunteer at one of the local hospitals, and nothing would do but for my daughter to seek the same appointment at that institution. This she did two days a week after her school day ended. It was a marvellous experience for Maha, for although she was forced to wear her *abaaya* and head scarf, she was not required to wear the hated veil once inside the hospital doors.

Once the war ended, Maha refused to go back to the old ways. She held tight to her newfound freedom and begged her father and me to allow her to continue her work at the hospital.

Our approval was reluctantly given.

One afternoon Maha was expected at the hospital, and our driver was waiting in the front drive. I decided to go and hurry her. By some whim of circumstance, I happened to enter Maha's room just as my daughter was strapping a small calibre pistol to a brown leather holster attached to her thigh.

I was struck dumb! A weapon!

Kareem happened to be home for the afternoon siesta, and upon hearing our raised voices, he came to investigate. After an emotional scene, Maha confessed that during the war, she and Aisha had begun to arm themselves, in the event that the Iraqi army broke through to Riyadh! Now that the war was over, she thought she might need protection from the morals police who had begun to threaten women on the street.

The 'morals' or 'religious police' sometimes called the *Mutawwa*, are members of the 'Committee for Enforcing Right and Forbidding Wrong'. During the Gulf War period, these men were instructed by King Fahd to relax their harsh enforcements against improper attire worn by females. Now that the foreign journalists had departed the kingdom, these zealots were more active than we could ever recall, initiating arrests and prosecutions against women in my country.

Maha and Aisha had decided that they would not endure the attentions of the zealots let loose upon innocent women.

I looked at my daughter in alarm and disbelief! Was she planning to fire upon a man of religion?

Kareem learned that the weapon belonged to Aisha's father. He, like many Arab men, had quite a collection of firearms and had not missed two pistols that his daughter and Maha had stolen.

Imagine our horror when we learned that the pistol was loaded, but had no safety-catch. Maha tearfully disclosed that she and Aisha had practised firing the pistols in a vacant lot at the back of Aisha's home!

To Maha's dismay, her enraged father confiscated the illegal weapon and bundled her into his Mercedes. Dismissing his driver, Kareem drove like a madman across the city of Riyadh to Aisha's home in order to return the gun and warn Aisha's parents of our children's dangerous activities.

The result of our bizarre discovery was a hasty conference called between ourselves and Aisha's parents. Both of our daughters were sent to Aisha's room.

Aisha's mother and I, covered still by our black veils, sat in our separate worlds and discussed the children to whom we had given life. Oddly enough, for once in my life I was pleased to be veiled, for I could stare in undisguised contempt at Aisha's father, a man I knew to be a molester of young girls. Surprisingly, he was a youthful man with a dignified appearance.

I thought to myself, beware of those who look like a rose, for even roses have thorns. With the main topic of the evening being our daughters, I had little time to dwell upon the dark secrets of the home we were visiting.

What Kareem and I uncovered that evening about our elder daughter's shocking convictions will haunt our memories until we cease to walk the earth.

While I question the unjust practices and cruel

customs inflicted upon the female population of Saudi Arabia by those who so rigidly interpret – and thus often misinterpret – the laws laid down by the Prophet, there is no doubt in my mind of the existence of one God as preached by his messenger, Mohammed. Our three children have been raised to revere the teachings of the Prophet and the Koran which was passed down from God. That a child of mine would curse God and denounce his word brought a chill to my heart and numbed me.

When the decision was announced to Aisha and Maha that their parents had arrived at the reasonable conclusion that the two girls should henceforth avoid each other's company, and seek out other friends and new interests, my daughter Maha yanked the veil from her face, raised her head in fury and displayed such a look of evil that she terrorized her own mother who had carried her in her womb and suckled her at her breast. If I had not heard Maha's words with my own ears, no person could convince me of their validity.

Her full lips tight with determination, our daughter yelled, 'I will *not* do as you say! Aisha and I will leave this land we hate and make our home in another place. We hate it here! We *hate it*! To be a woman in this awful country you must defile your life with the most tremendous injustices.'

Spittle dripped from Maha's lips. Her body moved with uncontrolled rage. Her eyes sought my eyes. 'If a girl lives modestly, she is a fool. If she lives normally, she is a hypocrite. If she believes there is a God, *she is an imbecile*!'

Unable to move, Kareem did manage to find his voice. 'Maha! You blaspheme!'

'Blaspheme? What is there to blaspheme? *There is no God!*'

Kareem jumped to his feet and squeezed Maha's lips together with his fingers.

Aisha's mother screamed and fainted, for such a statement can cost a life in the land of my birth.

Aisha's father shouted out for us to remove our unbelieving daughter from his home.

Kareem and I struggled with Maha, who suddenly had the strength of a giant. My daughter had lost her mind! Only the insane have such unnatural power! After much pulling and pushing, Kareem and I shoved our child into the back seat of the car and raced back to our home. Kareem drove while I tried to quieten my child, who no longer knew her mother. Finally, she lay still, as someone in a swoon.

An Egyptian physician, who was a trusted family doctor, was summoned. In a vain attempt to calm us, he said that there were many disorders in teen-age girls the world over, and proceeded to cite statistics on the strange malady that seems to affect females only.

The physician had his own theory. He claimed that at puberty, a girl often produces large doses of hormones, and such an event drives them crazy for short periods of time. He said that he had treated many such psychological cases within the royal family, without any complications or permanent effects. He grinned and stated that he had not lost a patient yet.

In the doctor's opinion, Maha should be kept sedated for a few days, and she would recover from the case of hysterics on her own.

Leaving us with an ample supply of tranquillizers, the physician said that he would return in the morning to check on his patient.

Kareem thanked the doctor, and walked him to the door. When he returned, we exchanged a long and thoughtful look. There were no words necessary between us.

While Kareem arranged for our private plane to be made ready, I telephoned my sister, Sara, and gained permission for Abdullah and Amani to stay with her until our return. Kareem and I were taking Maha to London. She was in desperate need of the best psychiatric care available. Sara was asked to keep Maha's condition a secret. If enquiries were made, our families were to be told that Maha was in need of dental care that required a number of visits to London.

Many members of the Saudi royal family routinely travel abroad for medical and dental treatment. Such a trip would arouse little curiosity.

While packing Maha's clothing, I came across disturbing books and documents that were hidden under her underwear. There were numerous writings on astrology, black magic, and witchcraft. Maha had underlined many passages detailing revelations and prophecies. Most alarming to my mind were malevolent items that were supposed to wreak dire evils upon people who had offended her, or induce love at a glance, or cause death by a spell.

I caught my breath when I saw a clothing item of Abdullah's wrapped around a black stone with some bits of loose, grey-coloured substance that I could not identify. I stood, hand to forehead, thinking. Could it be true? Had Maha plotted to harm

60

her only brother? If this were the case, then I was a failure as a mother.

In a state of upheaval, I moved about in a turmoil, collecting damning evidence of my child's barbaric interests. Confused, I traced in my mind Maha's activities from the days of her childhood. Where had my daughter learned of such matters, accumulating a treasure-house of dark paraphernalia?

I remembered Huda, my father's long-deceased slave, and her obvious abilities at predicting the future. But Huda had died before my daughter's birth. As far as I knew, there were no other freed slaves or servants from Africa in our homes who possessed Huda's power of sorcery.

I recoiled, as if hit, as I thought of my mother-in-law, Noorah. It had to be Noorah! Disappointed that her son had neither divorced me nor taken a second wife, Noorah had never ceased to hate me, although she was careful to hide her dislike under a thin veneer of false affections.

From Kareem's revelations to his mother, Noorah had detected with her eagle eyes that Maha was my weakest point. From a young age, Maha's mental life had been one of conflict and pain, and Noorah had seized on that pain and found it vulnerable.

It was plain to see that Noorah had always favoured Maha over her other granddaughters, and her attention had been gratefully received by the confused child. Maha had spent long hours alone with her grandmother. Noorah, an avid believer in the occult, had lost no time in teaching my daughter her own ominous beliefs. How could I, Sultana, be so stupid as to believe that Noorah had my best interests in mind?

I had been a fool, for my heart had been softened by Noorah's obvious delight in Maha, and I had often expressed my profound appreciation for her generous attentions towards my most troubled child. Noorah, in her dislike of me, had chosen to lead my emotionally fragile daughter deeper into the abyss.

I knew that I must confide my findings to Kareem. My actions would have to be delicate, for Kareem would have great difficulty in believing that his mother was capable of such a shameful deed. The truth could become twisted, and I, Sultana, might bear the brunt of his anger, while Noorah would sit contentedly in her palace gloating at her most hated daughter-in-law's failure as a mother and wife.

Chapter Three

LONDON

Not for ever can one enjoy stillness and peace. But misfortune and obstruction are not final. When the grass has been burnt by the fire of the steppe, it will grow anew in summer.
Wisdom from the Mongolian Steppe

Under the influence of strong medication, Maha lay as one dead, while her father and I attempted to make some sense of the precarious situation in which we found ourselves. On the aeroplane to London, Kareem sat like a stone, pale-faced as he handled the distasteful objects that I had brought in a small bag from Maha's room. He, like myself, was appalled at our daughter's fascination in the supernatural.

After a few silent moments, Kareem posed the question that I had been dreading. 'Sultana, where did Maha come across such madness?' His brow furrowed, and he wondered aloud, 'Do you believe it was that foolish girl, Aisha?'

I squirmed in my seat, not knowing how to

answer my husband. Recalling a wise Arab proverb spoken often by my gentle mother, 'A fly will never be able to enter a mouth which knows when to stay shut', I felt that this was not the time to implicate Noorah, my husband's mother. Kareem had endured too many shocks for one day.

Biting my lip and shaking my head, I answered him, 'I don't know. We'll tell the doctor what we found. Perhaps Maha will confide in him, then we'll know who or what is behind her knowledge of such matters.'

Kareem nodded his head in agreement.

For the remainder of the flight, we took turns sleeping, and watching our child, who appeared in her drug-induced sleep as sweet as an angel. For some unexplained reason, I was reminded of another Al Sa'ud royal, Princess Misha'il, a young woman who hid her deception of illicit love. When her secret was discovered, my royal cousin's life ended in the face of a firing-squad.

While Kareem slept, I watched Maha, and remembered Princess Misha'il.

Misha'il was the granddaughter of Prince Mohammed Ibn Abdul Aziz, the same Prince Mohammed who had been passed over for the crown, because of his father's ruling that the ferocious behaviour of a warrior had no place on a throne.

While I did not have a close friendship with Misha'il, I had met her at various royal functions. She was known in the family as a rather wild girl. I thought perhaps her unhappy temperament had something to do with her marriage to an old man, who failed to placate her. Whatever it was, she was miserable and became romantically involved with

Khalid Muhalhal, who happened to be the nephew of the special Saudi Arabian envoy to Lebanon.

Their love affair was hot and filled with the tension caused by the impossible social climate of Saudi Arabia. Many members of the royal family had heard of their illicit relationship, and when the young couple were on the brink of discovery, they made a fatal decision to run off together.

My oldest sister, Nura, was in Jeddah at the time, and heard the story firsthand from a member of Misha'il's immediate family. Misha'il, fearing the wrath of her family, attempted to stage her own death. She told her family that she was going for a swim at their private beach on the Red Sea. Misha'il piled her clothes on the shore, then dressed herself as a Saudi man and tried to flee the country.

Unfortunately, for Misha'il, her grandfather, Prince Mohammed, was one of the shrewdest and most powerful men in the country. He did not believe she had drowned. Officials manning all exits from the country were alerted to search for the granddaughter of Prince Mohammed. Misha'il was caught – intercepted trying to catch a flight from the airport in Jeddah.

Telephones were ringing all over the kingdom, with each royal professing to know more than the next. There was a rumour a minute. I heard that Misha'il had been set free and allowed to leave the kingdom with her lover. Then I was told that a divorce would be granted. Later, a hysterical cousin called and claimed that Misha'il had been beheaded, and that it had taken three blows to separate her head from her body. Not only that, Misha'il's lips had moved and had called out her lover's name, causing the executioner to run from the scene! Can you imagine, my excited cousin asked, words from a bodiless head!

Finally, the very real and ugly truth was made known. Prince Mohammed, in a fit of anger, said that his granddaughter was an adulteress and that an adulteress should submit to Islamic law. Misha'il and her lover were going to be executed.

King Khalid, who was our ruler during this time of tragedy, was known for his indulgent nature. He recommended that Prince Mohammed show mercy, but mercy was not an emotion that was agreeable to that fierce bedouin.

On the day of the execution, I waited with my siblings for news of the event. My sisters and I hoped for a last-minute reprieve. Ali, not surprisingly, expressed the opinion that adulterous women should submit to the laws of Islam and prepare themselves for death.

On that hot day in July of 1977, my cousin Misha'il was blindfolded and forced to kneel before a pile of dirt. She was shot by a firing-squad. Her lover was forced to watch her die. He was then beheaded with a sword.

Once again, unsanctioned love had cost two young people their lives.

The affair was hushed up, and the Al Sa'ud clan hoped that talk of a young woman murdered for the simple act of love would soon disappear. It was not to be. Though buried in the sands of the desert, Misha'il was not forgotten.

Many Westerners will recall the documentary about her death, called, appropriately *Death of a Princess*. As divided as our family was over her punishment, nothing compared with the arguments and hostility generated by the film.

Having comfortably mastered the role of dictators, the men in our family grew furious over their inability to control the news releases and films shown in the West. Offended to the edge of madness, King Khalid ordered the ambassador from Great Britain to leave our country.

I heard later from Kareem and Asad, Sara's husband, that our rulers had seriously considered forcing all British citizens out of our country!

International tensions ran high over the sexual misconduct and execution of one Saudi Arabian princess.

I despaired of the memory. I held my head in my hands. Now, I was the mother of a child who had gone mad. In her madness, what act might Maha commit that would disrupt our family and introduce the pain of young death into our home? My uncharitable father would surely insist upon the harshest of punishments for the child of my womb who had so spitefully and vigorously pointed out his shortcomings as a grandfather.

Maha stirred.

Kareem awakened, and once again we shared our tortured fears for our daughter.

While we were *en route* for London, as agreed, Sara had made the necessary medical arrangements by telephone. We called my sister from Gatwick Airport. Sara reported that Maha was expected at a leading mental institution in London and that her bed was waiting. Sara had thoughtfully arranged for an ambulance to transport us to the institute.

Once we had fulfilled the tiresome admission procedures, Kareem and I were informed by the hospital staff that Maha's physician would meet us the following morning after his initial consultation and his examination of our child. One of the younger nurses was especially kind. She held my hand and whispered that my sister had found one of the most respected physicians in the city, that he had years of experience with Arab women and their unique social and mental problems.

At that moment, I envied the British. In my land, shame over a child's madness would close the minds and mouths of my countrymen, and sympathy would never be shown.

Anguished at leaving our precious child in the hands of strangers, albeit capable strangers, Kareem and I walked sluggishly to the waiting car which would take us to our apartment in the city.

Aroused from sleep, our permanent staff at our London home were clearly not expecting us. Kareem was irritated, but I calmed him with the thought that our personal comfort was the last thing on Sara's mind. We could not fault her for not telephoning our servants prior to our arrival.

Due to the Iraqi invasion of Kuwait, and the recent Gulf War, it had been almost a year since we had visited London, one of our favourite spots in the Western world. In our absence, our three servants had grown slovenly and careless. Whether we were in London or Riyadh, they had strict instructions to maintain the apartment as if we were in the city.

We were too depressed over Maha's condition to complain. Kareem and I sat among the dust-sheets in the sitting-room and ordered strong coffee. Servants scurried about the place as best they could, considering they had been awakened at three o'clock in the morning.

I found myself apologizing for intruding on their sleep, and Kareem snapped at me, ordering, 'Sultana! Never apologize to those who are paid by us. You'll ruin their work habits!'

I felt peevish and wanted to retort that we Saudis could benefit from a little humility. Instead, I changed the subject and began to talk once again about our daughter.

I thought to myself that I too must be coming down with some form of insanity. Twice in one day I had chosen to avoid an argument with my husband.

After our bed was prepared, Kareem and I rested without sleeping.

Never had a night seemed so long.

The British psychiatrist was an odd-looking man whose head sat large on his small body. His brow was vast, and his nose slightly skewed to one side. I could only stare in surprise at the tufts of white hair that sprouted strangely from his ears and nose. While his appearance was disconcerting, his manner was encouraging. With his small, blue, penetrating eyes, I could tell that he was a man who took the problems of his patients very seriously. My daughter was in good hands.

Kareem and I quickly discovered that he was a man who spoke what was on his mind. Without caring about our wealth, or Kareem's princely status in the royal family of Riyadh, he spoke with fearless honesty of the system of our land that so hobbled the will of women.

Well-informed of the traditions and customs of Arab lands, he told us, 'As a child I was fascinated by the Arabian explorers: Philby, Thesiger, Burton, Doughty, Thomas, and of course, Lawrence. I devoured their adventures. And, quite determined to view what I had read about, I convinced my parents to send me to Egypt. It wasn't Arabia, but it was a start, anyway. To my misfortune, I arrived just as the Suez Crisis occurred. But, I was hooked.'

His eyes took on a faraway look. 'I went back years later . . . set up a small practice in Cairo . . . learned a bit of Arabic,' he paused, looking at Kareem, 'and found out more than I wanted to know about the way you fellows treat your women.'

Kareem's love of his daughter proved stronger than his love of honour. To my relief, he remained quiet, his face free of all expression.

The doctor looked pleased. He seemed to be thinking that 'here is an Arab who would not spout nonsense about the need to lock females in *purdah*'.

The worry in Kareem's voice told the doctor of his love of Maha. 'Will our daughter recover? Fully recover?' he asked.

I moved to the edge of my seat. I could hear my heart pounding in my ears.

The doctor clasped both hands together, rubbing them as if he were lubricating his palms. Looking from Kareem to me, he heaped drama upon an already dramatic situation. His face remained bland as he answered, 'Will your daughter recover? *Fully* recover? I have talked to her for just an hour. Therefore, it's difficult to summarize her case completely.' Looking upon my stricken face, he added, 'But, her case seems quite typical. I've treated a good number of Arab ladies who suffered from hysterics, women who were visiting our city. Generally speaking, given time and proper care, I would say that your daughter's prognosis is favourable.'

I wept in my husband's arms.

Maha's physician left us alone in his office.

For three months I remained in London while Maha underwent psychiatric tests and treatment. Once we understood that our daughter required lengthy care, that cure could not be pronounced in a matter of days, Kareem travelled back and forth to Riyadh, making a point of being in London on Tuesdays and Thursdays, the two days of the week that we were allowed to visit our child.

During our visits, we offered Maha peace, but she preferred to fight. It was as if a thousand terrors limited her ability to speak calmly and reasonably. Nothing we could say or do pleased her. Following the physician's instructions, Kareem and I refused to argue with our child. At those moments, Maha argued with herself, even going so far as to speak in two voices! Maha's doctor reassured us that the time would come when Maha's mental state would improve beyond our expectations.

How we prayed for that moment to arrive!

The intense visits wore poorly on Kareem. I could see my husband aging before my eyes. I said to him one evening, 'If nothing else, I have learned that aging has nothing to do with accumulation of years.

Aging is the inevitable defeat of parents by their young.'

A small twinkle came into Kareem's eyes, the first sign of joy that I had seen in many days. He claimed, in all seriousness, that it could not be so. 'If that were the case, Sultana, your long-suffering father would appear the oldest living man on the planet.'

Pleased that my husband showed a glimmer of life, I let the reference pass and leaned fondly on his shoulder, relieved that our family tragedy had brought us closer together rather than pushed us further apart. At that moment I reminded myself that no person leads an irreproachable life, and I forgave my husband for the trauma I had endured in his futile quest for a second wife. Full of emotions I had assumed I'd lost for ever, I congratulated myself on the worth of the man I had wed.

In time, Kareem and I witnessed a miracle.

Maha's doctor was, as I had expected, a man of genius and perseverance, a devoted physician whose natural abilities diluted my daughter's frightful demons. In happy obscurity, while locked in the drabbest of offices in the dreariest of hospital wards, he combined his medical knowledge with rich experiences learned in the world of Arab women, and gained my daughter's trust. With this trust, the physician opened her wounds, and torrents of jealousy, hate, and anger spilled from Maha's trembling hands onto the pages of an ordinary note-pad, producing an extraordinary journal.

Weeks later, while reading one of these short but disturbing stories from her notes, given freely from

Maha's hands to her parents, Kareem and I discovered the depths into which our child had plunged in a world more sinister than either of us could have ever imagined.

LIVING IN THE MIRAGE OF SAUDI ARABIA
or
THE HAREM OF DREAMS
by
Princess Maha Al Sa'ud

During the dark period of Saudi Arabian history, ambitious desert women could only dream of harems stocked with hard muscled men, well endowed with instruments of pleasure. In the enlightened year of 2010, when the matriarchal family ascended into power, with the most intelligent woman crowned Queen, women became the political, economic, and legal authority of society.

The great wealth accumulated during the oil boom of the year 2000, the boom that had crippled the powers of the United States, Europe, and Japan to that of third world powers, assured the land of Arabia plenty for generations to come. With little but time on their hands, women addressed social issues that had plagued the land for more years than they could remember.

A small minority of women voted to abolish polygamy, the practice of taking four husbands, while the majority, remembering the evils the practice had spawned when the kingdom was a patriarchal society, recognized that while the system was not the best that they could devise, it was the only social system that embittered women would receive. The pleasures of love that had been forbidden now wormed their way into the mind of every woman, even that of the waif-like Malaak, the daughter of the Queen of Saudi Arabia.

Malaak danced a hot dance of love, challenging her favourite lover, Shadi, with a gold sovereign between her lips, motioning with her head for the man to pull it out with his teeth.

Malaak was small and brown-skinned with delicate features. Her lover was large and heavy with muscles of steel. Wanting desperately to achieve his goal of being appointed the most influential man in the harem, Shadi moved his tongue over every part of Malaak's body, enticing her senses in an agony of passion.

In a frenzy of movement, Shadi removed the coin with his teeth, and lifted Malaak into his arms, taking her behind the flimsy curtains of his assigned section of the harem. There, the lovers pressed against each other, the warmth of their breath spreading over their faces, and down their necks, to their chests. Shutting out the world, they began to kiss.

Malaak opened her eyes to watch her lover perform his rhythmic movements. Her muscles tensed when she saw that the man Shadi had softened into a woman!

Life having produced a cynical soul, Malaak adjusted herself to the power at hand, and she became enamoured of the loveliness of the woman who shared her bed. Choosing between being feared without love and being loved without fear, Malaak could not sacrifice the love.

With Machiavellian subtlety, Malaak became what she had to be in the circumstances and atmosphere of her time.

With a pale, sickly look, Kareem laid the pages of Maha's journal on the doctor's desk. Bewildered, he asked, 'What does this mean?' He gestured towards the note-pad, his tone accusatory. 'You said that Maha was much improved. This writing is nothing more than the ramblings of a lunatic.'

I know not the source of my instinct, but I knew what the doctor was going to say before he said it. I could not breathe, I could not speak, I saw the room through a haze of blue. The doctor's voice came to me from a distance.

The doctor was gentle with Kareem. 'It's quite simple, really. Your daughter is telling you that she has made the discovery that men are her enemies, and that women are her friends.'

Kareem still did not comprehend what the doctor was saying. He was impatient in his ignorance. 'Yes? So?'

There was nothing else to do but to speak bluntly. The doctor verbalized what I already knew. 'Prince Kareem. Your daughter and her friend, Aisha, are lovers.'

Kareem was quiet for many minutes. When Kareem regained his senses, he had to be restrained, and kept from Maha's side for three days.

Muslims are taught that love and sex between two of the same is wrong, and the Koran forbids

75

experimenting: 'Do not follow what you do not know.' In Saudi Arabia, love and sex are considered distasteful, even between those of the *opposite* sex, and our society pretends as if relationships based on sexual love do not exist. In this atmosphere of shame, Saudi citizens respond to social and religious expectations by *saying* exactly what is expected. What we *do* is another matter altogether.

Arabs are by nature sensuous, yet live in a puritanical society. The topic of sex is of national interest to everyone, including that of our Saudi Government which spends enormous amounts of money employing countless censors. These men sit in government offices, searching out what they deem are odious references to women and sex in every publication allowed into the kingdom. Rarely does a magazine or newspaper make it past Saudi censors without losing a number of pages, or having sentences or paragraphs blacked out by the censor's ever-ready pen.

This form of extreme censorship against all conventional social behaviour affects every aspect of our lives, and the lives of those who compete to claim our business.

When one of Asad's companies contracted with a foreign film company to make a simple food commercial for Saudi Arabian television, the list of restrictions that accompanied the contract would have been amusing had it not been authentic. The list of restrictions read:

1. There can be no attractive females in the commercial.
2. If a female is included, she cannot wear

revealing clothing such as short skirts, pants, or swimming suits. No flesh can be exposed other than the face, and hands.

3. No two people can eat from the same dish, or drink from the same cup.

4. There can be no fast body movement. (It is suggested in the contract that if a female is used, she has to sit or stand without moving at all.)

5. There can be no winking.

6. Kissing is taboo.

7. There can be no burping.

8. Unless it is absolutely necessary to sell the product (it is suggested) that there be no laughter.

When the normal is forbidden, people fall into the abnormal.

That, I believe, is what happened to my daughter.

In my country, religious law prohibits single men and women from seeing each other. While inside the country, men socialize with men and women with women. Since we are prevented from engaging in traditional behaviour, the sexual tension between those of the same sex is palpable. Any foreigner who has lived in Saudi Arabia for a length of time becomes aware that homosexual relations are rampant within the kingdom.

I have attended many all-female concerts and functions where quivering beauties and suggestive behaviour triumph over heavy veils and black *abaayas*. An orderly gathering of heavily perfumed and love-starved Saudi women festers into spontaneous exuberance, bursting forth in the form of a wild party with the singing of forbidden love accompanied by lusty dancing. I have watched as shy-faced women danced lewdly with other women, flesh to flesh, face to face. I have heard women whisper of love and plan clandestine meetings, while their drivers wait patiently in the parking lots. They will later deliver them to their husbands who are at that same evening captivated by other men.

While the conduct of men is overlooked, the behaviour of women, even with other women, is often carefully guarded. This is apparent by the various rules and regulations governing females.

Some years ago I cut out a small item from one of our Saudi Arabian newspapers to show to my sisters. I was particularly irritated by yet another foolish restriction placed upon women. A ban on cosmetics had been announced in a girls' school. Recently I ran across this clipping while throwing out some papers.

This article reads:

COSMETICS BAN IN SCHOOL

The Director of Girls Education at Al Ras, Abdullah Muhammad Al Rashid, urged all students and staff of the school under the directorate to refrain from using cosmetics, dyestuffs, ornaments and other make-ups, inside the school compounds.

The Director added that some staff and students were noticed of late to have been using transparent garments and cosmetics as well as high-heel shoes, hence, such adornments are prohibited. While the students must keep uniformity in dress, the teachers should set good examples to the students. The authorities would not hesitate to take punitive measures against violators of school regulations, Al Rashid added.

I remember well what I had said to my sisters at the time. I waved the clipping angrily under their noses, raging, 'See for yourself! The men of this country want to regulate the wearing of our shoes, the ribbons in our hair, the colour of our lips!'

My sisters, while their anger did not equal mine, had sullenly complained that our men were obsessed with controlling every aspect of our lives, even that part of our daily living which was supposedly private.

In my opinion, the control fanatics that govern our traditional lives had driven my daughter into the arms of a woman! While I was greatly distressed and did not condone my daughter's relationship with another woman, in view of the harsh restrictions against those of her sex that she had inherited by the mere fact of being born female, I understood how she had come to seek solace with one of her kind.

Knowing the problem, I now felt more capable of seeking solutions.

Kareem feared that Maha's character was now marred by her experiences. As a mother, I could not agree. I told Kareem that the fact that Maha wanted to share her darkest secret with those who love her best pointed to recovery.

I was right in my assessment of the situation.

After months of professional treatment, Maha was ready for maternal guidance. For the first time in her young life, she drew close to her mother, wanting to communicate, tearfully acknowledging that from her earliest memory, she had hated all men but her father. She had no ready explanation for it.

I felt a twinge of guilt, wondering if my own prejudices against the male sex had seeped into the embryo to which I had given life. It was as if my daughter had been forewarned of the wicked nature of men, while lying cradled in my womb.

Maha confessed that the early traumas she had endured on the occasion of her parents' long separation had further eroded her trust in men. She asked, 'What was so wrong with Father that we had to flee from his presence?'

It had been many years since I had taken my children from their summer camp in Dubai and fled to safety into the countryside of France, not wishing to share my wifely status with another woman. France, with its humane people who shelter those in distress, had seemed the perfect spot to protect my young while I negotiated during those long months with my husband over his scheme to wed another woman. How I had tried to shield my children from the trauma of my own failing marriage, and our separation from Kareem!

What folly! As a parent, I know now that it is preposterous to believe that even minor parental conflict does not impinge upon the emotional well-being of a child. Hearing Maha say that my action in leaving her father had furthered her mental pain, allowing abnormal thoughts to creep into her consciousness, caused me more anguish than any previous agony I have known.

Maha confessed that even after Kareem and I had patched over our differences and we were united with our children again, our continuing strife had pierced the cocoon in which they lived.

When I prodded my daughter on her relationship with Aisha, Maha confided that she had not known that women could love women and men could love men. Such a possibility had never entered her mind, until the day that Aisha had shown her some magazines she had taken from her father's study. The magazines revealed photograph after photograph of beautiful women, in acts of female love. At first the photographs were a novelty, but later Maha came to see them as beautiful, sensing that the love between women was more tender and caring than the aggressive, possessive love of man to woman.

There were other disturbing revelations.

Aisha, a girl who had experimented with many social taboos before knowing my daughter, thought nothing of spying on her father's sexual misdeeds. The girl had made a small peephole in the study adjoining her father's bedroom. There, my daughter and her friend had watched as Aisha's father deflowered one young virgin after another. Maha claimed that the cries of those young girls had closed her mind to wanting a relationship with a man.

She told me an unbelievable tale that I would brush aside as fabrication, had my own daughter not witnessed the event.

Maha said that on one particular Thursday evening, Aisha had telephoned her, urging her to come over quickly. Maha said that Kareem and I were out so she had one of our drivers deliver her to Aisha's home.

Aisha's father had gathered together seven young

girls in his home. Maha did not know if he had wed the girls, or if they were concubines.

My daughter watched as those young girls were made to prance naked around the room, each with a large peacock feather stuck up her backside. With these feathers, the girls were forced to fan and tickle the face of Aisha's father. Over the course of a long night, the father had had sex with five of the seven girls.

Afterwards, Maha and Aisha had stolen a feather and had played together on Aisha's bed, giggling and tickling each other's bodies. It was then that Aisha showed Maha the pleasure that women could have with one another.

Ashamed of her love for Aisha, Maha cried in my arms, sobbing that she wanted to be a happy, well-adjusted girl with a productive life. She cried out, 'Why am I different from Amani? We came from the same seed, but we have blossomed into different plants!' She screamed, 'Amani is a beautiful rose! I am a prickly cactus.'

Not knowing the ways of God, I could not answer my child. I held her in my arms and comforted her with the thought that the remainder of her life would be that of a beautiful flower.

Then my troubled daughter asked me the most difficult question of my life. 'Mother, how can I ever love a man, knowing all that I know of their nature?'

I had no ready answer, yet it was with profound happiness that I understood that Kareem and I had another chance with our daughter.

It was time to go home to Riyadh.

We did not leave before Kareem offered Maha's

British physician a position in Riyadh as our family's personal doctor.

Much to our amazement, the physician refused. 'Thank you,' he said. 'I am honoured. Fortunately, or unfortunately, whatever is the case, my aesthetic sensibilities are too keen for Saudi Arabia.'

Undaunted, Kareem insisted upon rewarding the man with a large sum of cash. He even went so far as to try to put the money into the man's hand.

Maha's doctor firmly waved aside the offer, uttering words that had they not been spoken softly would have been a keen insult. 'My dear man, please, do not. The shallowness of wealth and power holds no appeal for me.'

While staring in awe at one of the least prepossessing figures I have ever beheld, I suddenly had the answer to Maha's earlier, unanswerable question! Later, I told Maha that she would one day meet a man deserving of her faithful love, for such men existed. She and I had met one in London.

Once back in Riyadh, the source of Maha's knowledge of black magic was revealed. It was as I had thought. Noorah was the culprit.

Maha told her father, in my presence, that it was her grandmother who had introduced her to the dark world of the occult. When we confronted her with Abdullah's clothing wrapped around a charm, Maha denied wanting to cast a spell on her brother.

Hoping that Maha had learned a great lesson, we did not press the issue.

I wanted nothing more than to confront my mother-in-law, spit in her face, and yank out her hair.

Kareem, wisely recognizing the dangers of pent-up anger, refused to let me accompany him when he went to confront her about her misdeeds. Nevertheless, I did coax my unenthusiastic sister, Sara, into paying a visit to our mutual mother-in-law's palace at the time of Kareem's visit.

Sara arrived at Noorah's villa shortly after my husband and waited in the garden until Kareem left. Sara said that she overheard Kareem's shouts and Noorah's pleas of mercy, for Kareem forbade his mother to visit his children unsupervised.

Long after my husband had left his mother, Sara said that Noorah's moans of despair could be heard in the garden. 'Kareem, most beloved, you came from my womb! Come back to your mother, who cannot live without your precious love.'

Sara accused me of being as wicked as Noorah, for I radiated much happiness when she told me of my treacherous mother-in-law's deserved wretchedness.

Chapter Four

MAKKAH

God, Great and Glorious is He, said: 'And proclaim among men the pilgrimage, they will come to you on foot and on every lean camel, coming from every deep ravine.'
Al-Haj, 22:27

There is no means of calculating the number of pious Muslims who have perished while making the gruelling journey across the deserts of Saudi Arabia since the time of Prophet Mohammed and the first pilgrimage, but the total of dead is estimated to be in the thousands. While I am pleased to report that it is no longer necessary for devout Muslims to do battle with raiding bedouin parties, or even to travel through Saudi Arabia on foot or on lean camels, in order to fulfil their fervent desire to perform one of the basic tenets of Islam, still, the annual pilgrimage to the holy city of Makkah remains a chaotic affair. Each year, hundreds of thousands of pilgrims converge on the cities, airports, and highways of Saudi Arabia for the rite of pilgrimage during the time of *Haj*. (*Haj* begins in Dhu al-Qida, the 11th month of the hegira calandar, and ends during Dhu al-Hijah, the 12th month of the hegira calendar.)

I performed the traditional pilgrimage many times in my youth, as a laughing child in my mother's arms, and later as a rebellious girl seeking communication with my God, whom I prayed would administer peace of mind to an unhappy child.

To my great dissatisfaction, since the moment Kareem and I wed, I had not worshipped in Makkah during the official time of *Haj*.

While Kareem and I, along with our children, have made the *Umrah*, or the lesser pilgrimage, which can be made any time of the year, never had we joined the multitudes in the massive annual celebration of *Haj*, a time that Muslims remind themselves of the lessons of sacrifice, obedience, mercy and faith, models of conduct that are required in the Islamic faith.

Many times over the years, I pointed out to my husband that our children should experience the moving occasion of the pilgrimage during the designated time of *Haj*. Much to my chagrin, Kareem was forever adamant that our family flee the pandemonium of Saudi Arabia during the annual pilgrimage, which brings the largest, and most concentrated gathering of human beings on earth into our country.

Each time I requested of Kareem the justification for his nonperformance of *Haj*, my husband would provide me with a multitude of lame explanations laden with contradiction.

Bewildered at his attitude and determined to get to the heart of the matter, I once purposely entangled Kareem in the discrepancy of his excuses, trapping him on the issue. Kareem was groping for a way out of his dilemma, when I plainly told my husband, a man who believes in the God of Mohammed, that it seemed to me that he abhorred the ritual that brings such joy to all Muslims. There was no other explanation for his bizarre behaviour.

I crossed my arms across my chest and waited for his response to an insulting charge that demanded clarification.

Kareem's face swelled with revulsion at the accusation so vile to a Muslim! Shocked at such a scandalous idea, Kareem swore to me that he did not abhor the pilgrimage!

In the manner in which all men respond when they are in the wrong, Kareem then yelled out that 'I was ugly to his eyes', and he turned his back to me in an angry effort to leave the room, but I ran around his side and with outstretched arms blocked the door with my body, demanding he be more specific.

I screamed out that I was displeased with what I had heard, and that I would wait for ever for a compelling explanation for his addiction to annual *Haj* flight from the kingdom. Sensing that Kareem was in a position of weakness, I became reckless and added a small lie, saying that, 'Others have noticed your strange distaste for *Haj*, and people are beginning to talk.'

When Kareem saw that I would not remove myself without physical force, he stared down at me and hesitated for a long moment. I could see that Kareem was examining and weighing the wisdom of his reply. Making a decision, he pulled me by the arm and forced me down on the side of the bed by pushing my shoulders with his hands. He paced for a short time to the balcony doors and back, and then his defences fell.

Kareem confessed in a rush that as a young man he had once suffered a realistic and terrifying nightmare that he was crushed to death in a crowd of Hajiis (people of the Muslim faith who attend *Haj*).

I made a sound in my throat. Many baffling episodes regarding my husband's odd behaviour were now clear in my mind. Since the time I had first met him, Kareem had seen crowds where there were none, interpreting the smallest groups of people as a mass of humanity. I shook my head in confoundment, at the perplexing intimacies of my husband's inner life that I had never known. So! Kareem was frightened of the masses of pilgrims!

Being a strong believer in the powerful message of dreams, I turned my attention once more to Kareem's words, my mood grim as I listened to his vivid description of the imaginary yet frightening experience that he had endured while sleeping.

My husband's face became pale as he described the graphic illusion of being asphyxiated under the trampling feet of frenzied worshippers. He told me that since the time of his dream, when he was twenty-three, that he had purposely avoided the congested conditions endured by the faithful in making the annual pilgrimage to Makkah.

Kareem so intensely felt that his nightmare would be fulfilled if he attended *Haj*, that I had little heart to haggle with a man and his visionary forebodings.

Once again, everything was as before, as our

family continued to depart the kingdom during the time of *Haj*.

When the very real and ghastly tragedy of the 1990 *Haj* occurred, as over 1,500 pilgrims were crushed to death in a mountain tunnel in Makkah, Kareem took to his bed in Paris and trembled for a whole day, declaring that the cataclysmic disaster was yet another extraordinary omen from God that he should never again worship at the Holy Mosque!

After the fateful accident of 1990, when hundreds of worshippers died, Kareem's extreme reaction to a dream began to annoy me, and I told my husband that his fears were inherently unsound. Nothing I could say or do at the time comforted my husband, even when I pointed out the obvious, that his dream had been realized in the death of others. In my opinion, the exact catastrophe was unlikely to occur again.

I saw that my observation failed to quieten Kareem's fierce apprehension when he replied that, evidently, he would be crushed as a singular tragedy if he failed to heed his dream, or the recent mishap, which to his mind was nothing less than a direct warning from God.

Since it is true that a number of Hajiis are trampled or crushed to death every *Haj* season, I could not reason further with Kareem. I wanted to dismiss Kareem's obsession with his nightmare, to ignore his terrors, but I could not. I struggled successfully to indulge his fears.

Sadly, I pushed the possibility of ever again making the happy journey of *Haj* far into the back of my mind, but not from my heart.

After our triumphant return from London, with a loving Maha in our arms, I felt an irresistible desire to embrace the ritual of glorifying God in unison with other Muslims. The time of *Haj* was upon us, and I gently approached the topic with my husband once again, suggesting that I take our children to Makkah. Since women of our country rarely travel without the protection of a male escort, I wondered aloud about the possibility of accompanying my sister, Sara, and her family to Makkah.

Much to my surprise, Kareem responded favourably to my ardent wish to undertake a journey to the city of Mohammed. My mouth fell open when he said that he would consider taking the journey to *Haj*. Kareem acknowledged that his change in attitude was in spite of his continued fear of personal harm, but that he, too, shared my need to give special thanks to God for the return of our precious Maha.

We were discussing the forthcoming trip with members of Kareem's family when we received a warning from Kareem's brother-in-law, Mohammed, who was married to Kareem's youngest sister, Hanan. Mohammed said that over two million pilgrims were expected to unite in our holiest city of Makkah, and of that total, 150,000 worrisome worshippers were expected from Iran, the Shiite country that makes an annual call to revoke King Fahd's exclusive custodianship over Islam's holiest places.

In 1987, the inflamed Shiites had gone so far as to lead a violent protest during the traditional holy event, and in the process of breaching Saudi laws, had desecrated the Holy Mosque, causing the deaths of 402 pilgrims. Two years later, in 1989, Tehran had instigated two deadly bombings, killing one and wounding sixteen others.

In Mohammed's view, *Haj* was becoming a dangerous religious ceremony for peaceful Muslims. Radical Muslims were on the move the world over, and they favoured the holiest of Islamic sanctuaries to make known their political grievances.

Mohammed, a prince of high authority in Public Security, a Saudi public service organization that strives to ensure the security of the Saudis and visiting Muslims to our country, was privy to knowledge that most Saudis do not have. Blind to my emotion, and absorbed only in our personal safety, Mohammed suggested that Kareem and I wait until the masses of pilgrims left the kingdom. Then, we could take our children and perform the sacred rites.

Kareem had a pale face and said little, and I knew that my husband was not in the slightest concerned over Iranian danger but was considering the dreaded effects of four million tramping feet.

Stubborn and determined to fulfil my personal desires, as is my way, I challenged Mohammed's warning, saying that, in my opinion, as a result of the Iranians' past capers, those pilgrims travelling from Iran would be so carefully screened and observed by Saudi Security, that they would be of little danger to *Haj* worshippers.

Mohammed, with a stern, and uneasy look on his face, said, 'No. The Iranians can *never* be trusted. Do not let yourself forget, Sultana, that we are dealing with Shiite fanatics who dream of overthrowing our Al Sa'ud-led Sunni Government!'

Seeing that my reasoning was not going to achieve the reassuring response that I was seeking,

I used a female tactic, mischievously asking Mohammed and my husband if they failed to remember that, according to Islamic teachings, to die while in Makkah ensures immediate ascension to heaven?

My husband and brother-in-law failed to see any humour in the current situation, and my religious argument made little impact with Kareem, but obviously, he too felt the wonderful release of anxiety regarding Maha's miraculous revival even more than I had imagined.

Kareem took a deep breath, gave a weak smile, and said, 'Sultana, I will face a thousand dangers if it will give you peace of mind. Together, we will take our children and go on the pilgrimage.'

Mohammed hid a disappointed face with a smile, and I gave my husband an unexpected kiss on the cheek, and began to pull on his earlobes, promising him that he would never regret his decision.

Mohammed looked scandalized at my affectionate display, and made some small excuse to leave the room. Kareem's younger sister, Hanan, who had been married for some years to Mohammed, gave us a knowing smile and said that we should ignore her husband's prudish façade, that Mohammed was the most loving, affectionate, and attentive of men behind closed doors.

I laughed aloud, wondering about their secret life of sweet sex, for Mohammed had always seemed strict and stand-offish, and in the past I had pitied my sister-in-law.

I looked at my husband and saw that his face had reddened at the idea of his sister's marriage bed. I thought to myself that our Saudi men are too uptight, and unbearably puritanical when it comes to married passion, even their own.

Remembering that we were soon going to Makkah, I kissed my husband again! I was elated!

Kareem and I invited Sara, Asad, and their growing brood to accompany our family on our long-awaited religious odyssey. Sara never failed to do *Haj* and was immensely pleased that our family was not going to travel abroad on our usual lengthy European holiday during the religious occasion.

We made excited plans to depart Riyadh for Makkah in two days' time.

Finally, it was the day of our trip to Makkah. There was much to be accomplished! Our plan was to meet Sara and her family at the airport in Riyadh at seven o'clock in the evening. Prior to that time, each member of the family had to enter *Ihram*, which is marked by an all-consuming intention of the heart to fulfil all the rites of pilgrimage.

During the time of *Ihram*, nothing involving normal life is acceptable. Hair cannot be cut, nails cannot be trimmed, beards cannot be shaved, perfumes cannot be worn, garments with seams cannot be worn, animals cannot be killed, sexual relations must be postponed, and direct contact between men and women avoided, until the sacred time of *Ihram* has ended.

Each member of our family started their rituals for the pilgrimage before leaving Riyadh. It was important for each person to enter into a state of purity even before the long awaited journey began.

Startling my Filipino maid, Cora, who was dusting in my bedroom, I entered my private quarters while chanting the famous cry uttered by all pilgrims as they perform the rites while in the holy city of Makkah, 'Here I am, God! Here I am! Here I am to do your bidding.'

After Cora recovered herself, I, in a happy frame of mind, explained the significance of our upcoming religious journey.

Cora, a dedicated Catholic, had little understanding of Muslim traditions, but as a girl of deep religious convictions, she did appreciate my delight at going on a pilgrimage.

I continued to chant my cry to God as a smiling Cora filled my bath.

I counted off on my fingers all the tasks I had to accomplish. My face had to be cleansed of all make-up, and I had to take off my jewellery, even the 10 carat flawless diamond earrings given to me by my husband the year before, pieces of jewellery that I rarely removed from my pierced ears.

After removing my earrings and placing them in the large bedroom safe that holds my collection of precious jewels, I submerged myself for hours in a hot tub, to cleanse myself symbolically of any impurities. While soaking, I prepared myself for the journey by repeating aloud God's command to Muslims to visit Makkah, 'And proclaim among men the pilgrimage, they will come to you on foot and on every lean camel, coming from every deep ravine.'

I put aside any and every thought of my family and myself, and concentrated instead on things of peace and feelings of love for my fellow man.

After my long bath, I wrapped myself in a seamless black garment and covered my hair with a lightweight black scarf. Facing the holy city of Makkah, I prostrated myself on the bedroom floor, and performed my prayers, appealing to God to accept the rites of *Haj* from me.

Finally, I was prepared for my journey.

I met my husband and children in the sitting-room downstairs. Kareem and Abdullah were immaculate in white seamless robes and plain sandals. Maha and Amani were dressed in modest, dark coloured garments that covered all flesh except their faces, feet and hands. They, as I, were not veiled. It is not necessary to cover female faces while doing *Haj*. 'The true veil is in the eyes of men,' runs a saying of the Prophet. Thus, women on pilgrimage are forbidden to cover their faces while on *Haj*.

As a child, I often queried my mother on the strange necessity of covering her face before man but not before God. My mother, reared never to question the authority of men, appeared baffled and confused at the sane logic put forth by her enquiring daughter, but having spent a lifetime under the rigid jurisdiction of men, hushed her child and made no answer to what I believe is still a justifiable question.

Now, looking at my daughters' faces in all their innocence, the memory came flowing into my mind.

I hugged each of my daughters, and said in an irritated tone, 'When man comes to share God's wisdom, you can discard the veils that you so hate!' I could not help but toss a glance of contempt at my husband and son.

Kareem moaned, 'Sultana,' admonishing me for what I had done.

I was struck with the horrible thought that I had

broken my *Haj* vow! I had lapsed into a moment of discord, thinking of wordly concerns, when I must rejoice in topics of peace and love.

Embarrassed by my indiscretion, I left the room in a rush, explaining that I must perform my rituals once again.

Kareem was smiling, and the children began to laugh, as they seated themselves on the chairs and sofas, patiently waiting for my return.

I prostrated myself on the bedroom floor, asking God to quieten my tongue and assist me in entering *Ihram* once again.

While I was praying, sad thoughts of my mother once again crept into my mind, and angry images of my father played across my eyes, ending the tranquillity so necessary in entering *Ihram*. With a frowning face, I had to begin my prayers again, from the very beginning.

I was on the verge of tears when I rejoined my family, and my husband gave me a tender look of love which I mistook for a sexual thought. I shouted at Kareem, and then burst into tears, declaring that I could not go to *Haj*, that my family would have to leave without me, for I could not calm my active and spiteful mind in order to enter the state of *Ihram*!

Kareem gave a nod to my daughers, for our flesh was forbidden contact, and Maha and Amani laughingly pushed me from the room into the waiting car. We were going to the airport.

Kareem calmed my protests by saying that I could go through my rituals once again on the aeroplane, or at our home in Jeddah before we made the short drive the following morning to Makkah.

*   *   *

Asad, Sara and their children were waiting for us in the royal waiting lounge at the King Khalid International Airport, which is a forty-five-minute drive out of the city of Riyadh.

I greeted my sister and her family with strained silence, and after Maha whispered in my sister's ear, Sara gave a knowing smile that told me she understood our delay.

Our family travelled by air in one of Kareem's private Lear jets to Jeddah. It was a quiet journey, with adults thinking of God, and their planned communication with him. The older children played quiet games, while the younger ones slept or looked through some books.

Respectful of my inability to control my tongue, I spoke not a word until moments before we landed, and then I spoke too much.

It was night when we arrived at the King Abdul Aziz International Airport at Jeddah, and I was pleased when Kareem instructed the American pilot to take us through the *Haj*, or Pilgrim's Terminal, which is a surrealistic tent city that covers 370 acres of land. The Pilgrim's Terminal is for incoming pilgrims from other lands, but our royal status made it possible for us to land wherever we might wish.

A few years before, Kareem had taken Abdullah to the grand opening of the terminal, but neither of my daughters had yet been inside the spectacular building.

Forgetting my earlier vow to remain silent until my feet touched the streets of Makkah, I felt an unexplained urge for my daughters to discover a sense of pride in their heritage, even if that pride were linked implicitly with economic wealth.

Initially, I spoke in a quiet voice that I knew would not be offensive to God. I explained to my daughters that the terminal had won an international award as a unique design and as an advanced engineering innovation. I felt a surge of pride in the infrastructure that Saudi Arabians had accomplished in one short generation. No longer feeling the shame of my ancestors' wrenching poverty, which had haunted me in my younger days, the old passions left me, and my sense of the past was sharpened. What had once seemed bleak and shameful was now lovely and of great value. I thought to myself: from a forbidding land where scarcely fifty years ago, warring tribes had fought over camels and goats, we Saudis have become an economic force. My own family had guided lawless tribesmen from a stark desert land into one of the wealthiest peoples and nations on earth.

While Western minds have always claimed that only the oil paved our way into prosperity, I paid that analysis little heed, for oil had been discovered in other lands, and the ordinary citizens of those countries had never enjoyed the substantial lifestyle experienced by all Saudis. The secret lay in the wisdom of the men who guided the proceeds from our resources. While I have always found much fault with the men of my family, particularly regarding their stance on women's issues, on this one subject I recognized and commended their clever and insightful leadership.

Thinking the opportunity was ripe to instil ancestral pride into those that I had given life, I became enthusiastic and began to talk loudly, reminding the children of past events and the virtues of the ones who came before us: the courage, endurance, self-reliance, and intelligence of our bedouin ancestors. Recalling the impoverished life lived by my parents, and then the extravagant life enjoyed by their children and grandchildren, a reversal which was nothing short of miraculous, I became animated, telling family tales with dramatic intensity, and convincing realism.

Thinking myself quite the storyteller, remembering happy moments spent at the feet of my own mother and older aunties, I was immersed in the drama of the founding of our country, when suddenly, I realized that I had no audience.

Sara, Asad and Kareem shared pained looks, but as I had quite forgotten the purpose of our journey, their expressions of disbelief at my conduct made no impact on my mind.

I glanced at our young ones, and I was keenly disappointed when I looked into the faces of our disinterested young, so absorbed in present activities. I knew at that moment that poverty not endured does not affect the privileged, and that the younger Al Sa'ud generation had fallen under the enfeebling influence of great wealth.

Plainly, the children were bored at the thought of the bedouin seed from which they had sprung.

Abdullah was playing a game of backgammon with Sara's oldest son, while the smallest children were cavorting with some small cars and trucks that Asad had brought back from his last trip to London.

Recalling the face of my loving mother and her

poignant stories of the wonderful grandparents that I had never known, my palms itched with the desire to slap the unresponsive faces of the descendants of those tender souls that had been dead for so very long. I looked around for someone to pounce upon, and just as I reached over to pinch the skin on Abdullah's arm, my eyes met Sara's, and she mouthed the word, *Ihram*.

Once again, I had failed to remember where I was going! Thinking, too late, I will perform my rituals once again when I reach my home in Jeddah, my thoughts strayed back to where they had come, and tears came without warning at the thought of the hardy and brave ancestors that we would see no more. Sara gave me a gentle smile of forgiveness, and I knew that my dearest sister knew my thoughts and forgave me my transgression.

Struck by the memory of an apt proverb, 'Only our own eyes will cry for us,' I was saddened at my family's ability to discard the memory of those who had come before us. I cried out in a forceful voice, 'Those that seem dead to you are alive to me!'

My family looked at me in astonishment, except for Kareem, who failed to control a fit of laughter. I glared at him as he wiped his wet eyes with a tissue and mumbled something to Asad that I tried to hear but could not, regarding the woman that he had wed.

To calm my emotions I turned my attention to my two daughters, and saw that they, at least, had heard something of what I had spoken.

Maha, preferring Europe and America over anything Saudi Arabian, was of little comfort. She had ignored my boastful commentary on our family history, and began to complain bitterly about the terminal, disbelieving that the designers had designed an airport terminal as a tent!

'Why dig up the past?' she muttered, with a tinge of dismay in her voice. 'It *is* the twentieth century, you know.'

Amani, though, was entranced by the spotlights which were mounted on the support pylons. They gave an amazing view of the striking engineering wonder, and she gave a squeal of delight.

Showing off his earlier knowledge of the terminal, Abdullah glanced at his youngest sister and casually remarked that, at the present time, the fabric roof of the tent covers the world's largest space, although there were plans in motion to cover a larger space in the city of Madinah.

Amani, my most sensitive child, squeezed my hand and smiled sweetly, saying, 'Mummy, thanks for bringing us here.'

I gave my daughter a happy look. All was not lost!

Who could have known that a journey made with virtuous thought and the desire to praise God for the return of my eldest daughter's lucidity would have significance for my youngest child, Amani, and enduringly disastrous consequences for her mother and father?

Chapter Five

AMANI

Makkah, 'the blessed', known as Umm al Qurrah, 'Mother of Cities', is the spot towards which every believer faces five times a day in prayer. For millions of Muslims, it is the goal of a lifetime to travel to Makkah for Haj. The city is strictly banned to non-Muslims, but non-believers feel the keen disappointment of what they are missing and want to know what lies within. As a Saudi, I have been personally selected by God to protect the true faith that got its start in the holiest city in the world that is located in my country.

The explanation given to the author by an elderly Saudi bedouin of why Saudi Arabians are the chosen people of God.

On the joyous occasion of Amani's birth, my sister Sara joined me in the pangs of delivery, giving birth to her second child, a daughter that she and her husband, Asad, gave the name Nashwa, meaning ecstasy. While Amani has brought bliss into our lives, Nashwa is a loud and obnoxious girl, and has often introduced havoc into Sara and Asad's happy home.

Many times I have secretly questioned Kareem on the fearful possibility that Amani was the true child of Sara and Asad, while Nashwa was of our blood, for Nashwa's character is remarkably similar to mine. Amani, though, bears a startling resemblance to her Auntie Sara, whom she doubles in lovely countenance and calm spirit.

Could the staff at the hospital have accidentally mistaken our two daughters? Our children were born eleven hours apart, but Sara and I occupied adjoining royal suites. Infant confusion seemed likely to my mind. Many times over the years, Kareem has attempted to push away my fears, quoting meaningless statistics showing that such mix-ups rarely occur, but each time that I gaze on my perfect child, I dread the thought that she belongs to another.

Amani, an absorbed and melancholy spirit, treasured books more than toys, and from an early age was an enthusiastic student of art and language. Unlike her elder sister Maha, Amani for the most part created little turbulence and instead generated tranquillity and affection in our home.

While Amani's sensitive soul had penetrated more deeply into my heart than that of her two older siblings, I nevertheless should have been alerted to the shadowed tenacity in Amani's complex temperament. My daughter's alarming attraction to animals caused open conflict with other members of our family. Her youthful devotion to all living creatures clashed with the Saudi male requisite to hunt and kill to extinction every creature which inhabits our land.

While Abdullah and his father gleefully joined other royal cousins in desert hunts, machine-gunning gazelles and rabbits by the light of huge spotlights mounted on specially equipped jeeps and open trucks, Amani crept into her father's hunting room, hiding ammunition, sucessfully dismantling weapons, and tossing expensive firearms into the garbage. Because of Amani's intense love of animals, she was willing to relinquish her strong desire for family harmony.

This humane but troubling trait showed up at an early age. Owing to Amani's fervour, our home was overrun with stray beasts of many species, sizes and colours.

Most Arabs, unlike many Westerners, feel little devotion for animals, and starving and injured cats and dogs run wild on our city streets. Since the early 1980s there has been an active government policy in Saudi Arabia of collecting strays and abandoning these creatures in the vast empty quarter of the desert to die slow and painful deaths. Yet many animals do outwit their slayers and manage to find a safe haven with those of a tender nature.

While I appreciated and sympathized with Amani's pressing compulsion to protect abused animals, Kareem and others in our home were greatly distressed that our property was becoming a sanctuary for strays. Not content with the mere act of saving their lives, Amani pampered these abandoned creatures as if they were rare and expensive breeds, and when they died, the animals were buried after having solemn funerals in our garden. The surviving strays that she had trained to be lap pets joined our family on our grounds and in our home.

Many times it seemed to me that Amani cared

more for animals than she did for members of her own family, but I am a mother that has difficulty in penalizing or restraining her young, and Amani was allowed her one unfortunate idiosyncracy.

Kareem employed two young men from Thailand to clean and disinfect after the animals and to train the dogs in obedience lessons. We even took the extreme action of building our own small zoo on the grounds, equipping the facility with spacious caged areas and purchased numerous breeds of exotic animals in the hope that Amani's personal zoo would satisfy her need to collect and coddle large numbers of animals. Next to the zoo area, Kareem had a sizeable area walled off for Amani's strays. He commanded his daughter to restrict those animals to that special section of the yard. After Amani shed many tears, Kareem reluctantly agreed that our daughter could select her ten favourite cats and dogs that would be allowed inside our home and free access to the general grounds area.

In spite of these efforts, our daughter remained alert to street strays, and these creatures invariably found their way to our door.

Once Kareem came home to a strange sight. Three Filipino men who worked for our neighbours were caught in the act of delivering five cats in a bag to one of the Thai zoo-keepers. Confronting the Filipinos, who were frightened into silence, Kareem was handed a poster that stated our household would reward the bearer 100 *riyals*[1] for each stray cat or puppy. Kareem flew into a fit of wild anger. After threatening the Thai employees with the sack,

[1]About £17.

they confessed to Kareem that Amani had instructed them to attach the reward posters to the walls of neighbouring palaces and villas. In addition, the two men had been told to roam the local streets, abducting cats and dogs, and to bring them to Amani. Our daughter had sworn the two men to secrecy, and since Kareem had employed them to work directly for our daughter, they had kept her confidence.

Kareem forced a head count of strays, and when he discovered that he was feeding over forty cats, and twelve dogs, he slumped to the ground in a daze. After a long period, without a glance directed at his family, my husband got to his feet and not speaking a word, left our home. We heard the wheels of his car spin as he left the neighbourhood. He was away for two days and three nights. I later learned that Kareem had been visiting his parents during this time. I heard from gossipy servants that Kareem had told his startled parents that he must have a few days' respite from the complex women in his life, or he would be forced to commit us all to an institution.

While Kareem was away, I decided that I must find some manner of dulling my daughter's extreme sensitivity to animals. I made many strange discoveries that had gone undetected. The forty cats were dining on fresh fish from the Red Sea, while the twelve dogs were treated to gourmet meats from an expensive Australian-supplied meat shop. Amani had been appropriating money from the weekly funds that are deposited in a small cash box in the kitchen, money that our servants used for our personal shopping. Our household expenses are so enormous that our bookkeeper had failed to notice the sum taken by our daughter to be used for her animals. When I discovered that Amani was using large amounts of money to purchase caged birds, in order to free them, I seriously threatened my child with visits to a psychiatrist, and for a while she became less involved with the animal kingdom.

I distinctly recall one dramatic occasion that involved my brother, Ali. In the past, Ali had made a point of complaining about Amani's pets. He would grumble to me that no self-respecting Muslim could enter my home for fear that the animals roaming at will would create a need for purification. Ali's unmistakable dislike of animals evidently made an impression on the psyche of Amani's greatly loved creatures, since the dogs generally made themselves scarce and hid behind bushes until my brother passed through the garden.

There was one particular incident that stands out in my mind. Ali dropped by our palace for a brief visit and had just entered the garden gate, when he stopped to order one of our servants to wash his car while he was visiting our home. While Ali was speaking, one of Amani's favourite dogs, Napoleon, chose to lift his leg on Ali's freshly laundered *thobe*. Ali, a vain man who is proud of his handsome and impeccable appearance, became speechless with rage. He kicked the poor creature brutally before Amani could rush to Napoleon's rescue. My daughter was so infuriated that she flung herself on her uncle, beating him on his arms and chest with her fists.

Urinated upon by a dog and physically asssaulted by his niece, Ali lost no time in leaving our home, shrieking to the smirking servants that not only was his sister completely mad, but that she had given birth to demented children who preferred beasts to humans for companionship!

From that moment, Amani hated her Uncle Ali with the same intensity that I had hated my unfeeling brother as a young girl.

In the Muslim faith, a dog is considered impure, and that fact was a factor in Ali's extreme anger and disgust. In the Islamic faith, if a dog drinks out of any container, it should be washed seven times, the first of which should be water mixed with dust.

Ali is my only brother, and in spite of our continued explosive differences, he chooses to maintain a relationship with my family. Kareem forced Amani to telephone and apologize to her uncle, but the episode with Napoleon kept Ali away from our home for over two months. When he finally recovered from his anger and embarrassment, Ali returned for a visit, calling ahead to insist that our servants shut away Napoleon.

I was apprehensive about Amani's anger, which I knew was thinly veiled, and was pleased with my daughter when she entered the sitting-room on the day of Ali's visit, playing hostess and offering her uncle a glass of freshly squeezed grapefruit juice.

With an expression of relief over the forgotten incident, Ali said that he happened to be quite thirsty.

Noting the similarities between Sara and Amani, I beamed with motherly pride when my beautiful child graciously handed Ali a glass of juice and a plate of almond cookies. Her demeanour was above reproach. I gave her a happy smile, thinking to buy her a special present the next time that I went shopping.

Ali smiled his approval and commented that Amani would, one day, make some lucky man very happy.

It was only after Ali left that I discovered Amani in her bedroom, laughing so loudly that the servants came from all around to learn the cause of her merriment.

Amani told an amazed audience that her uncle had drunk his juice out of a glass that had been licked clean by her entourage of stray pets. My daughter had filled the glass with cool water for her beasts prior to pouring juice for her uncle! Not only that, but she had given the recovered Napoleon a few licks on the cookies before serving them to Ali!

The servants grinned with satisfaction, for Ali is not a popular man with them.

While I tried to appear stern at Amani's unconscionable act, my lips paid no heed, and my face trembled as I struggled to control a laugh. Giving up the charade of parental guidance, I held my daughter in my arms and roared with uncontrollable laughter.

For the first time in her life, Amani exhibited traits that led me to hope that she was a child born of my body instead of my sister, Sara's.

I know now that I should have scolded my child for a deed that would have caused Ali a heart attack had he known the truth, but I could barely control my glee, and when I laughingly confided the story to Kareem, he had such a look of sheer horror at my amusement, that I knew that my husband feared for the sanity of those he loved.

Kareem's patience snapped at my revelation. Seething with Muslim anger at the prank and disturbed by Amani's preoccupation with animals, which he insisted was ruining our lives, Kareem demanded that we sit down with our daughter and have a frank discussion.

Before I could respond, my husband spoke into the house intercom and instructed Amani to come into our living quarters, immediately.

Together, Kareem and I waited for Amani in the sitting area that is attached to our master bedroom.

Amani's black eyes sparkled with interest as she swept with sprightly grace into the room.

Before I could diffuse the situation, Kareem bluntly asked, 'Amani, what is your object in life?'

Amani, with childlike serenity, replied without hesitation, 'To save all the animals from man.'

'Saving animals is nothing more than a pampered passion of rich Europeans and Americans,' Kareem angrily responded. He looked at me as if I were to blame and said, 'Sultana, I thought that your child would be more intelligent.'

Tears began to well in Amani's eyes, and she asked to leave the room.

Uncomfortable with female tears, my husband thought better of his sarcastic tactics. Kareem tempered his opinion, and spoke with perfect seriousness. 'And, Amani, after you save all the animals, of what consequence will you be to yourself, or to your family?'

Amani squeezed her lips together and looked off into space. Without responding, she gradually came back into our world. Unable to formulate her thoughts, she looked at her father and shrugged her shoulders.

Remaining wisely uncritical of her great love of animals, Kareem clarified the need for greater purpose in human life, to create and inspire those of our own kind. He reminded Amani that she could perform good deeds for four-legged beasts while still influencing civilization. He added, 'Advancing civilization is the responsibility of the minorities in a society, for only out of discontent with imperfection does mankind seek to better the society in which he lives.'

Amani scoffed at his message. She raised her voice and asked her father the obvious question, 'In Saudi Arabia? What can a female do that will make a difference in *this* country?'

My daughter looked at me and waited for my expected agreement.

Just as I was about to argue with Kareem, he interrupted me, and to my astonishment, Kareem pointed me out to our daughter, and said that I, as an unheard minority in Saudi Arabia, had not reconciled myself to the life of a royal idler, but that I had become educated and was utilizing my knowledge to further women's causes. He continued by saying that one day women's roles would develop, and our influence would be felt outside the home.

Dumbfounded at Kareem's words, I could add little to the conversation. Never had my husband acknowledged the righteousness of my vision of freedom for women.

After a discussion of more than an hour, Amani promised her father that she would look beyond her furry friends and find a second, equally challenging purpose in her life.

As affectionate a child that has ever lived, Amani kissed each of us goodnight, and said that she had much thinking to do. As she was closing our bedroom door, she turned back and, giving us a wonderful smile, said, 'I love you Dada, and Mummy, you too,' bringing back to mind the innocent girl that our youngest daughter still was.

Thrilled at what he declared a huge success, Kareem held me in his arms and spoke of his dreams for his daughters, as well as his son, saying that if it were up to him, 'All the ridiculous restrictions placed upon the heads of women would disappear, just like magic.' Kareem snapped his fingers in the air and gave me a tender look.

A thought cynically brushed my mind that there is nothing like a beloved daughter to induce a man to clamour for adjustments in an unfair world.

Longing for unaccustomed peace in a household of three lively children, I welcomed the idea of the peaceful family life that Kareem promised would come, now that Amani would surely get over her affair with the world of animals.

Shortly afterwards, the Gulf War occurred, followed by the culmination of Maha's mental instability. During this stressful period, a stymied and solitary Amani had no-one to help her search for a more fitting, fresh objective to life.

Now, retracing Amani's pattern of obsession with causes that held her interest, I, a woman schooled in philosophy, which is the critical study of fundamental beliefs, should have recognized that my youngest child possessed the traits often connected with those we deem fanatics, frightening people who eagerly embrace extremist convictions.

Perceiving the resolute earnestness of my daughter, I now reproach myself for initiating an impressionable and mentally disoriented child to that most religious occasion, *Haj*, at a time of maximum teenage upheaval.

During our pilgrimage to Makkah, by one of the strangest transformations in our family history, Kareem and I observed our daughter, Amani, arise almost overnight from her dormant religious faith and embrace the Islamic beliefs with unnerving intensity. I was nothing more than a mother tending her child, offering her the outlines of her heritage, but it was as if Amani's mind was caught by a high vision, a secret that was in herself, too intimate to reveal to her mother or father.

The morning after our arrival in Jeddah, we made the short drive in an air-conditioned limousine from that Red Sea city to the Holiest city of Islam, the city of the Prophet Mohammed, Makkah. I was thrilled to find myself at the *Haj*, with my most beloved family members in attendance. I tried to concentrate on my prayers but found myself peering out of the car window, thinking of ancient times when enormous numbers of the faithful had come by camel caravan or trodden with bare feet on rugged and rocky terrain in the eager quest to fulfil one of the five pillars of the Islamic faith.

I wanted desperately to share my thoughts with Kareem and my children, but I saw that each was busy contemplating God and his or her relationship with him. Maha's eyes were closed, while Abdullah was fingering his prayer beads. Kareem seemed glassy-eyed, and I hoped that my husband was not reliving his youthful nightmare of being trampled to death on this day. I leaned close and stared, but my husband studiously avoided my eyes. Amani was caught up in her solitary meditations, and I thought that my daughter's face seemed afire.

Satisfied, I smiled, and patted her hand, thinking that I had accomplished much good in bringing my family together for the holy event.

Soon we arrived in the city, which is enclosed by the Valley of Abraham and surrounded by two mountain ranges to the east, west and south. Makkah is set in a rugged landscape that consists mainly of solid granite, but the ancient city is the most beautiful of sights to all Muslims.

I chanted, 'Here I am, O God! Here I am!' Outside the Holy Mosque of Makkah, our family met a specially appointed official guide who would lead us through the rituals of *Haj* and would perform as our Iman, or minister, during our prayers. Sara and I remained with our daughters, while Kareem and Asad walked away with our sons. All around us other pilgrims called out their prayers to God as we pushed through the expansive marble steps of the Holy Mosque. Taking off our shoes at the entrance of the mosque, we continued to walk and to pray, 'God, You are the peace, and from You peace proceeds. O God of ours, greet us with peace.'

As the Prophet always moved with the right side of his body, I was careful to enter the white marble courtyard of the Holy Mosque by stepping through the Gate of Peace with my right foot first.

There are seven main gates that open into the immense courtyard, and crowds were surging through each of those gates. On the sides of the mosque, white marble columns rise high into the air, while elaborately carved minarets tower above the columns. There are red silk carpets that run the length of the courtyard, and here pilgrims were sitting and reading silently or meditating about God.

The cry of the *muezzin* rang out, and we were called to prayer. There is a section of the courtyard reserved for women only, but Sara and I, with our daughters, lined up in a row behind the men who were in the front, joining other Muslims in prayer, rising and falling in the prostrations so familiar to all Muslims the world over.

I felt myself humbled. I am of the royal family, but before the eyes of God, I was at one with all classes of people. To the side and back of my family were the poorest of God's people, yet they were as rich as I, in the eyes of God.

When the prayers finished, we streamed forward towards the Kaaba, which is a simple stone structure that has a single door six feet up from the marble floor. Fifty feet high and thirty-five feet long, the Kaaba is in the centre of the sacred mosque. This is the spot where three millennia ago, Ibrahim, known as Abraham to Jews and Christians, first dedicated a house of worship to a single God. In the Koran, God says that 'The first house of God that was built for people is the one in Makkah.' It is towards this structure that one billion people turn five times each day to bow down and pray.

A huge black velvet cloth embroidered in gold with verses from the Koran is draped over the Kaaba. I knew that at the end of the annual *Haj*, the cloth would be taken down and replaced by a new cloth that had been woven in a special mill in Makkah. Many pilgrims would pay large amounts of money to take a bit of the beautiful cloth to their country as a memento of their sacred journey to Makkah.

In a corner of the Kaaba is the Black Stone, which is the symbol of Muslim love of God. The Black Stone is framed in silver. The Stone had been honoured by Prophet Mohammed. The *Hadith*, or sayings and traditions of the Prophet, says that our Prophet kissed the Black Stone as he helped to place it in the Kaaba. For this reason, the stone is particularly sacred to all Muslims.

In our next sacred rite of pilgrimage, the *tawwaf*, or the circumambulation, people began to walk around the Kaaba.

Keeping the Kaaba on our left, we circle the Kaaba, while reciting, 'God is most Great. O God, grant us good in this world and good in the hereafter, and protect us from the torment of the fires in hell.'

After we completed this ritual, I saw Kareem. He motioned with his head for us to come. We were fortunate, for Kareem had arranged for us to be taken inside the Kaaba to offer additional prayers.

My family and I climbed a portable staircase that had been rolled up to the structure to enter through the door which is high above the ground. The door had been inscribed in silver with verses from the Koran. Inside the Kaaba is the most sacred spot in the world for Muslims.

The interior of the Kaaba was very dark, and I prayed in each corner of the structure, asking God to keep the devil away from my daughter, Maha, and to bless the other members of my family. In light of the recent Gulf War, I also requested that God assist Muslims in keeping the peace. Not forgetting my main focus in life, I prayed that God would guide the men of Arabia in their interpretation of the teachings of the Prophet, and to release their wives, sisters, and daughters from the bondage wrapped so tightly around us in our daily lives.

I heard the sobbing of a child and looking through the darkness witnessed my own daughter, Amani, weeping. Through her cries, I heard her ask God to help her divorce herself from the world of royal luxuries, to be better equipped to stamp out human wickedness. She pleaded with God to swallow up all the sins of mankind and to cure the ills of the world.

Amani was having a religious experience.

Amani's eyes were red, but she ignored my touch of love, tenderly given as we left the Kaaba.

Once we had departed the Kaaba, we walked to the Station of Ibrahim, which is located in the Holy Mosque, and there we performed two more prostrations. Bowing to God, we acknowledged to ourselves that the ritual of circling the Kaaba was not a worship of that structure, but a worship to God, the One and Only One, the Eternal and the Absolute, and none except God deserves to be worshipped.

We then left the courtyard of the Holy Mosque to begin our next rituals, which would take place at the Well of Zamzam, and the Mas'a, or the Running Place. This spot is in the plains that surround Makkah.

Once again, Sara and I separated from the male

members of our family. Though we would perform the exact rituals, we would so so with those of our own sex.

It was in the plains surrounding Makkah that Ibrahim, weary of Sarah's ill persecution of Hagar, allowed Hagar to leave with his son, Ismail. It was then that Ibrahim left with Sarah and Isaac to travel to Palestine. Christians and Jews know that Ibrahim's descendants in Palestine developed the Jewish faith, while his descendants in Makkah went on to establish the Islamic faith.

Thus, by one great man, Ibrahim, two of three great monotheistic religions, Judaism and Islam, are joined.

Hagar and Ismail travelled through the desert with nothing more than a bag of dates. Searching desperately for water for her young son, Hagar ran between the two hills of Safa and Marwa, seeking to find a well of water from which she could nourish her child. A miracle happened. The Angel Gabriel replenished a well that had gone dry, at the feet of Hagar's son, Ismail. Thus God saved Hagar and her son. This well, which was named Zamzam, still runs clear and fresh.

While Hagar ran over rocky terrain in the boiling sun, we pilgrims run between the hills of Safa and Marwa in an air-conditioned gallery. This convenience was built by the men of my family in order to reduce the number of annual casualties suffered each year at the *Haj*. Old, sick, and handicapped pilgrims carried on the shoulders of the faithful used to run seven times between the hills, regardless of the heat. Sunstroke and heart attacks were not uncommon.

There are signs posted in the gallery which tell men when to run and when to walk, while women are instructed to walk. While moving between the hills, pilgrims recite verses from the Koran and chant, 'God is great'. After seven trips, my daughters and I drank the waters of the Zamzam and sprinkled drops of the liquid on our clothing. The mountain spring is no longer visible, as the waters of the well are now delivered to pilgrims through hundreds of water taps that are covered with a beautiful marble vault.

Just as we were about to depart the waters of Zamzam, we heard a loud commotion that swept through the crowd of pilgrims. Curious, I walked towards a group of Muslim women from Indonesia and asked them in the English language if they knew the source of the excitement.

One of them replied, 'Yes!' Three men had fallen and been trampled upon, and they had heard that two of the men had died!

I could not catch my breath! I could think of nothing but my husband Kareem! Had his nightmare come true, after all?

I ran back to my sister and our daughters, my eyes wild with terror, with my incoherent words making no sense.

Sara grabbed my shoulders and demanded to know what was the trouble.

'Kareem! I have heard some men have been trampled. I fear for Kareem's life!'

Thinking that I had viewed his body, my daughters began to moan, and Sara raised her voice, demanding to know why I thought one of the dead men might be Kareem.

I told Sara. 'A dream! Kareem suffered a dream

that he would be crushed at *Haj*! Now, some men have been trampled to death in the area where he was last seen.'

Sara, like me, has learned that there is much in life that is not for our understanding, that unexplained forces move through our lives. She was concerned, though not yet as hysterical as I.

Just as we were about to split into three groups to search for our men, we saw that two stretchers with bodies covered in white sheets were being carried through the crowd. I ran as fast as I could, and screaming, ripped the sheets from the bodies of the dead, first one, and then the other.

The four hospital workers from Makkah stood frozen to the spot, not knowing what to expect next from a woman who was clearly deranged.

Neither of the dead men was Kareem! Both were old, and it was easy to see how they could be pushed to their deaths.

I held the sheet in my hand, and stood over the body of one man, crying out in great relief that I did not know the dead. I was standing in that position just as Kareem, Asad, and our sons followed the sounds of shouting women to see what calamity had occurred.

Kareem could not believe his eyes! His wife was laughing with joy at the sight of a dead man! He pushed through the crowd and caught me by the wrists, pulling me from the scene.

'Sultana! Have you gone quite mad?'

Sara quickly explained what I had feared, and Kareem's angry look softened. Embarrassed, he had to speak in great detail of his fearful nightmare that he had shared with his wife.

The atmosphere was electric with emotion. The crowd began to mumble and menacingly look in my direction, as the wives of the two now dead realized their tragedy and learned that I had laughed like a hyena at the deaths of their husbands.

We hurriedly left the area, while Asad revealed our identity to some guards. With their protection Asad gave a gift of 3,000 *riyals*[2] to each of the families and told them that we were members of the royal family. He quickly explained my fear of Kareem's dream and pacified the angry crowd.

After we escaped the scene, my family began to laugh nervously, and later, as time erased the shame of my conduct, we came to think of the incident as hilarious, and it has amused us ever since.

Our rituals were completed for the first day of *Haj*.

We then returned to our palace in Jeddah which is situated beside the Red Sea. During the drive, in an attempt to put the experience of the men trampled out of our minds, each of us shared our profound experiences of the day. Only Amani was strangely quiet and withdrawn.

I thought to myself that there was something perplexing about my youngest child's demeanour.

The feeling of impending doom would not leave me, and once we were back in our home, I followed Kareem around until I could focus my thoughts and articulate what was in my heart and on my mind. I accompanied him from the entrance hall to our bedroom out onto the balcony, and then back into the bedroom and into his library.

[2]About £500.

An abyss divided our moods.

Looking at me in exasperation, Kareem finally asked, 'Sultana, what can I *do* for you?'

Unsure of what my concerns were, I had difficulty expressing myself. 'Have you noticed your daughter, Amani, today?' I asked. 'Amani is worrying me. I feel that a strange mood is oppressing our daughter. I don't like it.'

In a weary tone, my husband insisted, 'Sultana, stop looking for danger where there is none. She is at *Haj*. Aren't all pilgrims engrossed in special thoughts?' He paused and then added in a malicious tone, 'Except *you*, Sultana.'

Kareem then stood silent, but he gave me a withering look that spoke clearly of his desire for solitude.

Irritated, I left Kareem in his library. I searched for Maha, but she had retired to her bedroom and was sleeping. Abdullah was not around. He had gone with his Auntie Sara to their villa. I felt terribly alone in the world.

I decided that I would go to the source of my worry. I walked to Amani's bedroom, and when I heard her mumbling voice, I held my ear to the door and tried to understand the words that she was saying. My daughter was praying, and her voice pleaded with God with an urgency that awakened my memory of another that I had eavesdropped upon from behind a locked door. Suddenly, the memory of that other voice in another time struck me as to why I was so tormented with anxiety. Lawand! Amani was praying with the same sort of isolated longing that I had often heard from the locked room of her cousin, Lawand!

The atmosphere that had surrounded Amani from

the moment of our participation in the first ritual of the day had seemed vaguely familiar. Now, on this day, Lawand's insanity had re-emerged in the chilling intensity of Amani's eyes.

I told myself that Amani was going the way of her cousin, Lawand!

While still a teenager, Lawand, who was a first cousin of Kareem on his father's side of the family, had attended school in Geneva, Switzerland. Her parents' decision to send her abroad for schooling had proved a grievous mistake. While in Geneva, Lawand had disgraced her family by becoming involved with several young men. In addition to her sexual involvements, Lawand had become addicted to cocaine. While moving secretly out of her room one evening, Lawand was captured by the headmistress, who called her father in Saudi Arabia, with a demand that he come and collect his wayward child.

When the family got a whiff of their daughter's activities, Lawand's father and two brothers had flown to Geneva and had taken the girl to a drug rehabilitation centre in that country. Six months later, when her treatment was completed, she was brought back to Saudi Arabia. The family was exhausted with shame and fury, and as punishment a decision was reached to confine Lawland to a small apartment in their home, until they were satisfied that she had realized her reckless offence to Muslim life.

When I heard the verdict, another came to my mind. Through the blur of distance, I could think of little but Sameera, my sister Tahani's best friend. Sameera was a brilliant and beautiful young woman, who so long ago had been deprived of her freedom and forced into the dark prison of the 'Woman's Room'. While Lawand would one day secure her freedom, only death would remove Sameera from her incarceration.

Now, within my thin sphere of expectations, I found myself thinking that Lawand was fortunate! Relieved that Lawand's father was not of the unfeeling character that could confine his daughter to life imprisonment, or to death by stoning, I experienced sad relief in lieu of passionate anger.

How fortunate is the human being who has no memories, for memories often remould the victim of suppression into the image of their suppressor! With terrifying seriousness, I listened as the men of my family mouthed the law of obedience, saying that the calm structure of our conservative society rested upon the perfect obedience of children to their parents, and wives to their husbands. Without that obedience, anarchy would rule the day. The men of my family firmly stated that Lawand's punishment was fair.

I visited the family on many occasions, listening with profound sympathy to the grief of Lawand's mother and her sisters. Often, the women of the family talked to Lawand through the locked door. Initially, Lawand begged for forgiveness and pleaded with her mother to set her free.

Sara and I smuggled notes of encouragement to this cousin, advising her to recall the wisdom of silence and to read the books and play the games that female members of the family placed through the small opening that had been constructed for the delivery of food and for emptying the pail containing body wastes, but Lawand had little interest in occupying her time with quiet pursuits.

After several weeks of confinement, Lawand returned to God and began to pray, declaring that she had seen the error of her ways, and swearing to her parents that she would never again commit a single wrong.

Taking great pity on her daughter, Lawand's mother beseeched her husband to set her daughter free, saying that she felt certain Lawand would now return to the pious life.

Lawand's father thought perhaps that Lawand was speaking with deceit, since he had told his daughter that her confinement would end when her mind once again embraced the proper thoughts of a believing Muslim.

Before long, Lawand prayed all of her waking moments, failing to respond to our worried voices. I could easily see that Lawand was hallucinating, for she spoke to God in her prayers on an equal basis, shouting out that she would represent him on earth, teaching his followers a new moral code of which only she, Lawand, had knowledge.

After one particular visit, when Lawand's mother and I overheard her madly rejoicing in the confines of her room, I told Kareem that I was certain that Lawand had lost her mind.

Kareem spoke to his father, who in turn, visited his brother's home. As the eldest brother of Lawand's father, Kareem's father had authority over the family. On my father-in-law's advice, Lawand's father opened the locked door and released his daughter from her prison. Lawand would now be allowed to rejoin her family in a normal life.

Lawand's eleven-week confinement had ended, but the family tragedy ripened rapidly. During the course of her prison sentence, Lawand had disciplined herself to ascetic austerity, and came out of her imprisonment seething with Islamic fervour, claiming that a new day had dawned for Islam.

On the day of her release, Lawand informed her family that all Muslims must denounce luxury and vice, and promptly pounced upon her two sisters for wearing kohl (black powder) on their eyes, rouge on their cheeks, and nail polish. After she made her sisters cower on the sofa, Lawand ripped an expensive necklace from her mother's neck and rushed to throw precious stones down the kitchen drain. The women of the house could barely restrain her, and the family disturbance resulted in various minor injuries. Lawand was given a shot by one of the palace physicians and a prescription for drugs that calm the mind.

Violence hid its face for a while, but nevertheless survived, and from time to time Lawand would lash out with blunt passion, directing abuse at whoever was handy.

After she ripped Sara's gold earrings from my sister's ears, shouting out that to wear such gleaming finery hurt the eyes of God, I thought to protect myself by purchasing a small canister of mace while I was on holiday in the United States. I hid the item in my luggage, even from the eyes of Kareem, and began to carry it in a small bag when I visited Lawand's home.

As is my disastrous misfortune, Lawand selected an afternoon when I was paying a visit to demonstrate her renewed religious fervour.

Lawand, her mother, two sisters, and I were having a pleasant chat while sipping tea, eating pastries and discussing my last trip to America when Lawand suddenly became restless, her eyes flashing about, seeking some affront to God.

In her temporarily disordered mind, she began to criticize her mother's choice of clothing, which Lawand stated was much too immodest for a believing Muslim. In fascination, I watched as Lawand carefully folded her table napkin and very courteously covered her mother's neck with the fabric. Then, without warning, Lawand began to curse. She made a sudden wild leap in the air, twisting her body in mid-air to face me.

I saw that Lawland was eyeing my new pearl necklace, and remembered too late Kareem's warning that I should not wear jewellery in her home.

Lawand's pale ascetic face, twisted in passionate and divine conviction, awed me, and I felt the acute danger that she posed. I quickly dug in my small bag and brought out the mace, warning my cousin that she should quit the room or sit down immediately, or I would be forced to defend myself.

Lawand's mother began to scream and to tug on her mad daughter's sleeve. I braced myself for an attack when Lawand pushed her pawing mother from her side and rushed at me, forcing me into a small corner between a lamp and a chair.

The worst was yet to come.

Sara, who had agreed to meet me at Lawand's home, entered the villa at that exact moment. I saw that Sara held her youngest child in her arms.

Sara's jaw dropped when she saw that Lawand had cornered her youngest sister between a chair and a lamp, and that I was holding a weapon in my hand.

Knowing Lawand's weakness, Sara quickly regained her composure and subtly attempted to persuade Lawand to stop her foolishness. For a short moment, Lawand, with feline deception, pretended to submit to Sara's wisdom. She dropped her aggressive stance and began rubbing her hands together nervously.

Not trusting someone who is known to be a lunatic, I yelled for Sara to take her baby and run from the room! At the sound of my excited voice, Lawand turned back to me and then with all the fury of one who is insane, bounded towards me with outstretched hands, making for my pearl necklace.

I squeezed the mace container with both hands and Lawand dropped to her knees. In the back of my mind, I remembered reading that it takes double power to disable the insane, so in my excitement, I emptied the container and maced not only Lawand, but her mother and one sister, who had come to Lawand's aid.

Lawand recovered from the mace attack rapidly, but had lost her will to fight.

Her father finally realized that his daughter needed long-term professional attention, which she received in France and within a year enjoyed a full recovery.

Lawand's mother and sister required immediate medical attention. The Pakistani physician summoned to treat the women had difficulty in maintaining professional seriousness, when informed that one royal princess had maced three other princesses who were members of her family.

Everyone in Kareem's family thought that I had acted with haste in macing my opponent, but I refused to let myself be crucified for defending myself against a woman who had lost her mind, and I told them so. Indignantly, I added that instead of criticism, I deserved their appreciation for my deed, for the event had led their daughter to recovery.

While there is a tendency of some to dismiss my actions as those of a female of excitable emotion, I am a woman of deadly seriousness when it comes to women's issues.

A wise man was once asked what was the most difficult truth in life to uncover. His reply was: 'to know thyself'. While others might harbour doubt, I know my own character. Undeniably, my personality has been doused with an overabundance of spontaneity, but it is in this exuberance that I gain my power to do battle against those in command of females in my land. I can claim some degree of success in bending the bonds of tradition.

Now, in my memory of Lawand's temporary and unhinged obsession with unhealthy fundamentalist fervour, I attached great significance to my daughter's extreme infatuation with our religion.

While I believe in and honour the God of Mohammed, it is my considered opinion that the masses of humanity who are engaged in loving, struggling, suffering, and enjoying are living life as God intended. I have no desire for my child to turn her back on the rich complexity of life and reaffirm her future through the harsh asceticism of a militant interpretation of our religion.

I ran to my husband. I said, in a rush of words, 'Amani is praying!'

129

Kareem, who was quietly reading the Koran, looked at me as though I had finally lost all reason. '*Praying?*' he asked, his voice tinged with disbelief at my reaction over another's communication with God.

'Yes!' I cried. 'She is exhausting herself with prayer.' I insisted, 'Come! See for yourself!'

Regretfully, Kareem laid his Koran on his desk and with an expression of incredulity, humoured his wife by following me from the room.

As we entered the hallway leading to Amani's door, we could easily hear the sound of her voice, rising and falling with the intensity of her words.

Kareem left my side and burst into Amani's room. Our daughter turned, displaying a face lined with pain and haggard with sorrow.

Kareem spoke softly. 'Amani, it's time for you to take a small rest. Go to bed. Your mother will wake you in an hour for the evening meal.'

Amani's expression appeared stricken, and she did not speak. Still bound to Kareem's influence, she lay across the bed, fully dressed, and closed her eyes.

I could see my child's lips as they still moved in silent prayer, uttering words that were not meant for my ears.

Kareem and I quietly left our daughter. Drinking coffee in our sitting-room, Kareem confessed that he had a small degree of concern but was sceptical of my exaggerated fears that Amani was sinking into a medieval passion, darkened with thoughts of sin, suffering and hell. He sat quietly for a short while and then announced that my apprehension was directly linked to Lawand's unhinged denunciations of human wickedness. He told me that Amani's religious revival did not result from insanity, but was essentially linked with the overpowering joy of *Haj*.

'You'll see,' he promised. 'Once we've returned to the normal routine of life, Amani will lapse again into the habit of accumulating wandering beasts, and her religious fanaticism will seem another age.' Kareem smiled and asked a small favour. 'Sultana, please, allow Amani some peace to turn from her daily problems to a oneness with God. It is a duty of all Muslims.'

With a grimace, I nodded my head in agreement. Somewhat relieved, I hoped that Kareem was right.

Still, not leaving such importance to chance, in my prayers that evening I indulged in long hours of pleading with God that Amani would once again be the child she had been prior to our attending *Haj*.

I suffered varying nightmares throughout the night: I dreamt that my daughter, Amani, left our home to join an extremist religious organization in Amman, Jordan, that doused gasoline on the clothing of working Muslim women, setting alight and burning to death those women whom they deemed non-believers.

Chapter Six

HAJ

*Arab lands will now go the way of Iran. Egypt will
not be the first to fall, nevertheless it shall fall. The
women will be the first to suffer loss of human rights.
We women were offered our rights as human beings
first by Nasser then by Sadat. The courts have
already struck down the humane law giving women
the right to divorce husbands who take second
wives. Egyptian women cringe to think of
what is yet to come, often joking that soon
we shall share the unfortunate fate of our
Saudi sisters.*
Comments of an Egyptian feminist pilgrim made
to Sara Al Sa'ud, during the *Haj* of 1990

I thought that God must have heard my stirring
appeal, for the following morning Amani seemed
her usual self. It was as if sleep had erased the
apotheosis of human suffering that I had witnessed
on my daughter's face the day before. She giggled
and joked with her sister, Maha, as they ate their
breakfast of fresh yogurt and melon and munched

on pieces of kibbeh that had been left from our evening meal.

Our driver delivered us to the Valley of Mina, which is approximately six miles north of Makkah. We would spend the night in Mina, in an air-conditioned and well-equipped tent for which Kareem had made arrangements. The children seemed quite excited at the prospect, since we had never performed that particular ritual in the past.

Along the way, we passed hundreds of buses carrying pilgrims to the valley. On the sides of the highway, thousands of the devout were slowly walking the six-mile journey. Muslims of every colour and nationality were performing their duty by attending *Haj*. I carefully watched their contrasting faces as we slowly passed them by, and there was no doubt that God's name was on every lip.

Thinking that Amani had returned to normal, I once again found myself glad that I was a part of this wonderful gathering of the faithful, and I happily looked forward to the last days of *Haj*.

It was while we were in the Valley of Mina that Kareem met an old friend of his from youthful days spent in England. The man, Yousif, was from Egypt. One moment Kareem was standing by my side, and the next he was heartily embracing a man none of his family had ever seen.

Looking at the man from a distance, I saw that he had a long, slightly curving nose, projecting cheek-bones, and a curly beard. What most caught my attention was the indisputable and concentrated scorn that blazed in his eyes when his gaze fell upon the females in Kareem's family.

Kareem called out the man's name in a loud voice, and I remembered hearing of this person from my husband. Thinking back, I recalled some of what Kareem had told me about this particular acquaintance. During the years of our married life, each time we had visited our villa in Cairo, Kareem's memories had been stirred regarding his Egyptian schoolmate. His plans were to look up his old friend and share the pleasure of exchanging life's joys and pains. On each occasion, the fullness of our family life had prevented Kareem from seeking out his old friend.

Now, after a quick view of the man, I was glad that Kareem's plans had never materialized, for I felt myself in invisible conflict with a malevolent character that, to my eye, had been conspicuous in his dislike for women.

I wondered what had produced such changes in Yousif's life, for I distinctly recalled that Kareem had told me that Yousif had such attractive manners that women had found it hard to resist him and that Yousif had never slept alone.

Kareem and Yousif had known each other during their student days when they had resided in a land not their own. While in London, Yousif had been a carefree, happy individual who was interested in little more than merrymaking with Western women in gambling casinos. Kareem had said that the man had been noticeably brilliant and had little need to study his lessons, and that had been a good thing, for Yousif introduced a different girlfriend each week. In spite of Yousif's insatiable lust for female company, Kareem had predicted a great future for his friend in the legal and political system of Egypt, for Yousif had a quick mind and a pleasing manner.

Yousif had graduated from law school one year ahead of Kareem, and they had not seen each other since that time.

As Yousif and Kareem began to share their news, my daughters and I stayed in the background, which is our way when the man is not of our family, but we could overhear all that Kareem and Yousif were saying.

Apparently Yousif had changed radically from his years as a student, for after a short conversation, it was evident that he and my husband no longer enjoyed much in common.

Yousif was strangely reticent regarding his career, and when Kareem pressed him on his profession, the man would say little more than that he had changed from the youth of Kareem's memory and had become more attached to the traditional ways of Islam.

Yousif proudly told Kareem that since they had last met, he had married and divorced one woman, who had given him two sons, and had married a second woman, fathering five sons in that union. The man delighted in boasting about the joys of having seven sons. Yousif did mention that he had full custody of the first two children, and that the boys had been forcibly taken from the influence of his first wife, who was a modern woman who insisted upon working outside the home. She, Yousif said, with ill-concealed disgust, was a teacher with new ideas about women and their station in life.

Yousif spat on the ground when he mentioned his

first wife's name, and said, Praise to God, Egypt was returning to the teachings of the Koran, and Egyptians would soon have the law of Mohammed ruling their lives, rather than the unsettling system of secular law that encouraged women to come out of *purdah*, or complete seclusion.

At this bit of information, I began to come to life and was about to intrude on their conversation and tell the man some of my thoughts, when I was struck dumb by further revelations from Kareem's friend.

Yousif proudly told Kareem that his greatest blessing from God was that neither of his marriages had been cursed with the birth of daughters, and that truly, women were the source of all sin, and if a man had to waste his energies in guarding women, he had little time for performing other, more important duties in life.

Without waiting for Kareem's response to his shocking comments, Yousif launched into a story of a man whom he had met while in Makkah. He said that the man was an Indian Muslim and that this Muslim was thinking of remaining in Saudi Arabia since there was a warrant out for his arrest in India. Two days after his departure to Saudi Arabia, the authorities in India had discovered that he and his wife had murdered their baby daughter by pouring scalding water down her throat.

Yousif asked for Kareem's opinion on the matter, and before my husband could speak, he resumed his loud, rude speech, and said that he, himself, thought that the man should not be punished, since he was the father of four daughters and had desired a son to the point of madness. While

Yousif acknowledged that the Prophet had not condoned such a practice, he thought that in such a case the authorities should not intervene on a private matter that had harmed no-one but the baby girl.

Yousif wondered if Kareem could offer assistance on obtaining a work visa for the man, and possibly offer him a job in Saudi Arabia so he would not have to return to his country and face trial.

Yousif had not bothered to discover the sex of Kareem's children, and Kareem had begun to breathe heavily. Knowing Kareem's thoughts on such matters, I thought that my husband might strike his old friend and fling him to the ground.

The back of Kareem's neck turned red, so I knew that my husband blushed in anger. I decided that he could see from the back of his head, for he motioned with his hand for me to stay away. Kareem curtly informed his old friend that he, himself, had been blessed with two beautiful daughters and one son, and that he loved his daughters as he did his son.

A man with thick skin, Yousif gave his condolences to Kareem over the life of our girls, saying that it was too unfortunate that Kareem was the father of daughters. Without taking a moment to breathe, Yousif began to argue the benefits of sons, and wondered why my husband did not take another wife? Kareem could, after all, allow me to keep the daughters, and he could raise our son.

Kareem responded with the calm demeanour of a man who is very angry by reminding Yousif of the teachings of Mohammed. He asked, 'Yousif, you say you are a practising and good Muslim. If so, do you not recall the words of the Blessed Prophet when a man entered the mosque and approached the Prophet?'

I knew the story well, since I have always quoted the fairness of the Prophet with regard to women, in fighting the extremists in my land.

Yousif listened with a blank face, and it was evident to my eyes that here was a man who had no interest in the words of the Prophet if those words did not agree with Yousif's thoughts on life.

Kareem plunged ahead, a man intent on teaching another a good lesson by using intellect, and the teachings of a man appointed by God to spread his word, instead of resorting to brute force. Frankly, I desired to see Yousif be beaten and bloodied by my husband's fists, but I did have a moment of pride when Kareem spoke with the passion of a *muezzin* reminding the faithful to come to prayer, as he told the true story of Prophet Mohammed's reminder to all fathers about the equal value of their children, regardless of the sex.

A man entered the Mosque and approached the Prophet. He sat down and began to talk. After some time, the man's two children, a boy and a girl, followed their father into the Mosque. The boy came in first, and received much praise and a loving kiss from his father. The boy settled on the man's lap, while the man continued talking to the Prophet.

Some time later, the man's daughter arrived at the Mosque. When she approached her father, he did not kiss her, or put her on his lap, as he had done with his son. Instead, he motioned for the little girl to sit in front of him, and went on talking to the Prophet.

The Prophet was greatly concerned when he saw this. Why, he asked, do you not treat these children equally? Why did you not kiss your daughter as you kissed your son, and let her, also, sit on your lap?

The man felt ashamed when he heard the Prophet say those words. He understood that he had acted in an improper manner towards his two children.

Sons and daughters are both gifts of God, the Prophet reminded him. Both are equally great gifts, and so they should always be treated equally.

Kareem glared at Yousif, his expression seeming to say, now, what do you have to say to that!

This Yousif fellow was a rude man. Ignoring Kareem's obvious discomfort at his attitude towards women and the message of the Prophet's words, he started his tirade against women once again, quoting remarks from the *Green Book*, written by President Qadaffi of Libya, a man who was known to cling to the strictest interpretation of the proper role of women in Islam. Seeing that he had not won over Kareem to his way of thinking, he concluded his efforts by reminding Kareem of the breakdown of the family unit in the Western countries, stating that, 'God has assigned a specific duty for men and for women. Women are created for procreation, nothing else! Kareem, come now, who can deny that by nature all women are exhibitionists? This tendency cannot be changed, but it is a man's duty to keep her away from all men, otherwise, she will squander her beauty and give to any man that asks, her charms . . .'

Furious, Kareem turned his back and walked away from his friend Yousif. His face was an ugly mask as he led his women from the scene.

In a loud voice, he said to me, 'That Yousif has become a dangerous man!'

I glanced back at Yousif. Never have I witnessed such evil in another's face.

Kareem called his brother-in-law Mohammed on his portable telephone, and asked him to make some delicate enquiries about the activities of Yousif, telling Mohammed that the man was extremely radical and possibly an instigator of violence.

Within hours, Mohammed returned Kareem's call and said that Kareem was on the mark, that the man was a skilled lawyer whose clients were members of the Gamaa Al Islamiya, an Egyptian Islamic extremist group formed in the early 1980s that was responsible for militant violence in Egypt.

Kareem was astonished. Yousif represented men that were attempting to overthrow the Egyptian secular government! The Egyptian internal security authorities had told Mohammed that there had never been charges lodged against the man but, when in Egypt, he was kept under careful surveillance. Mohammed added that he had placed Saudi Security around Yousif to ensure that he did not incite security problems while in Saudi Arabia.

A little less than a year later, Kareem was saddened but not surprised at the news that Yousif had been arrested in Assiut, in southern Egypt, as a principal leader of the Muslim extremist group. While watching a news programme, Kareem spotted

Yousif's face – his old friend was looking out on the world from a cage. Kareem followed his case closely and seemed somewhat relieved that Yousif had not been sentenced to death, while I thought that the world was a more dangerous place with such men among the living and would have welcomed his demise.

In spite of the fact that we were at *Haj* and knew we should not concentrate on worldly matters, the man Yousif had made such an impression on our daughters' moods, that Kareem thought it best to talk the matter through and give our daughters the comforting knowledge that men like Yousif were only a passing phase in the long history of Islam.

After the dinner hour, our family sat and discussed the man, Yousif, and what he represented in the Muslim world.

We asked each of the children their thoughts on what they had heard that day.

Abdullah spoke first. Our son was plainly disturbed, saying that Islam was on the move and that it would affect each of our lives, for the extremist groups were calling for the downfall of the Saudi monarchy. He envisaged Saudi Arabia going the way of Iran, with the disposal of the rulers with a man like Khomeini leading our country. Abdullah predicted that his generation of Al Sa'uds would live out their lives on the French Riviera, and such a thought was distressing to our son.

After hearing what the man had to say about females and their value, Maha was spitting mad and wanted her father to have Yousif arrested, and charged as a spy. She would have liked to see him beheaded, even if it was on trumped-up offences!

Amani was reflective and said that Muslim love of all things Western was making men such as Yousif gain power in Muslim countries.

Kareem and I looked at each other, neither of us liking our youngest child's turn of thought.

Maha pinched her sister, accusing her of supporting the man's words.

Amani responded to the charge and said 'no', she did not, but she did consider the possibility that life was simpler when women's roles were more defined and not open for discussion and change. She mentioned that in the bedouin life prior to the building of cities, men and women were not so confused as they were today.

It was as I had feared! My daughter's thoughts were harking to the past. She seemed to be losing pride in her femaleness, and I wondered what I could do to reinforce her worth as a modern woman in an advancing civilization.

Abdullah was unfeeling and began to laugh, asking Amani if she longed for the time that female babies were buried in the sand! It was not too late to take up the practice, he said, the man Yousif could introduce us to such a man who had recently killed his own daughter!

Knowing Amani's mental state was delicate, Kareem gave his son a stern look and said that the matter was no joke, that the evil practice was a terrible problem in India, Pakistan and China. Kareem told us that he had recently read an article in a foreign newspaper that quoted statistics that were startling. Kareem said that tens of millions of females were missing in those lands, and no-one seemed particularly interested in finding out the fate of those victims.

My husband felt so strongly about the matter that he insisted upon discussing further the evils of the practice of infanticide, by telling our children a story that I was not aware my husband knew in such detail.

The children moaned and said that they were too old for stories from their father, but my husband insisted, saying that while statistics made little impact on our emotions, individual tales of horror bring tears to eyes and generate action on social issues in the world community.

With new thoughts about my husband, I listened to Kareem as he told the famous Muslim tale that had been passed down by professional storytellers from the time of Prophet Mohammed.

Kareem said that, 'Prior to the founding of the Islamic faith by Prophet Mohammed, there was a tribe in Arabia that practised the inhuman deed of burying alive their baby daughters, in much the same manner that baby girls are murdered today in other countries.

'Qais bin Asim was the chief of this tribe. When Chief Asim embraced Islam, he confessed a dreadful tale to Prophet Mohammed.

'"O Messenger of God! A daughter was born to my wife when I was away from my home on a journey. My wife was fearful that I might bury the child alive, and after nursing her for a few days, sent this child to her sister so that she might be cherished by another. My wife prayed that I might be merciful to the child when the girl became older.

'"When I came home from the journey I was told

that my wife had given birth to a dead child. Thus, the matter was forgotten. During the time, the child remained being loved by her aunt. Once I went out of the house for a whole day, and my wife, thinking I would be out much longer, thought it safe to call her daughter home and enjoy her company for some time in my absence.

'"Unexpectedly, I changed my mind and came home earlier. When I entered my home I saw a very beautiful, neat little girl playing in the house. When I looked at her I suddenly felt a surge of strong and spontaneous love for her within me. My wife sensed my feelings and thought that my blood had called to my own blood and my fatherly love and affection had sprung up naturally for the girl. I asked her, 'Oh, my wife, whose child is this? How charming she is!'

'"Then, my wife told me about the truth of the girl. I could not control my joy and eagerly took the girl in my arms. Her mother told her that I was her father and she began loving me dearly, and calling out to me, 'Oh my father! My father!' At those moments I felt an indescribable pleasure when this girl child put her arms around my neck and showed me affection.

'"Days went by in this way and the child remained being nourished by us and was free from any worry or discomfort. But, there were times when this girl caught my attention and such thoughts came to my mind: I have to give this girl to another man in marriage. I will have to bear the insult that another man will know my daughter as his wife. How will I be able to face other men, knowing that my honour is ruined when this child is bedded by a man. These thoughts took hold of my mind and I was tortured incessantly. At last these thoughts aroused my indignation and made me devoid of patience with the girl. After some time of thinking, I decided that I had to do away with the stigma of shame and humiliation for me and for my ancestors.

'"I decided I had to bury the girl alive.

'"I could not confide this plan to my wife, so I asked her to get the child ready, that I was going to take her to a feast with me. My wife gave the girl a bath, clad her in pretty clothes, and made her ready for the feast. The little girl was excited, bubbling with cheerfulness, believing that she was accompanying her father on a joyful occasion.

'"I left the house with the girl. She was leaping with joy and pleasure, holding my hand every now and then, and running ahead of me, prattling to me with squeals of innocent laughter and gaiety.

'"By this time I had become blind to the girl, and was impatient to get rid of her as soon as possible. The poor child was unaware of my sinister intentions and followed me merrily.

'"At last I stopped at a lonely spot and began to dig into the ground. The innocent girl was surprised to see me doing this and asked repeatedly, 'Father, why are you digging in the earth?'

'"I paid no attention to her questions. She could not know that I was digging a pit to bury my own beautiful daughter with my own hands.

'"While digging in the earth, dust and sand fell upon my feet and clothes. My lovely daughter would clean the dust from my feet and clothes while saying, 'Father, you are spoiling your clothes!'

'"I was like a deaf person and did not look at her, and pretended that I heard nothing she said. I continued my task and finally had dug a pit large enough to serve my purpose.

'"I grabbed my daughter and threw her into the pit, and began to fill the pit with great haste. The poor girl was looking at me with frightened eyes. She began to cry frantically and screamed, 'My dear father, what is this? I have done no wrong! Father, please, do not hide me in the ground!'

'"I kept on doing my work like a deaf, dumb and blind person without paying attention to her pleadings and entreaties.

'"O Great Prophet of God! I was too heartless to have pity on my own child! On the contrary, after burying her alive, I heaved a huge sigh of relief and came back satisfied that I had saved my honour and pride from humiliation."

'When Prophet Mohammed heard this heart-rending story about an innocent girl, the Holy Prophet could not control himself and tears fell upon his cheeks. He asked the Chief of the Tribe of Asim, "This is too cruel! How can one, who does not pity others, expect to be pitied by the Almighty God?"'

Kareem looked into the faces of his children. 'Prophet Mohammed, upon hearing this story, became very gloomy, and he related another story that was similar in its horror.'

A man came to Mohammed and told him that he had once been very ignorant. He said that he had no knowledge and no guidance until the Prophet came and made God's wishes known.

This man said, O Messenger of God! We

worshipped idols and killed our children with our own hands. I once had a little and very charming daughter. When I would call her she would run into my arms laughing with joy and pleasure. One day I called this girl to me, and she readily came. I asked her to follow me, and she did. I walked too rapidly, and this girl came running with her small steps. There was a deep well at a short distance from my home. When I reached this well, I stopped and the child came to the well, trotting after me. I caught hold of that child by the hand and threw her into the well. The poor child cried and called out for me to save her. Father, was the last word on the child's lips.

'When the man finished his story, the Prophet wept for a long time, and the tears were so plentiful that they wet his beard. Our ignorance about females was washed away by the shedding of his tears, and today, it is considered a vile and cruel act for a man to bury alive, to throw down into wells, or to harm their female children.'

I hugged each of my daughters. In our hearts, it was as if the Prophet himself were near us, and it seemed as if the tragic tale of the two young girls had occurred in the present and not centuries prior to our existence. Who could doubt that our Prophet had done much to abolish unjust practices and cruel customs? He had been born in an evil time, when pagan Gods were worshipped, when men took hundreds of wives, and the practice of infanticide was common. Prophet Mohammed had great difficulty in abolishing these evil practices, and what he could not abolish, he restricted.

I told my family that, in my opinion, the remaining traditions of that era were what kept us women in bondage, and not the Koran. Few people know the facts, that the Koran does not call for veiling, nor the restrictions women endure in the Muslim world. It is the traditions passed down that so hinder us from moving forward.

A lively discussion ensued as to why the position of women was one of subjection to men, with Maha insulting her brother Abdullah by reminding him that her marks at school were better than his in every subject.

Just as Abdullah opened his mouth to respond, I warned my children not to make the conversation personal.

Then I brought up the obvious, that the physical vulnerabilities of a woman can be traced to that most important function of human accomplishments, the absorption of her strength in carrying, nursing and rearing children. I have always known that this one fact doomed females to a subordinate status in all societies. Instead of attaining honour for being producers of life, we are penalized!

To my mind, this fact is the scandal of civilization!

Abdullah, whose favourite instructor at school was a Lebanese philosophy professor, showed off his knowledge by giving us a history lesson on women's slow climb from the beginning of life until the present moment. That women had been nothing more than beasts of burden in the earlier days, tending to the children, gathering wood for the fire, cooking the meals, making the clothes and boots, and working as pack animals when the tribes were on the march. The men, Abdullah said, risked themselves in the capture of the game, and their reward for providing the tribe with meat was to rest the reminder of the time.

Teasing his sisters, Abdullah flexed his muscles, and said that brute force kept men to the fore, and if his sisters were truly interested in equality, then they should work out with his weights in our exercise studio, rather than read books in their spare time.

Kareem had to restrain our daughters, to keep them from piling on top of their brother. Maha dodged her father's arms and gave a kick to Abdullah's private parts, and Kareem and I both were astonished at her knowledge of his weakest area.

I smiled at my children's antics, but nevertheless my heart was gloomy as I thought of how we women had suffered from the moment of creation. From the beginning of time, we were used as slaves to do the work, and that practice still continued in many countries of the world. In my own country, women were now considered nothing more than things of beauty, sexual toys for man's enjoyment.

I have personal knowledge that women are equal to men in endurance, resourcefulness and courage, but I was ahead of my time in the backward land of Arabia.

Kareem became quiet. Then he broke the silence and said that he was remembering his old friend, Yousif, and the wrongful path that he had chosen.

I was pleased that Kareem had witnessed Yousif's disintegration as a civilized man, for it was as if my husband finally became what I wanted him to be, in his recognition of the evil that sprouts and takes hold in society when such men gain power.

Kareem mulled over his thoughts. 'Sultana, you know, it is unsuccessful men, such as Yousif, who mould the myth that women are the root of all evil. I know now that it is a paralysing disillusionment that is so attractive to men, but this disillusionment regarding women does nothing more than create a hateful barrier between the two sexes.'

Kareem looked at his son and said, 'Abdullah, I hope that you will never accept such obstinate resistance to the worth of women. It will be up to your generation to abandon the subjugation of women. I am sad to say that the men of my generation have given new form to women's oppression.'

I could only imagine what my daughters were thinking, since I did not know, but Maha seemed bewildered and angry that she was born into a society so reluctant to adjust to social change, while Amani, recently attached to her consoling faith, appeared burdened by the traditional sanctions that favour the subjugation of women.

Weary of men such as Yousif and of the life they envisage for women – all of whom they consider wicked and therefore strive to control – I could not reconcile myself to the dark years ahead when women would be forced to protect themselves from the growing movement of extremists who called so loudly for their banishment from a normal life.

As I prepared myself for bed, I felt that the sparkle had gone from the occasion of *Haj*. This, in spite of Kareem's new-found philosophy that spoke of enlightened liberation within our family walls.

The following morning, our faces were drawn from

our late evening. Silent throughout our morning meal, we prepared ourselves for the most important day of *Haj.*

We were driven five miles north to the hill of Arafat. This was the spot where, according to history, Adam and Eve united after their wanderings. It was also on this site that Ibrahim had been ordered by God to sacrifice his son Isaac. Lastly, this was the place where Prophet Mohammed had delivered his final sermon. Four months later, he was dead.

Disheartened, I barely moved my lips as I uttered the words of the Prophet: 'You have to appear before your God, who shall demand from you an account of all your actions. Know that all Muslims are brothers. You are one brotherhood, no man shall take from his brother unless by his free consent. Keep yourselves from injustice. Let him who is present tell this to him who is absent. It may be that he who is told this afterwards may remember it better than he who has now heard it.'

Walking up the steep side of Mount Arafat, I cried, 'Here I am, O God! Here I am!' This is the day when God erases all our sins and confers his forgiveness.

For six hours, my family and I, with the other pilgrims, stood in the heat of the desert. We prayed and read from the Koran. My daughters, like many other pilgrims, held an umbrella over their heads for shade, but I felt the need to suffer the effects of a baking sun, as a testimony of my faith. Many men and women were fainting all around me, and they were carried off on stretchers to the sunstroke vans, manned by hospital attendants.

At dusk, we moved to the open plain between

Mount Arafat and Mina. We rested for a while and then once again began our prayers.

Abdullah and Kareem gathered small stones for the following morning's rituals, and without family communication, for each of us showed signs of physical weariness, we rested fitfully that last night and prepared ourselves for the final day of *Haj*.

The last morning, we chanted, 'In the name of God Almighty I do this, and in hatred of the Devil and his pretence! God is Great!' We each cast seven sets of the small stones gathered by Kareem and Abdullah at the stone pillars that symbolize the Devil. These pillars stand along the road to Mina. This is the very spot where Ibrahim drove Satan away when the Devil tried to tell him not to sacrifice Isaac as God had ordered. Each of the stones represented a bad thought, or temptation to sin, or burden endured by the pilgrims.

We were cleansed of our sins! Now, in the final ritual of the *Haj*, we travelled to the plain of Mina. There, sheep, goats and camels were being butchered to commemorate Ibrahim's willingness to sacrifice his beloved son to God. Butchers roamed throughout the crowd of pilgrims, offering to butcher an animal for a certain sum. Once paid, they held the animal with care, and faced its head toward the Kaaba at the Holy Mosque, while praying, 'In the name of God! God is Great!' After their prayer, the butchers quickly slit the throat of the animal, allowing the blood to drain prior to skinning the beast.

Hearing the cries of the poor beasts and watching the blood run freely, poor Amani screamed as one insane, and dropped to the ground in a faint.

Kareem and Abdullah carried our daughter to one of the small trailers which were alongside for the faint of heart and the weak.

They soon returned, saying that Amani was resting comfortably but was still crying, paralysed with grief at what she deemed was the senseless slaughter of many beasts.

Kareem gave me an 'I told you so' look. I felt some small degree of happiness that a recognizable part of Amani's personality had survived intact and hoped that Kareem was right in his assessment that once we departed Makkah that our daughter would be her old self.

As we watched the violent activity, I reminded myself that it was an important ritual, that the animals are sacrificed to remind the pilgrims of the lessons they have learned at *Haj*: sacrifice, obedience to God, mercy to all men, and faith.

Since a child, I had always been fascinated with the skinning process, with the butcher cutting a thin slit in the leg of the animal, then pumping air through the slit to separate the skin from the flesh. The animals grew larger and larger before my eyes, while the butcher struck the body of the animal with a strong stick to distribute the air evenly.

The four days of celebration now began in earnest. I knew that Muslims all over the world were joining us in the celebration, their hearts longing to be at the Holy city of Makkah. Shops were closing, families were receiving new clothes, and vacations were being taken.

As a close to our pilgrimage, we cut off locks of our hair and then exchanged our plain garb for colourful dresses, while the men put on clean cotton *thobes*, the white of the garment shining as brightly as newly spun silk.

That afternoon, the actual feast started. Amani was still pale but had recovered sufficiently to join in the festivities, though she refused to partake of any meat.

Our family gathered at our tent, and we exchanged small gifts and congratulated each other. We said our prayers, and then sat together at a long table and ate a wonderful meal of lamb with rice.

What remained of our feast was given to the poor. While many pilgrims would pray and repeat their rituals over the next few days, our family decided to return to our home in Jeddah to celebrate further.

We prepared for our departure.

My children were now entitled to place the honoured title of *Hajii* before their first name. In spite of the fact that I knew they would not do so, this term of respect reminds all Muslims that a person has fulfilled the fifth pillar of Islam. I knew that we had pleased God by doing *Haj*.

Now, I prayed for God to please me by releasing my daughter, Amani, from the fundamentalist leaning that seemed to grip her soul. I knew that mental instability could lend sanctity to the most extreme doctrine. I did not want my daughter sacrificed to the militant ideals so common to many religions, that I had struggled diligently against from the moment of understanding.

It was not to be. Whether I had pleased God or not, his decision concerning my daughter failed to please me.

The trip to Makkah would later prove to be both

fortunate and misfortunate for my family. While Kareem and I grew closer than we had since the first few years of our marriage, and Maha and Abdullah sought to live the lives of responsible citizens of our land, Amani became a gloomy recluse.

My deepest fears became reality.

Chapter Seven

EXTREMIST

*Let us imagine a desert country lying in absolute
darkness with many living things swarming
blindly about in it.*
Buddha

Haj was completed and summer was upon us.
The hot desert air had nagged us little during our
pilgrimage to Makkah, for our minds were on other,
more important matters connected to our spiritual
oneness with God.

From Makkah we travelled to our palace in
Jeddah, thinking to return to Riyadh the following
day. It was not to be. While I was organizing the
palace staff for our departure, Kareem entered the
room and said that he had cancelled our flight: air
traffic control had informed him that a particularly
turbulent sand storm was on the way from the
Rub Al-Khali desert and moving towards Riyadh.
Even without sandstorms, nearly 4,000 tons of sand
routinely settles on Riyadh every month. Wanting to
avoid this terrible storm of sand that stings the eyes,

fills the pores, and covers everything, I was pleased to remain longer in Jeddah, in spite of the fact that Jeddah's humid temperature is more oppressive than the dry desert heat of Riyadh.

Once the children had heard the news, Abdullah and Maha became excited at postponing Riyadh and their normal routine for a few days. Our two eldest children pleaded with us that we take a small holiday while in Jeddah. I looked at my husband and smiled. The smile faded from my face when I noticed that Amani was sitting off by herself in the corner of the room, her nose in the pages of the Koran. Amani was rapidly becoming a gloomy recluse and seemed unconcerned as to where she might be. It appeared to me that my youngest child had raised barriers against a normal desire for harmless fun, for in the past nothing thrilled Amani more than to swim in the lapping, warm waters of the Red Sea.

Determined not to allow Amani's activities to depress me further, I nodded my head, yes, in response to Kareem's questioning eyes. So, in spite of the humidity and the heat waves that were dancing in the air, Kareem and I decided to remain in Jeddah for an additional two weeks, for we could see that our two eldest children were sorely tempted by the blue mirror of the Red Sea waters that we could see from the walls of our palace.

Like many members of the royal family, I preferred the lively port city of Jeddah to staid Riyadh. I was looking forward to taking my daughters shopping in Jeddah's modern shopping malls and entertaining family friends who lived there, and the holiday loomed pleasantly before my mind. Had not Amani chosen this time to expand the growing gap between herself and her family, it would have been a perfect time in an otherwise imperfect life.

I was down on my knees in the long corridor which connected the various wings of the palace, when Maha made the discovery that her mother was attempting to overhear the voice of her sister, Amani, through a small crack in the door onto the Turkish baths and indoor garden area.

'Mummy! What are you doing?' Maha called out in a loud, laughing voice, even as I tried to wave her away with my hand.

From inside the room, Amani stopped speaking, and I heard my daughter's determined footsteps as she made her way towards the door. I made a desperate attempt to spring to my feet so that I could move myself away from the door, but my high heel caught in the hem of my long dress. I was struggling to free myself when Amani flung the door open and stood staring down at her obviously guilty mother.

I was unnerved by my daughter's accusing face, for her piercing eyes and tight lips made it plain that she clearly understood the situation.

Unable to acknowledge my despicable deed, I began to rub my fingers against some red threads that were worked into the hall carpet, and with what I hoped was a lilt to my voice, began to lie with the intensity of one who knows that their listeners see through her lie.

'Amani! I thought you were in your room!' I exclaimed.

I returned my gaze to the carpet at my feet,

seriously studying the red of the carpet. 'Darlings, have either of you noticed the red stains on this carpet?'

Neither of my daughters responded.

With a frown, I gave the red threads a few more rubs, and with my heel still caught in my dress, I stood up hunched over and limped down the corridor. Short on explanation, I mumbled, 'The servants have become quite lax. I fear that the stain is permanent.'

Amani, unable to allow me the pleasure of believing that my small lie had been convincing, spoke to my back. 'Mummy. This carpet is *not* stained. Those are red roses woven into the pattern of the carpet!'

Maha could not restrain herself, and I heard her as she began to giggle.

Amani called out, 'Mummy, if you wish to hear my words, you are most welcome. Please, come into the room where I am speaking.' The door leading to the garden room slammed with a thunderous clap.

Tears formed in my eyes and I rushed to my bedroom. I could not bear to look at my beautiful daughter, for since we had returned from Makkah, she had begun to clothe herself from head to toe in black, even going so far as to wear thick black hosiery and long black gloves. In the privacy of our home, only her face remained uncovered, as my child wrapped her beautiful black hair in a stiff black headcovering that reminded me of something a goat-herding Yemeni woman would wear. When Amani ventured outside our palace walls, she added a veil of thick black fabric that hindered her vision, even though the religious officials of Jeddah were much more relaxed in pursuing women with unveiled faces than were those of Riyadh. Our desert capital is known throughout the Muslim world for its diligent morals committees, which are composed solely of angry-faced men who harass innocent women on the city streets.

Nothing I could say or do could persuade my daughter to dress in greater comfort than the heavy black cloak, veil and headdress, a forced manner of female dressing that strikes most Muslim believers in other Islamic lands as nothing less than ridiculous.

I could not control my sobs. At great risk to my happiness, I had battled most of my life for my daughters to have the right to wear the thinnest of veils, and now, my dear child dismissed my small victory as if it had no value.

And, that was not the worst! Not content with her new-found discovery of our faith, Amani felt a missionary zeal to convert others to her new way of thinking. Today, Amani had invited her closest friends, along with four of her younger cousins to our home, to hear her read from the Koran and to speak to those girls of her interpretation of the Prophet's words, which sounded distressingly like the interpretation I had so often heard from the Government's Committee for Commendation of Virtue and Prevention of Vice.

The intonation of Amani's childlike voice was ringing in my head as I closed the doors to my private quarters and lay crossways on the bed, wondering how I was going to tackle this latest crisis of motherhood.

While eavesdropping, I had overheard Amani as she had read from the holy Koran:

Do ye build a landmark
on every high place
to amuse yourselves?

And, do ye get for yourselves
fine buildings in the hope
of living therein forever?

and when ye exert
your strong hand
do ye do it like men
of absolute power?

Now fear God and obey me
And follow not the bidding
of those who are extravagant,
and make mischief in the land,
and mend not their ways.

My knees shaking, I had listened in horror as
Amani stressed the Saudi royal family's similarity to
the ostentatious sinners in the verse of the Koran.

'Look around you! Witness the wealth of the
home from which I speak! A palace fit for a God
could be no finer! Are we not discarding the very
words of God in embracing opulence of costly in-
dulgence that no human eyes are fit to see?'

Amani's voice went soft, as if she were speaking
in a whisper, but I had closed my eyes and leaned
closer, listening with great care. I could barely hear
Amani's words. 'Each of us must banish extravagance
from our lives. I will set the first example. The jewels
that I have received from the wealth of my family
name, I will give to the poor. If you believe in the

God of Mohammed, you, too, must follow my example.'

I did not hear the audience's response to their leader's outlandish demand, for at that moment, my elder daughter, Maha, had made my unwelcome presence known.

Now, remembering Amani's promise to divest herself of her jewels, I pushed myself from the bed and hurried to my daughter's bedroom. There, I opened the safe that she shared with her sister, and removed a large quantity of expensive necklaces, bracelets, earrings and rings, locking those items into the safe in Kareem's office. I had taken Maha's cache of jewellery along with Amani's, for who knew what offence Amani might commit in her turbulent religious state.

I knew that the total value of Amani's jewellery alone was well into millions of dollars, and it had been given her by people who loved her and wanted to provide economic security for her future. I promised myself that if Amani genuinely desired to provide for the poor, then money would be given to her for this purpose.

Feeling depressed and unappreciated for our generosity, I remembered the millions of riyals that Kareem and I have quietly donated over the years to the poor of the world. In addition to the required *zakah* liability, or percentage of our annual income not needed for our daily living expenses, Kareem and I contribute an extra fifteen per cent of our income for education purposes and medical care to various Muslim countries less fortunate than Saudi Arabia. Never have we forgotten the words of the Prophet, 'If you give alms openly, that is well, but if you give them to the needy in private, it is even better for you, and will atone for some of your bad deeds. Allah is aware of all you do.'

Thinking of the funds provided to build medical clinics, schools and private dwellings in the poorest of Muslim lands, I felt a keen desire to remind Amani of the enormity of the financial contributions made by her parents. Had my child discarded our charitable activities as meaningless? Or was her true desire to turn our family into beggars, like those who had benefited from our great wealth?

Returning to my bed, I lay quiet for over two hours, thinking thoughts, discarding wild ideas, not knowing how to do battle with a force that is higher than any man.

Darkness had fallen over my room when Kareem came home from his Jeddah offices.

'Sultana! Are you ill?' Kareem switched on several lamps and walked to my bed, peering down at my face with concern.

'Your face is flushed. Do you have a fever?'

I did not answer my husband's questions. Instead, I took a deep, tortured breath. 'Kareem, one of your flesh and blood is plotting the overthrow of the monarchy.'

Kareem's face turned from pale brown to bright red in a matter of seconds. 'What?'

I feebly waved my hand in the air. 'Amani. Today, our daughter held a meeting of young princesses and good friends. I accidentally overheard her speaking. She's using the Koran to turn her young cousins and acquaintances against the leadership of our family.'

Kareem clicked his tongue in the Arab manner

that denotes disbelief. He laughed. 'You're crazy, Sultana. Amani is the least likely of our children to incite violence.'

I shook my head. 'No more. Religion has strengthened our child. She's beginning to resemble a hungry lion rather than a gentle lamb.' I repeated to Kareem what I had overheard.

Kareem made a face. 'Sultana. Believe me when I say this latest passion is nothing more than a passing phase. Ignore her. She'll soon tire of her excesses.'

It was clear that Kareem himself was tired of the topic of Amani's religious conversion. I had talked of little else during the past week. Amani's passionate embrace of all things extreme in our religion tortured her mother, while her father dismissed his daughter's fervour with a joke and a prediction that it would be short-lived.

My hopes were dashed that Kareem and I would share and resolve this latest crisis, unlike our unity in Maha's case. I felt the fight ease from my body. For the first moment since giving birth to Abdullah so many years before, I grew weary of motherhood, and wondered how many more generations of women could be enticed to burden themselves with the solitary and thankless production, nourishing and guidance of the human race.

With a rasping sound in my throat, I cried out to my husband, 'How lonely a woman's life is!'

Fearing that I would react in an unsettled manner to my grief, Kareem patted me tenderly, and asked sweetly if I would like my dinner served to me in private in our quarters. He said that he would take the evening meal alone with our children, if that were the case.

With a sigh of martyrdom, I decided not to stay alone. I had been in solitude for many hours, and I did not want to give Amani the idea that her mother was sulking. I pushed myself off the bed and told my husband that I would freshen up for dinner and see him downstairs.

Kareem and I met in the small family sitting-room, and since we were an hour early for dinner, I asked my husband to go for a stroll with me in the Turkish bath and garden area.

Remembering the evening that we had shared before, Kareem thought that I was feeling romantic, and his eyes brushed my face with tenderness.

I returned his smile but, in reality, I wanted to examine the garden area and see what evidence, if any, my child had left of her religious meeting with her friends and her royal cousins.

We entered our large beautiful courtyard that had been designed by a famous Italian fashion designer, and over the years, many of our royal cousins had attempted unsuccessfully to copy the loveliness of this unique 'Turkish room'. The first thing one sees is a flowing waterfall at the back of the room. Clear water falls from it into a large circular pool full of exotic fish. A stone path encircles the pool and beautiful flowers, tenderly cared for by our staff of gardeners, line the walkway. There are two raised sitting areas to left and right. Lush, green foliage that was imported from Thailand drapes over the rattan furnishings which are scattered with pastel-coloured cushions. Glass-topped tables are set about in the sitting areas, and it is a most pleasant spot for our family to enjoy morning or evening coffee.

The walls are made of special tinted glass, but the

greenery is so abundant and dense that we are shaded from the hot rays of the sun. A pathway leads around the waterfall, and Kareem and I walked on these stones, which are carved with the faces of wild animals. I felt sad as I walked on the face of a giraffe, for I remembered that Kareem had the stones especially carved for Amani, as a surprise for our animal-worshipping child.

The walkway took us to the Turkish bath area. Our home in Cairo has such a room too, and I had requested the Italian designer to study that design and duplicate it at our palace in Jeddah.

The Turkish bath house contains four baths, each one set in a different style and size. There are steps that lead to each bath, and over one of the larger baths is an arched bridge made of stone. Steam was rising from the water and dissipating in the cool air.

My family have enjoyed many wonderful times in the Turkish baths, and Kareem and I, just the evening before, prior to our evening of romance, had soothed ourselves by enjoying a lengthy steam bath.

There was nothing visible to the eye to indicate that Amani had held a religious meeting in our home. Yet my head still thundered with the words that I had overheard. I desperately wanted Kareem to acknowledge the seriousness of Amani's new passion, for our daughter was now talking of becoming a female Imam, a woman who would minister to other women's religious needs. While I wanted my daughter to live the life of a good Muslim, I had no desire for her to further the bondage of women under the strictest interpretation of the traditions that so hobbled females in our land.

Sensing correctly that Kareem was not burdened by Amani's passionate attraction to everything that I had fought against since an early age, I thought to remind him of where such religious passion could lead, for I knew that my husband was sensitive on the subject of the Al Sa'uds' legitimate claim to the throne and the wealth and privilege that accompanied our envied position.

Knowing my husband's life was firmly centred in a fashionable life of luxury that could hardly be afforded without the vast wealth of our country's oil fields, I gestured at the lovely décor of the Turkish bath. 'This', I said to Kareem, 'is what our daughter believes is a great sin, to enjoy what God has seen fit to provide our family.'

My husband made no response.

I needled him further. 'Kareem, we must take action. Or, do you want your own flesh and blood to lead the revolt that will bring down the house of Al Sa'ud?'

Kareem, still not believing his daughter capable of serious mischief, refused to analyse Amani's disenchantment with our royal status any further, saying only that our daughter should be left to her consoling faith, even if it was against her mother's obstinate resistance.

Holding me tightly by my shoulders, Kareem forbade me to mention the subject again, making a ridiculous statement.

'Sultana,' he said, 'I decided long ago that each of us must respect each other's delusions, or there will be no peace in our home. Now! Drop this disagreeable subject!'

*　　*　　*

After days of soul-searching, I finally reached the understanding that I was not to blame for my daughter's new direction in life. I reached the conclusion that Amani's zeal for a cause was the direct result of Saudi Arabia's horrendous poverty that had been relieved by sudden and enormous wealth. To get to the heart of the matter, I had to go back in time.

Many people, Muslims and Christians alike, despise Saudis for their unearned wealth. Yet, few bother to understand the wretched poverty endured by all Saudi Arabians until the mid-1970s. I highly resent this hasty analysis of our current situation.

Many years passed after the actual discovery of oil under the sand of the desert before our people benefited from the riches guaranteed by oil production that had been organized by American companies. In the beginning, King Abdul Aziz, my grandfather and the founder of Saudi Arabia, trusted the smooth-talking men who made false promises, not understanding that the deals struck put millions into the pockets of the Americans and paltry sums into the coffers of Saudi Arabia. Only when the American oil companies were forced to be fair did they behave in a principled manner.

Thus, due to the disproportionate method of dividing the proceeds from the oil wealth, it took many years for the bedouin desert tents to be replaced by luxurious villas and palaces to house our people. Meanwhile people of Saudi Arabia suffered greatly. Infant mortality in Saudi Arabia was among the highest in the world, for there was no money, doctors, or hospitals to treat the sick. Saudi diets consisted of dates, camel milk, and goat and camel meat.

I can remember seeing the desperate look in the eyes of one of the wealthiest men in the kingdom, as he shared the horrifying tale of his early years. A brilliant and highly respected man of business, he spent the first fifteen years of his life going from door to door in the mud-hut village of Riyadh, in an attempt to sell small bags of goat's milk. He was the man of the family when he was only seven years old, for his father had died from a slight infection he had contracted from his sword when slaughtering a camel for the *Haj* feast. The infection had turned to gangrene, and his father had ended his life screaming in great pain.

As was the custom of the day, the young boy's mother was wed to a surviving brother of his father, a man who had many children of his own. The young boy felt responsible for his five younger siblings. Four of them were buried by his own hand, their death a result of poor nutrition and medical facilities. His brutish climb to prosperity was a tale of Dickensian horror.

After a youth spent amid dire poverty, it was quite natural for the first Saudi generation to use the power of wealth to pamper their offspring, showering them with everything money could buy. While Kareem and I grew to adulthood without need in our lives, we understood the vital force of poverty, since the vestiges of poverty in our parents' generation made a lasting impact on our youth. However, the children born from our generation never knew deprivation, even secondhand, and so did not realize what it really meant to be poor.

Civilization followed a natural course, for concentrated wealth balanced insecurely upon a lost heritage may at any moment be dismissed as of no value. It was only a matter of time before shaky foundations would begin to tumble.

The conventions and traditions accepted by past generations were questioned by my generation. The generation that followed mine often followed their animal instincts wholly without restraint. This primitive rejection of social order brought forth a natural backlash of religious fanaticism and disdain for extravagant wealth.

Now, those who are fanatical are the offspring of my generation. Having never known life without great wealth, and spared the knowledge of the consequences of wrenching poverty, our children and the children of our acquaintances are scornful of the economic ease of our lives and are searching for a greater purpose than the accumulation of additional riches.

My child, Amani, became a leader of a group of women who strove and still strive to be even more militant than the men who lead the faithful to overturn the throne claimed by the Al Sa'ud clan.

While Amani sought to save the souls of those she knew as relatives, or claimed as friends, she brought forth a confession from her cousin, Faten, the child of Ali, that none of us could ever have imagined.

No man has been haughtier with women than my brother, Ali. As a child, he treated his ten sisters with contempt. As a young man living in America, he bedded and casually discarded hundreds of Western women. As a husband, he treated his wives as slaves, caring little about their happiness, careful to wed girls at first puberty so that they knew little of man's nature and accepted his perverse behaviour as normal. In addition to four wives, Ali settled one concubine after another into his home. As a father, he virtually ignored his daughters and showered affection on his sons.

It was only natural that his son, Majed, Faten's brother, grew into a sadistic youth who considered women nothing more than sexual objects.

Looking back, I know now that Majed would have been beheaded, or shot to death by a firing-squad, had his crime become common knowledge. Nothing could have saved Majed this fate, not even the fact that he is the son of a high-ranking prince, for his sin was without precedent in the Al Sa'ud family.

We had returned to our home in Riyadh, where each afternoon after school Amani continued her daily Koran sessions with those relatives who were interested in returning to the times of darkness, when women would remain silent on all issues of life that did not occur within the confines of their homes.

It was a Wednesday afternoon, and I watched from my bedroom balcony as one after another of my daughter's friends and relatives left our driveway in the safety of their chauffeur-driven limousines. Faten, my brother Ali's daughter, was last to leave, and I thought it odd that she and Amani talked for so long, and exchanged passionate embraces on more than one occasion. Sadly, I guessed that Faten, in her desperate unhappiness as daughter of my unfeeling brother, had fiercely seized the cause my child had offered her.

Desperate to return to a normal relationship with

my child, I cautioned myself not to introduce the topic of religion ever again with Amani, to let God lead her where he wanted her to go. Still, I hoped to interest Amani in a game of backgammon, or cards, to see if I could focus her mind on something other than her faith.

When I timidly knocked on my daughter's door, there was no response. I heard the sound of weeping and entered her room. A sense of irritation swept through me, for there sat Amani, holding the Koran in one hand and wiping tears with the other. I wanted to shout that religion was not meant to bring sadness, but I resisted the urge and knelt at my child's feet. I patted her knee and calmly began to question her on the cause of her grief.

Expecting to hear that she had received some message from God not meant for my ears, I was startled when she replied, 'Mummy, I am truly grieved by what I must do!'

Then my child threw herself in my arms and wept as one who has heard the most devastating news!

'Amani! Daughter! What is this?'

'Mummy!' A spasm went through her small frame as she sobbed. 'A terrible sin has been committed. I have learned a loathsome secret. God has told me to make this sin public.'

'What sin?' I shouted, alarmed that Amani had somehow heard of Maha's unnatural love relationship with her girlfriend, Aisha, knowing that if their affair were made public, that my daughter and our family would suffer greatly.

Amani looked at me with her big eyes. 'Faten has confided a secret that is troubling her soul. This sin is too terrible to reveal, yet I must.'

Mollified that Amani was not speaking of her sister, Maha, I speculated on the latest of Al Sa'ud scandals that might be plaguing my child. In a family the size of the Al Sa'ud clan, there is much gossip regarding the ungovernable conduct of the young princes, and on rarer occasions, the youthful princesses. Male members of the family will often be featured in foreign newspapers after a great gambling loss or being caught in a sexual mis-adventure with foreign women. After family holidays in the West, more than one princess has returned to the kingdom expecting an illegitimate child. Rarely is the complete truth revealed, as the various relatives rush to cover their child's misdeeds, in order to prevent their personal mis-fortunes from becoming common knowledge throughout the Al Sa'ud clan.

Amani blurted out, 'Mummy. It's Majed. Majed has commited a sexual sin.'

I had difficulty in maintaining a serious face. 'Majed? Amani, Majed is his father's son.' I pulled my daughter's face to mine, warning her, 'If you speak of this matter, the men of our family will do nothing more than share a laugh at your expense. Ali is proud of his son's success with foreign women.'

Everyone in our family knew that Majed, Ali's second son, participated in foreign activities in our country, attending parties in foreign compounds, dating non-Muslim women from the hospitals and foreign airlines. This activity was generally frowned upon by Muslim families, but Ali thought it a perfect opportunity for his second son to enjoy sexual freedom in a land where such activities are strictly forbidden between people of the Muslim religion.

My heart ached when I saw the seriousness of Amani's expression as she explained further. 'No, Mummy. You don't understand. Majed has performed a sexual act without the consent of the woman.'

I had no idea of what my daughter spoke. 'Amani, what do you mean?'

My daughter began to cry again. Between her convulsive sobs, she asked that I go and find her father, saying that she needed his guidance in her decision on whom to inform of Majed's terrible conduct.

Hurt that Amani desired her father's opinion over my own, I nevertheless went through the house, looking for Kareem. When I finally located him with Abdullah and Maha in the games room, playing a lively game of pool, I felt a twinge of jealousy, thinking to myself that all three of my children preferred their father to their mother. I had to bite my tongue to avoid blurting out Kareem's distressing character flaws in an attempt to redirect my children's devotion.

All three members of my family jumped when I loudly yelled, 'Kareem! Amani needs you.'

'Just a moment. It's my turn.'

'Kareem. Your daughter is weeping. Come, now.'

My husband gave me a filthy look. 'What have you said to her, Sultana?'

Already testy and wrongly accused, I used my hand to knock each of the brightly coloured pool balls into the holes at the side of the table. I walked away, unconcerned with the disappointed moans coming from Kareem and Abdullah.

'Now,' I shouted over my shoulder. 'The game has ended. You've won. Now, perhaps you can tend to your child.'

Kareem was on my heels as we entered Amani's room. The tears had gone from my daughter's eyes, and she had the fixed look of one who has made a decision.

Kareem spoke first. 'Amani? Your mother said you needed to tell me something?'

'Father, Majed has to be punished for what he's done. I've carefully read everything that is written on such matters, and there's no other way. My cousin *must* be punished.'

Kareem sat on a chair and crossed his legs. He had a squeezed, funny look on his face, as though for the first moment he realized that Amani had gone too far in her religious quest.

His voice quiet, he asked, 'What has Majed done that's so terrible?'

Still an innocent girl, Amani's face turned a bright red. 'I'm ashamed of what I have to say.'

'Just say it,' Kareem prodded.

Embarrassed at speaking thus in the presence of a man, even her own father, whom she had purposely requested to share the confidence, Amani stared into her lap. Her face was clear and innocent as she told us a tale of evil blackness.

'One evening Majed attended a party at one of the Western compounds. I believe that it was the compound for Lockheed employees. While there, he met an American woman who took an interest in the fact that he was of the royal family. As the evening went on, Majed became drunk, and the woman thought better of her promise to go with

Majed to a friend's apartment. When Majed understood that he had wasted his evening and that there
would be no sex that night, he left the compound in
an angry mood. On the way home, he went to visit
a friend who happened to be in hospital with minor
injuries from a car accident. While at this hospital,
Majed became angrier, and in his drunken condition, he slipped from room to room searching for
a blonde or foreign woman whom he could coax or
pay to have sex.

'It was after midnight, and there were few
employees who were not sleeping.'

Amani's bottom lip began to tremble, and Kareem
had to persuade her to continue. 'And . . . what
happened then, Amani?'

The accusation tumbled from my daughter's
mouth. 'Majed had sex with a woman in the hospital
who was a patient, a woman who had been seriously
injured, and was not conscious.'

I could not move. As one who had been turned to
stone, I listened as my daughter and my husband
continued to speak.

Kareem shook his head in disbelief. 'Amani. Faten
told you that?'

'Yes, Father. And, more.'

'Amani. No. Faten is imagining this. It can't be
true. It's too sick to be real.'

'I knew you would resist the truth,' Amani
accused. 'There's proof.'

'Proof? What proof? I would like to know.'

'Well, there was a man from Pakistan working in
that area of the hospital. He discovered Majed
leaving the room, and when he examined the
patient, he saw that the sheets on her bed had been

176

disturbed. He followed Majed and threatened to call the authorities. When he was told that Majed was a prince, he demanded money. To shut him up, Majed gave him what he had in his pocket.'

'Amani!' Kareem, highly dubious, cautioned his daughter. 'Watch the words that come from your tongue. Rape! Blackmail! This is too much to believe!'

'It's true! It's true! You'll see! Now there's going to be trouble.' Amani's words rushed out, one atop the other, as she tried to convince her father. 'Now, it's been discovered that the woman who was in a coma, a Christian woman from another land, is with child! Even though she's been in hospital, unconscious, for six months! She's three months with child! There's a big investigation in that hospital, and Majed is afraid that his name will be made public in the scandal.'

Thinking for the first time that there might be some truth to the story, for the details were many, I began to breathe heavily, wondering how we could avoid this scandal.

Amani tearfully completed her tale of horror, 'Faten caught him trying to break open the safe in their father's office, in order to steal cash. When cornered, Majed confided in his sister that the Pakistani has demanded a lot of money. This man wants 1,000,000 *riyals*[1] to remain silent about Majed's royal identity. Majed can't ask his father for that amount of money without an explanation, and the man's going to name him. Majed's been given one week to come up with the money.'

[1] Roughly £172,000.

Kareem and I stared at each other, wondering if what we were hearing was the truth.

I recalled terrible words that Majed had once used to Abdullah, ridiculing my son for his refusal to have sex with what Abdullah had claimed was a particularly ugly American, a woman who was twice my son's age but had been willing to have sex with a young prince for money. Majed had accused Abdullah of being a man who did not like women, saying, 'A true man can become excited over a she-camel!' I vaguely recalled that Majed had then told Abdullah something about the woman looking better than the last woman he had 'ridden' – a woman who had been unconscious and had not known what fun she was missing.

When discussing the incident, we had assumed that the woman must have been drunk. Now, in the light of what Amani was saying, had that woman been unconscious from an injury? Had Ali's son raped a woman who had no ability to speak for herself? The timing of Abdullah's confidence now fitted in with Amani's story.

I wanted to ask Kareem about that conversation, for Abdullah had told him about it, and he had shared the story with me. I remembered that from that time onwards Kareem had forbidden Abdullah to accompany his cousin Majed to foreign parties.

Kareem came to when Amani said, 'Majed has to be punished. I will have to tell Wijdan to inform her father of Majed's misdeed.'

I heard Kareem's teeth as they ground against each other. He, as I, knew that Wijdan's father was a religious man who worked out of the royal mosque. While he bore no special animosity towards members of the royal family, he was a man of religion who followed his conscience. He would be a difficult man to buy off, and if nothing else, would insist on discussing the matter with the religious council and the King. The last thing our family needed was for that particular man to be told of the situation.

Besides, I still hoped in my heart that a mistake had been made and Majed was innocent of such unspeakable and indecent behaviour.

Kareem instructed his daughter, 'Amani, this is not a topic for young girls to be discussing. I'll investigate these charges, and if they're true, I give you my word that Majed will be punished. Now, I must have your promise that you will tell no-one of what you've said.'

Expecting Amani to disagree, I was pleasantly surprised when my child seemed relieved to discharge the problem to her father. She promised him all that he had asked.

Within three days, Kareen had discovered the ugly truth. Indeed, there was a Christian woman in a local hospital who had suffered a serious head injury in a car accident within the kingdom seven months prior to Kareem's investigation. She had been unconscious for that length of time. Now, the hospital staff and the family of the woman were in crisis, for the medical staff at the hospital had discovered that the woman was four months' pregnant! There was an ongoing inquiry at that institution to find the guilty party.

Amani's horrifying story was true!

Kareem said that Ali must be told, and my husband requested that I accompany him to my brother's home. For once in my life, I experienced no glee regarding my brother's misfortunes.

My stomach churned as we entered the side gate into the enormous compound that housed Ali's four wives and seven concubines. As our car entered the gateway, I caught sight of many women and numerous children gathered on the portion of the lawn partly hidden by green foliage. The children were playing, while the women were gossiping, playing card games, or knitting.

How strange, I thought, that over the years the women that my brother had wed, along with the concubines he kept, had developed close and loving relationships. It was rare that so many women attached to one man could maintain such a successful and friendly rapport.

I could not imagine sharing Kareem with one woman, let alone ten. I thought perhaps that the lack of love in my brother's manner caused the women to seek friendship and companionship with those of their own kind. Or perhaps my brother inspired no love at all from his women, and each one welcomed the intrusion of another to seduce Ali away from the marriage bed.

That thought brought a smile to my face.

But when I remembered the tragic reason for our visit to my brother's home, my smile vanished.

Ali was in a jolly mood, and he extended a friendly welcome to our unexpected and unexplained visit.

After an exchange of pleasantries, and our third cup of tea, Kareem broke the news. It was not an easy exchange, and, as Kareem informed Ali of what he had learned, Ali's expression changed from that of a contented man to one lost in sorrow. For the first time in my life, I felt sympathy for my brother, recalling words I had often heard spoken by those wiser than me. 'Those whose hands are in the water should not expect happiness from those whose hands are in the fire.'

Ali was a man with his hand in the fire.

Majed was summoned, and the boy's arrogant countenance cracked when he saw the furious look on his father's face. I wanted to hate the boy, but I remembered an incident that had occurred when I was but a child. After being corrected for some minor infraction, Ali once called our mother an 'ignorant bedouin' and had moved to kick at his own mother. When my sisters and I had begged our mother to beat Ali with a big stick, our mother had sadly responded, 'Why blame a young boy for resembling his father?'

Now, just as Ali had resembled our father in character and behaviour, Majed was the image of Ali.

Kareem and I left my brother and his son when Ali began to strike Majed with his bare hands.

A week later Ali confided to Kareem that the problem had been 'handled'. He reported that he had located the Pakistani orderly and had made the man very rich. With the cash he was given, the Pakistani invested his money in Canada, and with Ali's assistance would soon receive a passport to that country. Our family would hear no more from that troublemaker, Ali had declared.

Shaking his head in bafflement, Ali had told Kareem, 'All this disruption, for a woman.'

Neither the hospital nor the family of the woman raped by Majed was ever aware of the truth of the matter, that the guilty party was a royal prince.

Majed was sent away to school in the West.

Amani, convinced that no punishment could be worse than banishment from the land of the Prophet, was pacified.

Once again, wealth had abolished family responsibility for a crime committed.

I suppose I should not have been angry or suprised, for as my brother said, it was only a woman.

It seemed that nothing disturbed the male domination of my country, even when one of their own was guilty of the most heinous crime.

Chapter Eight

LOVE AFFAIR

When love beckons you, follow him, though his ways
are hard and steep.
Kahlil Gibran

Amani and her sister, Maha, awoke me from a pleasant afternoon nap. Through the thick doors leading into my private quarters, I could hear my daughters screaming at each other.

What had Amani done now? I thought to myself, as I quickly dressed. Since Amani's religious conversion, she liked to tell people what she thought of them, never hesitating to enumerate her brother's and sister's immoral acts, searching endlessly for a pretext to censure her siblings.

My son, Abdullah, was loath to fight. Dreading Amani's incalculable, and apparently unappeasable wrath, Abdullah, more often than not, simply ignored his sister. On the rare occasions that Amani's demands were simple to fulfil, he capitulated.

Amani did not find such agreement possible with Maha. With her older sister, Amani was dealing with a female character who was at least as strong as herself, for Maha's violent temper had characterized her from her first breath.

I followed the sound of my daughters' shouts. Several of the servants were standing in the doorway of the kitchen, but they were disinclined to interrupt what to their eyes was lively entertainment.

I had to push my way into the room.

I had arrived at an opportune moment. Maha, who is twice Amani's size and much fiercer than her younger sister, had reacted violently to Amani's latest regulation. As I rushed towards my daughters I saw that Maha had her younger sister pinned to the floor, rubbing her face into the pages of the morning newspaper!

It was as I had thought!

Just the week before, Amani and her religious group had come to the conclusion that the kingdom's daily newspapers were made holy since the pages contained the word God, the sayings of the Holy Prophet, and verses of the Koran. The committee had decreed that newspapers were not to be walked upon, eaten upon, or thrown into the trash. At the time, Amani had given notice to her family of the religious decision, and now she had violently apprehended Maha committing an irreverent act – heedless of her noble instruction.

The result had been predictable.

I shouted, 'Maha! Let your sister go!' Spurred on by her anger, Maha seemed not to hear my excited command. I made a futile attempt to pull Maha away from her sister, but my daughter was determined to teach Amani a lesson. Since Maha was stronger than Amani and me together, she was the victor in our three-way struggle.

Red-faced and breathing with great effort, I looked to the servants for assistance, and one of the Egyptian drivers moved quickly to intervene. The man had strong arms and was successful in separating my daughters.

One battle always invites another. Verbal insults replaced physical force. Maha began to curse her baby sister who was weeping bitter tears while accusing her elder sister of being a non-believer.

I proposed to mediate but could not be heard above the mayhem. I pinched the skin on my daughters' arms until they were silenced. Maha stood in smouldering sullenness. Amani, still on her hands and knees, reached to straighten the pages of the ripped newspaper. My daughter kept her devotions to the end!

The causes for religious fervour are many, and the results are endless. I had a thought that some people appear at their worst in their religion. Certainly, that was the case with Amani. In the past, I had felt both doubtful and hopeful that religion could, in time, soothe rather than incite Amani. But now I felt with dull certainty that would not be the case.

My patience did not equal my anger, and I led my daughters by their ears into the sitting-room. With a firm voice, I called for the servants to leave us to ourselves. I glared at my children, thinking ungallantly that I had made a grievous mistake in inflicting such troublesome characters upon the world.

'The wailing of the newborn infant is nothing

more than a siren of warning sung for a mother,' I said to my daughters.

My face and glance must have shown me as a madwoman, for my daughters' expressions were stricken. They held a curious respect for their mother's moments of insanity.

Thinking to avoid a second larger quarrel with three participants rather than two, I closed my eyes and took a deep breath. Once calmed, I told my daughters that each of them would have an opportunity to speak but that there would be no more violence.

Maha burst out, 'Too much! Too much! Amani is driving me insane! She will leave me alone, or . . .' I could see that Maha was searching through her mind for the worst possible insult, 'I'll slip into her room and rip up her Koran!'

Amani gasped in horror at the thought.

Knowing how spirited and daring Maha could be when she was determined to do a thing, I forbade my daughter the irreverent act.

Her fury unleashed, Maha continued. 'This stupid idea of not discarding old papers! We'll have to build a large storeroom to house them.' She looked at her sister, 'You've lost all good sense, Amani!' Maha looked back at me and charged her sister with dictatorship, 'Mother, from the moment we departed *Haj*, Amani no longer feels my equal but my master!'

I agreed completely with Maha. With impressive speed, I had seen my daughter's religious beliefs pass from confusion to a flourishing vision. Her sense of divine righteousness was producing ridiculous household sanctions that excluded no-one.

Just a few days before, she had discovered one of the Filipino gardeners proudly displaying a pair of rubber sandals that had been imprinted with the name of God on the sole of the shoe.

Instead of receiving anticipated praise for his purchase, Amani had shrieked in rage, grabbing the poor fellow's shoes and accusing him of blasphemy, threatening him with severe punishment.

In tears, the young man had confessed that he had purchased the shoes in Bahtha, a popular shopping souq located in the downtown district of Riyadh. He had thought that his Muslim employers would be pleased to see that the name of God was printed on his shoes.

Calling the shoes the work of the devil, Amani had called a special meeting of her religious group and had stunned them all by revealing the sacrilegious shoes.

Word had spread to other religious groups, and pamphlets had been distributed in the city, advising people not to buy or wear such shoes.

The shoes were rather shocking, since Muslims are taught not to walk on any item bearing God's name, even going so far as to forbid our shoes from lying sole up, in case that might be some insult to our maker. Yet, Amani's reaction had been somewhat drastic since the young Filipino was not of our faith and not acquainted with our truths. My daughter had been cruel in her angry denunciations.

Since an early age, I have been drawn to the idea of a kindly God, a being that does not find sin in every human delight. I knew with certainty that my child was not acquainted with the God of Mohammed, as taught to me by my loving mother. I sent a questionable prayer to my maker, asking that Amani's gloomy devoutness take a holiday.

My thoughts returned to the present crisis, and I looked upon my daughers.

With Maha's threat of defacing her Koran looming as a real possibility, Amani promised to refrain from inspecting her siblings' habits.

Maha declared that if Amani would only leave her to her own inclinations, however distracting they might be to her sister, she would commit no further violence.

I hoped that the truce would stick, but I had my doubts, for Amani was readily moved to judge all before her, never really happy except when making religious war. And Maha was not one to bear the taunts of her sister timidly.

My two daughters, trapped in a family unit, were too volatile a mixture for everlasting peace.

I abandoned desolation and yielded to motherly affection. With the deepest love, I embraced each of my daughters.

Maha, always quick to anger and prompt to forgive, gave me a genuine smile of peace. Amani, slow to pardon those she deemed in the wrong, was stiff and did not yield to my affection.

Exhausted by the responsibilities of motherhood, I wistfully observed my girls as they went their separate ways.

All at once, the room was empty of their mad energy, but the consoling quiet was not comforting. I felt edgy, and told myself that I was in need of a stimulant.

I rang the bell for Cora and asked that she bring me a cup of Turkish coffee. Then, without knowing my reason, I abruptly changed my mind and asked instead, that she mix me a strong drink of bourbon and Cola.

Cora stood open-mouthed with surprise. It was the first occasion that her mistress had requested a drink of alcohol during the daylight hours.

'Go on,' I demanded.

I sat, reading the newspaper without absorbing the news. I admitted to myself that I was looking forward to my drink with discomfiting anticipation, when Abdullah arrived at home.

Abdullah moved with speed through the door into the hallway. I caught a glimpse of my son's face and did not like what I saw. Accustomed to his gentle character, I saw by his dark expression that he was torn by agony.

I called out, 'Abdullah!'

Abdullah strode into the room. Unasked, he let his anguish be unconfined.

'Mother! Jafer has fled the kingdom!'

'What?'

'He's run away! With Fouad's daughter, Fayza.'

Staggered by confusion and scepticism, I could not speak. With my mouth hanging open, I sat and stared at my son.

Still in his early twenties, Jafer Dalal was a young man admired by all who knew him. He was both handsome and strong, with a serious but kindly countenance bespeaking quiet wisdom and calm strength. He was a charming conversationalist, a gentleman of refinement and courtesy. Jafer was one of but a few young men that Kareem trusted completely with the women of his family.

Jafer was Abdullah's dearest and most cherished friend.

Often I told Kareem that I would like to have known Jafer's parents, for never has a man been better raised. But that could never be, for Jafer's mother died when he was only twelve and his father was killed in the Lebanese civil war when Jafer was seventeen. Jafer's one brother, four years his senior, had been critically wounded in the Lebanese war and was a permanent resident of a nursing facility located in the south of Lebanon. Orphaned while still a teenager and without any siblings to offer him shelter, Jafer moved from the only home he had ever known and travelled to live with an uncle in Kuwait, who managed some businesses for a wealthy Kuwaiti.

As a Palestinian Sunni Muslim born and raised in the refugee camps of Southern Lebanon, Jafer did not have an easy life.

After the Iraqi invasion of Kuwait, the PLO stood behind Saddam Hussein. It was not surprising that after the war ended there was much resentment by Kuwaiti citizens towards the large Palestinian population. While Jafer's uncle and his family had remained loyal to their Kuwaiti sponsor and could have remained in Kuwait, there was such a backlash of dislike towards anyone with a Palestinian identification that the Kuwaiti sponsor recommended that the family move to another land. The kindly man did not want such a fine family to risk danger by remaining in Kuwait. 'Let a few years pass,' he promised, 'and the crisis will pass.'

This Kuwaiti sponsor co-owned a business with Kareem, and he suggested to my husband that

Jafer's uncle would make an excellent employee for a particular job opening in that company's offices in Riyadh.

As there was some bitterness at the time between our king and Yasser Arafat with regard to the Gulf War, there was a political move in Saudi Arabia to avoid employment of people with Palestinian nationality. As a high-ranking prince, Kareem could do as he pleased. On the recommendation of his Kuwaiti partner, he employed Jafer's uncle.

After the man arrived in Riyadh, he became one of Kareem's most entrusted employees, assigned with difficult tasks and responsible posts. Jafer accompanied his uncle and so impressed my husband that he was given a management position in Kareem's law offices.

From the moment Abdullah was introduced to Jafer, the two young men became fast friends, Abdullah claiming Jafer as the brother that he never had.

Jafer came into our lives only two short years ago, yet he quickly became a beloved member of our family.

Conspicuously attractive, Jafer drew much female attention wherever he went in the city. Abdullah claimed that women passed his friend notes of invitation while in hotel restaurants. Once when Jafer accompanied Abdullah to the King Faisal Specialist Hospital and Research Centre to visit a royal cousin hospitalized there, three foreign nurses volunteered their telephone numbers to Abdullah's friend after the briefest of conversations.

I thought Jafer wise beyond his years, for it appeared that he lived a life of celibacy, in a land that frowned upon illicit relationships between men and women.

Sensing that the young man was lonely and was of an age to settle down, Kareem reproached Jafer for persistent bachelorhood. Making serious offers to introduce Jafer to Lebanese or Palestinian contacts, men who might introduce him to marriageable Muslim women from those countries, Kareem declared that it would be a tragedy if Jafer avoided love, adding that even good men could be ruined by too much virtue!

With a wink in my direction, Kareem mischievously added that all men should experience the pleasures and tribulations of female companionship.

In jest, I made a threatening move towards my husband, for I knew the truth – that Kareem, a happy father, could not have borne a life without children.

Kareem failed in his attempt to provide female company to a young man whom he had grown to respect and love. Jafer never accepted Kareem's generous invitation to meet women.

Abdullah added to the mystery by saying that his friend was polite but firm in refusing all offers of female companionship.

I was puzzled but so consumed by the problems presented by my daughters, that I thought little more of Jafer's private life.

Looking back, how could we have thought that a full-blooded, sensual man like Jafer scorned all that love had to offer?

The truth as to why Jafer had deferred marriage was made known in a most devastating manner that threatened to end tragically.

*　*　*

My thoughts returned to my son.

Abdullah, who had loved Jafer with perfect sincerity, let his grief overflow. There was something disarmingly childlike about my son as he complained, 'Jafer never told me about Fayza.'

It was the darkest time of Abdullah's young life. My son's dishevelled innocence pierced my heart.

At that moment, Kareem arrived, as angry as Abdullah was sad.

'Abdullah!' he shouted. 'You've risked your life and the lives of innocents!'

Kareem told me that when Abdullah had been informed of Jafer's disappearance, he had become distraught and had left Kareem's offices in a dangerous mood. Fearful for his only son's safety, Kareem had followed in hot pursuit. My husband claimed that Abdullah had driven his car through the streets of the city at high speed. Kareem said that at one point Abdullah's car crossed the centre lane and forced a line of drivers from the road.

'You could have been killed!' So agitated at the possibility, Kareem reached across and slapped his son's face.

The sharp slap shocked and silenced my husband.

Over the years of my children's turbulent growth, I have pinched and slapped all three of our offspring with irresistible pleasure.

Never had Kareem struck one of our children!

Kareem was as stunned by his action as I was, staring down at his offensive hand as though it were not his own.

He embraced his shivering son and apologized, saying that in the course of following Abdullah's reckless path, he had gone out of his mind with worry.

The room was filled with emotion, and it took many moments for the mystery of Jafer and Fayza's hidden romance to be completely revealed.

Fayza was the daughter of Fouad, Kareem's partner in three foreign businesses. Fouad was not of the Al Sa'ud family but weakly related by marriage to a daughter of a royal.

Many years before, Fouad had been allowed to wed into the royal family, even though he was not from a clan of the Najd, nor was his tribe particularly close to the Al Sa'uds. Generally, Al Sa'ud women were wed out of the family for political or economic reasons. While Fouad was from a prosperous Jeddah trading family, his family had bitterly fought the Al Sa'uds during the early days of the formation of the kingdom.

Anxious to unite his family with the rulers of the land, Fouad had offered an immense dowry for Samia, a princess who, we often said in kindness, had been spared the distracting handicap of being a great beauty.

No-one in the royal family could believe Samia's good fortune, for she was long resigned to remaining a spinster, cruel gossip about her bad skin, small eyes, and bent back having stripped away all possibilities of marriage.

Fouad, determined to attach himself to the respected Al Sa'ud clan, had heard of Samia's lack of attraction through women who knew her family, but his only desire was to marry a woman of many virtues. He had been forewarned by the lurid stories that were bandied about by his female relatives telling of alluring women who made the most miserable wives, for carefully coiffured and richly garbed women could think of little besides expensive homes, many servants and endless jewels.

Fouad knew sound advice when he heard it. Denouncing the lure of beauty, he said that he desired a woman of humour and warmth. The particular princess he sought, while uncongenial to a poet's dream, was one of the more popular royals, well loved for her charm and grace.

Thinking that Fouad was a fool, Samia's family had accepted his offer, and a wedding was held.

Fouad was well pleased with his wife, for she had a sense of humour that Fouad knew would see them through the tribulations of marriage. His new bride facilitated matters by falling deeply in love with her husband. Theirs was the happiest of unions.

Fouad was a Saudi man who adored his one and only wife and was the proud father of three sons and one daughter. In one of the stranger quirks of nature, Fouad, a plain-faced man, and Samia, a woman who was pitied for her appearance, produced the most dazzling offspring. Their three sons were strikingly handsome, while their only daughter was a ravishing beauty.

Fayza was the only girl I have ever seen who rivalled Sara's youthful splendour. Stories about her fair complexion, wistful dark eyes, and long coal-black hair stirred the blood of Saudi Arabian men who could only imagine the girl's physical attractiveness from hearsay.

Fayza had other irresistible qualities. She had inherited something of her mother and was a girl of rare, dry wit and often livened our female gatherings.

I was sorry that Fayza was older than my son, for I thought Abdullah would have loved her intensely, had he the opportunity.

Beautiful, witty and smart, Fayza was a university student at a women's school in Riyadh. She was in the first courses of pre-dentistry and had aspirations to open a children's dental facility.

Fouad confided that while he wanted his daughter to obtain a degree, in reality she would have little need for working skills. He proudly confided in Kareem that at the completion of his daughter's education, Fayza would be married into a wealthy family. Meetings had already been conducted, and Fouad had his pick of three influential families. When his daughter graduated, he would allow her to have supervised meetings with each of the three young men in question, allowing his child to have a say in her future.

When Kareem told me Fouad's plans for his child, I felt great joy, thinking how far we have travelled since the days of my youth! None of my sisters had a voice in the choice of their husbands. And, Sara! Who among us could forget the nightmare that Sara endured in her first marriage to an evil man. It had been a cruel union that had scarred my sister, almost claiming Sara's life.

In my family I was the only daughter privileged to meet my husband before he became my intimate partner in life, and that decision had resulted from nothing more than the actions of a spirited girl, combined with the determination of a curious suitor.

Now! A man raised in the strictest of times was casually speaking of allowing his child the opportunity to take part in the selection of her husband.

How happy I was at the news!

Yet I did not let myself rejoice for too long, for I knew that most women in my land were still used as nothing more than political or economic prizes. Nevertheless, I assured myself, each individual battle won would eventually lead to widespread and enormous victory!

And, now! Fouad's dreams for his daughter's future had come to nothing. His only daughter, a beautiful woman sought by the wealthiest of men in my land, had eloped with a penniless Palestinian refugee!

'How did this happen?' I asked my husband.

With their lawyers' minds and information gathered by Samia, Kareem and Fouad had pieced together the drama of the two lovers.

Weeks after Jafer had begun his work at the firm, Fouad's family had come into the office to sign some papers. Fouad had acquired some rather large business interests abroad, and he had put some of those businesses in the names of his children.

Jafer was responsible for the clerical aspects of the documents. When Fouad's family arrived, they were ushered into Jafer's office, where the young man was able to obtain the necessary signatures. As our religious customs demand, Samia and her daughter, Fayza, were veiled. Feeling protected in a locked office, in the presence of a trusted employee, both women had thrown their veils off their faces, onto the top of their heads, for the purposes of reading and signing documents.

Now, in the midst of the controversy, Samia had the dimmest recollection that her daughter and Jafer had stared at each other for too long a time.

Samia, innocent in her inherent goodness, had not connected her daughter's nervous behaviour and crooked signature with the medley of incredible fancies that were playing upon her child.

At the time, Samia had listened without hearing and looked without seeing.

The handsome young man, Jafer, had offered them tea, and Samia had watched her daughter as she gratefully received the attentions of the man, their hands lightly brushing in the innocent exchange of pens and cups of tea. She told her husband that, at the time, she had thought that the touches were accidental.

Kareem reported that Fouad had screamed insults, blaming his wife, telling her that all men are by nature villains, and that she, the mother of an innocent girl, should have been more astute to Jafer's evil nature! Fouad had moaned, claiming that Jafer was nothing more than a man with a poem on his lips and a dagger in his pocket!

Samia could recall nothing more, other than that her child had seemed flushed and feverish while in the company of Jafer.

Fayza's personal Filipino maid, Connie, knew many details. She was carefully questioned by Kareem and Fouad. The two men discovered that there was no end to the intrigue of the two lovers, and according to Connie, it was Fouad's daughter, rather than Jafer, who had pursued the affair.

Connie reported that, from that first day, Fayza had been stricken by a great love. A weakening love that made the girl forget to eat and sleep. Torn between loyalty to her family and drawn by sexual desire for Jafer, Fayza had confessed to her maid that love was the victor, that she would have the man, Jafer, or no man at all.

Connie said that she had never seen a girl so taken by a man.

Knowing the plans of Fayza's parents for their lovely daughter, Connie found herself in an unenviable position. She could not report the truth about her young mistress, yet she knew that she should. Connie swore to Fouad that she reminded Fayza that the daughter of a wealthy Saudi family, with close connections to the Al Sa'uds, could not end up with a Palestinian clerk.

Such a situation could only lead to misfortune.

Having a tendency to lapse into criticism of our male-dominated society, I thought of where the blame might be placed. Thinking of Saudi Arabia's restrictive social customs, I interrupted Kareem and told him I had come to a conclusion, that Fayza's over-reaction to a charming, handsome man made a mockery of our system. My voice thick with frustration, I declared that if men and women could only meet each other under normal circumstances, delusions of instant love would be more infrequent.

While I do believe that great attractions lead to genuine love, such as it had with my sister, Sara, and her husband, Asad, such a happy outcome is rare. When life is filled with harsh social restrictions, when young men and women rarely have the opportunity to enjoy the other's company in ordinary social occasions, spontaneous emotions are quick to rise to the surface, often ending in terrible personal tragedies.

With an irritated look on his face, Kareem said he would quit the room if I insisted on burdening the conversation with my well-known theories of the subjugation of females in the Saudi culture!

Abdullah looked at me with longing, his eyes begging me not to make a scene. For the sake of my son, I agreed to be quiet.

Kareem, subtly pleased, continued to tell of the drama.

Fayza, telling Connie that her heart had been a willing recipient of love, knew that Jafer had loved her too, but that he was vulnerable in his low position to her elevated status. She feared that he would never take the initiative.

Fayza boldly called Jafer at his office, asking him to meet her, promising that her family would never know.

Jafer, while acknowledging to Fayza that no woman had ever affected him as she had, refused the tempting offer, telling the girl that what benefit there could be would be only temporary bliss, for when the relationship ended, unbearable mental torture would ensue.

Fayza gleefully confided to Connie that Jafer was snared, that she was certain she would soon see him, for their telephone conversations had become hot with passion, with Jafer warning her that if he ever had her, he would never give her up. His words were delightful to hear!

Fayza persisted. After two weeks of increasingly intimate telephone conversations that only served to further their desire, Jafer's resolve had weakened. They agreed to meet at the Al-Akariya, a large shopping mall in the city of Riyadh.

At last, a veiled Fayza, masquerading as a relative of Jafer, walked beside the man whom she had sought. The two walked from shop to shop, getting to know the other. They aroused little suspicion, for they appeared to be nothing more than an Arab man with a veiled woman, a common sight in our city.

Their walking relationship was unnatural, but they were too fearful to seat themselves at a restaurant to share a meal, for they knew that restaurants in our country are the principal target of the active and increasingly familiar morals committees that harass people of every nationality who live in Saudi Arabia.

Such committees are composed of menacing men who unexpectedly surround and enter eating establishments, demanding identification of the restaurant patrons. If proof is not forthcoming that the men and women sharing a table are not husband and wife, brother or sister, or father and daughter, these frightened people will be arrested and escorted to a city gaol, with punishment freely given. The legal penalties vary according to the nationality of the 'criminal'. Muslim offenders can be flogged for their social misconduct, while non-Muslims are gaoled or deported.

In the beginning, Jafer and Fayza adjusted their morals to the situation.

Over time, Jafer located an apartment where they could meet in privacy. A sympathetic Lebanese friend offered his place. Since Fayza, as a woman, was not allowed to drive, she was forced to trust a family driver. Knowing that his participation could result in deportation or worse, Fayza lessened his hesitation by offering the man a large sum of money.

Out of this tempting attraction a great love blossomed. The lovers accepted they could never love another. Jafer asked Fayza to marry him. Just as they were building up their courage to make their love known to their families, a crisis occurred. One of Saudi Arabia's wealthiest men approached Fouad for the privilege of the beautiful Fayza to wed his eldest son. Pressure mounted for Fayza to agree. Fouad declared that the prospective bridegroom was matchless.

'How long I have toiled to build a perfect relationship that my father would so readily destroy!' Fayza had cried out to Connie.

The desperate lovers made their decision to flee the country.

Fouad had been tricked, his honour tarnished, and now he would stop at nothing to find his only daughter!

Knowing how difficult it was for females in Saudi Arabia to travel freely, I asked, 'How did Fayza manage to leave the kingdom alone?'

'She didn't', Kareem replied, 'leave alone.'

I was pleased to hear that Fayza had not committed the sin of travelling alone. Saudi women are forbidden by our religion to travel without a male member of her family as an escort. This particular restriction is taken directly from the words of the Prophet who said: 'She who believes in Allah and the Last Day (meaning the Day of Judgement) must not travel any distance which is normally covered by one day's and one night's travelling unless accompanied by a *mahram*.'

A woman's *mahram* is any of her relatives to whom she cannot be married, such as her father, brother, uncle, nephew, stepfather, father-in-law or son-in-law. She is allowed to travel with her husband as a matter of course.

I discovered that Fayza had talents in the art of treachery. She told her parents she needed some time away from the mounting pressures on her. She hinted to her mother that a positive response would be forthcoming to the marriage proposal if she could enjoy a small holiday. She thought she would like to visit her cousin, a girl who had married a man from Dubai. Could she be rewarded with a weekend before she pledged herself to marriage?

Samia was bedridden with a sprained back, so Fayza's younger brother was taken along as his sister's required male escort.

Why should a connection be made that Jafer had taken his annual holiday during the same period? In their wildest imagination no-one in the family linked the young man with Fayza.

Once in the safety of Dubai, removed from the dangers of Saudi Arabia, Fayza had out-manoeuvred her younger brother, slipping her passport from his travel bag while he was in the shower, and making an ordinary pretence to shop with other females. Her brother volunteered to drive, dropping them at the Al Ghurair Centre on his way to meet a Saudi friend who was staying at the Chicago Beach Hotel, located on one of the most beautiful beaches in the Emirates.

From the Al Ghurair Centre, a popular shopping area, Fayza had whispered to her cousin that she had to seek a toilet but that she would soon return. Her cousin, intent upon selecting perfume, had thought little of the deception, promising Fayza that she would wait for her in the shop.

Fayza was not seen again. To her cousin's horror, she had disappeared.

A frantic search had ensued, with Fouad and his wife fearing the worst for their daughter's safety. Had their child been kidnapped, raped or murdered? While such crimes were rare in the Emirates, occasionally violent acts were committed.

When Connie learnt of her well-loved mistress's strange disappearance, she collapsed into a weeping fit and confessed Jafer and Fayza's activities.

A father's love knows no reason. Not believing that his innocent daughter could be so devious, all blame fell upon Jafer's head.

Neither Kareem nor I had ever heard of Fouad resorting to abuse or force. Fouad was known to all as a soft-spoken, kindly man. This was not the case in the emotional upheaval he suffered after his daughter's flight with a man. He fired the unfortunate Connie, putting her on the next flight to Manila. In his wild rage Fouad burst into Kareem's offices, and physically assaulted Jafer's uncle. There was a terrible scene, with Fouad threatening the life of the man if his daughter were not returned unharmed, still a marriageable virgin.

The police were summoned by a frightened Indian secretary in a neighbouring office.

In Saudi Arabia, liability for public disorder falls upon the foreigner, never upon a Saudi. Fouad was questioned by the police and apologies were made for their interference in a private matter. Had Kareem not been higher in rank and influence than Fouad, Jafer's uncle would have been imprisoned.

Everyone in my family felt saddened by the insoluble problems of human life, and no-one knew the appropriate action to take.

Sara and I visited Samia in her home. Muttering that 'life without love would be a mistake', I said everything wrong, causing poor Samia's ugly face to grow uglier still, while Sara knew how to express intense feeling in her own quiet way.

Bewildered by her child's rash flight, Samia had difficulty speaking and began to stutter anxious responses to Sara's kind sympathy. She appeared prematurely senile in her inconsolable grief.

When we left Samia's home, I asked my sister, 'How can the outworn traditions of our society be changed, without painful destruction of the older generation's expectations?'

In my opinion, I believe that marrige brought about by love is most natural and rewarding, while most inhabitants of my land scorn love and look only for respect and companionship after marriage.

How would we Saudi Arabians ever reconcile our differences?

Unable to determine his daughter's whereabouts without professional assistance, Fouad contacted private investigative agencies in France and America. One week after his child disappeared, Fouad discovered that she was in Nevada, registered in a hotel as Jafer's wife!

The moment the information came to Fouad, he travelled with his three sons to America, vowing to bring Fayza home. He promised his wife that their daughter would not remain with a Palestinian. Caught up in his tyrannical affection, he said that Fayza's death would be preferable to his shame.

This bit of news created a furore in our household.

I bit my nails until they bled.

Abdullah fell into a melancholy that threatened his health, sensing that nothing would ever be the same again.

Praying for the souls of the lovers, Amani glumly predicted that her prayers would not be answered, that the lovers had foolishly taken their paradise on earth, and that fires of molten hot metal would welcome them as they exited this earth.

Abdullah glared at his sister and cuttingly remarked that perhaps Jafer felt Fayza's feminine perfection was worth quitting heaven for.

Caring deeply for both Jafer and Fayza, Maha became hostile to anyone who criticized the lovers, declaring that no man or government should have authority over true love.

Hearing the news that Fouad and his sons were *en route* to the United States, Abdullah and I pleaded with Kareem to make contact with Jafer, to warn him to flee. I told Kareem that Fayza's male relatives needed additional days to accept the crucial fact that Fayza now belonged to another. Their extreme anger could not prevail, time would ease their rage.

It was not to be. My husband infuriated me, remaining true to the Saudi male policy of accepting any injustice, if that injustice involved a man's obsession with his women or the family honour. Thinking to incite him to action, I insulted Kareem, telling him that I was disappointed to learn that I had wed a man who failed to probe into the deeper complexities of life, but who, instead, was a dull, unfeeling type who tended to remain on the surface of things.

As I left my husband standing open-mouthed in amazement at my attack, I could not resist one final incivility. 'Kareem, how can you have no conflict between logic and feeling? Aren't you human?'

Silently I retreated, but secretly I had Abdullah take action. At my urging, he searched Kareem's office and brought forth information that had been provided by the investigative services.

Triumphant, we were careful to hide ourselves from Kareem or Amani, making our telephone call during the long evening prayer, knowing that Kareem was in the mosque and Amani was locked in her room, facing Makkah, saying her prayers.

With shaking fingers, Abdullah punched the number of the Mirage Hotel in Las Vegas, Nevada, where Jafer and Fayza were known to be registered.

As I watched the brooding face of my beautiful son patiently waiting for the hotel operator to ring the room, I was possessed by the fever a mother has for her children, desiring for Abdullah's pain to leave his body and enter mine.

Jafer answered the telephone!

Abdullah tortured himself trying to find the right words to make Jafer understand that he was in great danger.

His friend was dismayed at their rapid discovery but felt secure in his married state. 'What can they do now?' he asked Abdullah.

When Abdullah shared his words, I grabbed the telephone from my son's hand. 'They can do plenty, Jafer,' I yelled. 'Fouad's honour has been attacked, his only daughter vanished with a man not thought suitable! Don't be a fool! You're an Arab, you're aware what reactions such anguish will bring an Arab father!'

Jafer tried to soothe my fears, claiming that their love would see them through any persecution.

Fayza came to the telephone, speaking softly into the receiver that Jafer still held in his hand. Fayza's sultry voice told of the wonderful love that had prevailed, in spite of the substantial hindrance of the laws of our land.

'Fayza, you're still only twenty and have broken free from our inflated traditions. Your father can't do this. Fouad is a man of desert mentality, and he can only flow down the main stream. In his mind, you've committed a shocking offence. Leave that place! Have a meeting with the men of your family at a later date!'

My pleas for the lovers to vanish made no impact. How weak my words were to their brave spirits. Courageous, Jafer said that he would face the fury of Fayza's family.

I returned the telephone to my son, thinking that I had done all that I could do.

I thought, is it a glory or a disaster that they have no suspicion yet of the extent of their tragedy? I realized the narrow limits of their lovers' vision. Jafer and Fayza were blinded, believing that the strength of their great love could conquer the challenge of her furious and disapproving family.

Fretting in hopeful silence, I could only hope that Jafer and Fayza could delay destiny for a while.

It was four days before Fouad returned to the kingdom.

His voice low and uneasy, Kareem called me from his offices and reported that Fouad and his sons had returned from America.

My throat closed around the words that I could not ask.

After a dry pause, Kareem added that Fouad had returned with his daughter but without her husband.

My voice returned. 'Is Jafer dead?' I asked, wondering already how we would break the cruel news to Abdullah.

'No. Jafer isn't dead.' Kareem answered, his voice causing me to doubt his words even as he spoke them.

I was quiet, waiting for news that I was not sure I wanted to hear.

'Sultana, I'm coming home. We'll tell Abdullah what has happened together.'

'What happened?' I screamed, thinking that I could not bear to wait for Kareem to make the twenty-five-minute drive from his office to our home.

I heard a click and then a dead line. I told myself that my husband's news must be dreadful, for Kareem, like most Arabs, had a habit of putting aside unpleasant truths until the last possible moment.

Fouad had told my husband little, only that there had been a minor physical scuffle in the hotel room, and that Jafer had been left unconscious but without serious injury.

Fayza? Naturally, his daughter had been traumatized by the incident and was now at their palace under sedation. Without the influence of Jafer,

Fouad believed that his daughter would hasten to submit to her true self.

I looked at Kareem and announced with certainty, 'Jafer is dead!'

'Nonsense. They were in America.'

Two weeks later we received a telephone call from Jafer. He had returned to Lebanon. We finally learned the truth of the matter.

Jafer's words to me were, 'All is lost.' He paused. 'Except for my skin, which is safe.'

'Abdullah!' I called out. 'It's Jafer! Come quickly!'

Kareem, Maha and I stood round Abdullah as he spent long moments quietly listening to his dearest friend, comforting the caller with reassurances. 'What could you do? You had no choice.'

With a start, I heard my son say, 'I'm coming!', that he would soon be on his way to Lebanon, that nothing could keep him from his friend's side.

I grabbed Abdullah's arms and began to shake my head, 'No', vigorously.

My feet left the floor as Kareem yanked me from my son's face.

Abdullah hung up the telephone. With tears running down his face, my son buried his head in his hands and began to weep bitter tears. His words were muted, difficult to understand. 'Jafer's ruined! He's ruined!'

'What is this about Lebanon?' I enquired, too agitated at the thought of Abdullah travelling to that country to consider Jafer's condition.

'Hush, Sultana,' Kareem ordered.

Abdullah finally calmed himself and explained how Fouad and his sons had taken Fayza from Jafer.

A telephone call had awakened them in the night. Fayza's father and brothers were in the lobby. 'Could they come up please?' Fouad's tone was civil, Jafer was encouraged and felt no fear of physical assault.

When Jafer opened the door, he felt pleased and smiled.

Fouad and his sons took no time to talk. Provoked by Jafer's smiling face, which he now feared they had mistaken for a smirk, Fayza's brother set upon him. Caught by surprise, Jafer was no match for four men.

Jafer said that he was hit on the head with a heavy object, and blackness overcame him.

Hours later, when he revived, his new bride and her male relatives were gone.

Jafer said that he knew all was lost once they had stolen Fayza away from him. He was well aware that it is illegal in Saudi Arabia for a Saudi girl to marry a man not a Saudi national. He could receive no legal assistance in claiming Fayza as his own, despite their married state, for their union was not recognized in Saudi Arabia. Had Jafer been a Saudi and Fayza a Palestinian, there would have been no difficulties, for Saudi men can marry whom they wish.

In spite of that knowledge, Jafer had flown to London, making a desperate attempt to re-enter the kingdom, but had been told that his resident's visa for Saudi Arabia was no longer valid.

Jafer, having feared Kareem's scorn, now overcame his fear and asked to speak to my husband. He wondered if Kareem, with his princely status, could help?

Kareem said that he could but would not. Now that he knew Jafer was alive, he had no intention of placing him in a position that ensured his murder. Kareem warned Jafer that for certain Fouad and his sons would kill him if he returned to the kingdom.

Kareem had never said so, but I knew that my husband would never forgive Jafer his deception. Kareem had suffered acute embarrassment that an employee he had trusted had conquered and stolen the beloved only daughter of an old friend and business associate. His intense love for Abdullah had kept him silent.

Never one to promise more than he could give. Kareem recommended that Jafer try to find a life for himself in Lebanon, that it seemed the country was finally returning to peace.

'How sad,' I said. 'It is the end of a magnificent love story. And, now Jafer stands alone against an overwhelming power.'

Standing quietly to the side of the room, my son was an unforgettable figure clad in his white thobe. He was straight and tall and suddenly looked a man. His face was sad, and with dramatic intensity, Abdullah said no, that was not the case. Jafer would never be alone, for he would not forsake his friend. He was going to visit him in Lebanon.

Kareem and I refused our son permission to travel to that country, but Abdullah seemed to care not for our consent and said that he would go nevertheless.

Such a trip would invite a thousand calamities! I was miserable as I prepared myself for bed, plotting to stop my son from his sentimental journey.

I should have known I would fail, for it is impossible to rule a son in blossoming manhood, for such youthful vitality does not easily accept defeat.

Chapter Nine

ABDULLAH

*We will give it unto our children, and they unto their
children, and it shall not perish.*
Kahlil Gibran

After the distressing incident with Jafer and Fayza,
I underwent a persistent and depressing change,
retreating into myself, for my son, Abdullah, plotted
his trip to Lebanon with such inspired devotion that
I came to believe him when he said that nothing
would hinder the potentially perilous journey.

Kareem cautioned me to restraint, for he said that
our son's ardour would cool as the difficulties of
travel to Lebanon became apparent.

I grew cross with my husband, and with a voice
raised in disbelief asked how he could remain calm,
while those to whom we had given life tortured my
mind with grief.

With a mysterious half-smile, Kareem reminded
me that Abdullah's passport was locked in the safe.
It would be impossible for our son to leave the
kingdom.

For these reasons, my resistance to Abdullah's plan was sporadic, unorganized and ineffectual. In a matter of days, my one close relationship with my son became one of strained silences.

Everyone who lived in our palace fumed and despaired. While Abdullah packed his suitcases, his sister Amani mourned to see how little she could do to improve the morals of her brother and older sister. Spurred on by her faith, Amani began to spy on our employees. Horrified by what she called the looseness of our staff of sixty servants, for there are many secret romantic encounters among those who serve us, Amani set herself out with blunt directness to reform our Christian and Hindu servants into the superior Muslim faith.

After a hundred quarrels with my daughter's inconsiderate and indiscriminate vigour against those who practise a different religion from our own, I finally acknowledged that I had met my match in Amani, who continued to distance her mother in sheer perseverance.

I spent many hours in the solitude of my room, mulling over the lives of my children.

When my three offspring were infants, they gave my life great joy and meaning. In the days of their early childhood, only Maha generated chaos, and I had no reason to anticipate peril at every turn. In those pleasurable times, moments of parental happiness vastly overshadowed the dark intervals of fear and worry over the fate of these small beings to whom I had given life.

Now that my children were nearing adulthood, I came to the frightful conclusion that the only prerequisites to motherhood seemed to be a precarious dependence upon chance, for nothing I said or did altered my children's unpredictable behaviour.

As one who has enormous difficulty in adjusting to failure, I took to my bed, complaining to Kareem that nothing in my life was progressing as I had hoped. My psychological decline came at a time of Kareem's busiest period of business expansions, and as his free moments were limited, he was ill-equipped to console and liberate my soul from melancholy, that mental interloper which had intruded and dismantled my joyful pursuit of happiness.

I felt increasingly alone. Suppressing every display of emotion other than self-sympathy, I began to sleep poorly and overeat, gaining unwanted pounds. Continually ignored by family members whom I was attempting to manipulate, I became progressively bad-tempered with my family and the servants. I even acquired a disgusting habit of twisting, pulling and biting on my hair. The length of my hair became shorter, and the thickness became thinner until Kareem, after noticing my habit, sarcastically commented that he had thought I had employed a new, and more enthusiastic hairdresser, when in reality I was behaving like a child by pulling it out.

I was quick to snap an ugly retort, unfairly accusing Kareem of loving none but himself, that I, alone, had to keep watch over our children.

Gently impatient, Kareem's eyes took on a distant look, and I felt that he left me without leaving the room. When his spirits returned, he said that he had laboured to remember a comforting verse that he had once read about the rearing of spirited children.

Kareem recited, 'You may give your children love, but not your thoughts, for they have their own thoughts.'

'Kahlil Gibran,' I said.

'What?'

'That verse, it is from *The Prophet*. And, it was *I* that read that particular verse to you while we were awaiting the birth of our firstborn.'

Kareem's stern face softened as a smile parted his lips, and I wondered if he was remembering the happy moments so long ago that we had spent with our infant son.

That was not the case, for he complimented me by saying, 'Sultana, you're an amazing creature. How can you remember such a thing?'

Kareem had always marvelled at my memory, for once I'd read or heard something, my recall never failed in accuracy.

I was pleased with his recognition, but the cause of my discontent was too deep and varied to be so easily dissolved. In a collision with my children, my mad passion had blinded me to my husband's clear and logical mind. With no-one else to battle, I continued to snarl at my husband. In contempt I compared Kareem with Nero, the mad fiddler of Rome, blind to disaster even when his kingdom was aflame.

Angered by repeated insults, Kareem thought better of his solicitous sympathy and left me alone to consider his parting observation, which was not comforting. His spiteful words were, 'Sultana, you have it all. Yet, you fear everything, and understand nothing. I predict that you will, one day, be committed to an institution for the insane.'

I hissed like a snake and Kareem left, not to return for two days.

Shortly after our heated exchange, I was unconsciously twisting my hair with one hand, while idly thumbing through one of my many foreign publications, when I read an article featured in an American magazine that told of a rare disease that strikes only females, causing women to pull their hair out until they become completely bald. Once bald, those unfortunate women then progressed to eating their eyebrows, eyelashes and body hair.

I let go of my hair. Did I have that disease? I ran to view my image in the mirror, and to search through my scalp for bald spots. My hair did seem thin. Now I was truly worried, for I had never cured myself of vanity, and had no inclination to be bald! Besides, in the Muslim religion, it is forbidden for a woman to be bald.

Time proved that I did not have the disease, for unlike the women in the article, my attachment to beauty quickly helped to cure myself of that habit.

In spite of my success in retaining my hair, I feared that my passion for life was cracking, and I told myself that if my debilitating depression were not conquered, I would be overcome by premature old age. Feeling sorry for myself, I imagined that I would have a slow death through the gradual diminution of my senses.

I was saved from my self-destructive behaviour by my dearest sister.

Sara, a contemplative genius, was sensitive to my blunted lust for life, and she began to spend many hours by my side, humouring me with her undivided attention. Sara understood my feelings perfectly, and knew that worry over Abdullah and Amani now ruled my life.

My sister looked upon me with great pity when I tearfully told her that, 'Sara, if I have to live my life over again, I do not believe that I could survive it.'

Sara's mouth broke into a half-smile, as she wryly observed, 'Sultana, few of our family will survive if *you* are to live your life again.'

Our laughter filled the room.

My sister was so dear. Sara was not without problems of her own. Her life was disturbed by the actions of an unruly child, yet she found time to come to my aid in my moment of great need. While four of my sister's five children strived for perfection, Nashwa, Sara's teenage daughter born on the same day as Amani, relished controversy.

In strictest confidence, Sara told me to be thankful that Amani had attached herself to religion, for Sara had the opposite problem with Nashwa. Her daughter was wildly attracted to members of the opposite sex, and twice Asad had discovered Nashwa meeting Saudi teenage boys in a music shop at a shopping centre in the city.

Tears streamed down Sara's face as she confided in me that her daughter flirted outrageously with every male that entered their palace grounds. In a voice filled with disbelief, she said that the week before, Nashwa had begun an explicit sexual conversation with two of the younger Filipino drivers. One of Nashwa's brothers had overheard the conversation and, when confronted, Nashwa boldly acknowledged her action, stating that she had to do *something* to interrupt the monotony of life in Saudi Arabia.

Asad had been forced to fire those young drivers, and employ older Muslim men from Egypt who would respect the Muslim way: to ignore the wilful women of the house.

Just that morning, Sara had overheard her daughter speaking with a female friend on the telephone; the two girls were discussing in great detail the girl's eldest brother's good figure. It seemed to Sara that Nashwa had a crush on this boy, and now my sister had to reconsider or regulate her daughter's visits to that home.

Sara's face was drawn with worry over the outcome of Nashwa's loose morals and unbecoming conduct, saying that she had often heard that one of the oversights of nature was that beauty and virtue often arrive in separate packages. Nashwa, my sister said, was an innocent-faced beauty who was sadly lacking in virtue.

I had to agree that my difficulties with Amani paled in comparison with my sister's problems with Nashwa. There was some consolation in the knowledge that Amani's piety had the approval of the religious authorities, while Nashwa's activities could embroil Sara and Asad in that never-ending web of the Saudi religious and legal system.

Once again the thought came to me that Nashwa was my true child, while Amani must be attached by blood to Sara. I thought to ask Sara about the matter, but had a moment of speculation that an exchange of daughters might result from my baseless confidence to my sister. I reminded myself that in my country, it is better to wrestle with a persistent religious fanatic rather than the problem of a young girl habituated to sexual stimulus.

In an effort to raise my sister's spirits, I told her that too often when dealing with our children, a parent sees little but the defects. I thought to mention some of Nashwa's good traits, but could find nothing to say.

Sara and I were still for a time, looking at each other. We knew instinctively that we understood each other perfectly.

With her daughter in mind, my sister began to ponder the progress of civilization, and questioned the theory of how it had been possible for animals to turn into humans, for our children had been sheltered from all worldly concerns, lavished with creature comforts, provided with intelligent pursuits and moral guidance, yet the careful organization of their lives had made little impact on their development.

Sara said that she had come to the conclusion that human outcome was linked to nothing more than genetics, and her children might as well have grown like weeds, instead of meticulously tended plants. 'Besides,' she said with a laugh, 'the radicals of one age become the reactionaries of the next, so who's to know what will eventually happen to our offspring?'

Since it always lightens one's burdens to be reminded of the details of another's troubles, even if that person is one greatly loved, I felt more cheerful than I had in days.

I laughed and agreed with my sister, saying that the seeds we had planted had not all flowered. Thinking that all of life is in God's hands anyway, I promised myself that I would worry no longer.

Sara went to enquire of her youngest children,

who were playing in our palace playground located next to Amani's zoo, while I promised to bathe and dress myself for a visit to Fayza. Neither Sara nor I had seen the poor girl since she had been forced to return to the kingdom, though we had heard, with some surprise, that she had recovered and was now seeing close friends and relatives.

Enjoying uncommon peace for the first time in days, I was unprepared for a shocking telephone call from my husband.

His voice was alarmingly intense. 'Sultana, go to the safe and locate Abdullah's passport.'

'Why?' I asked.

Kareem told me to shut up and do as he said.

Thinking the worst, I dropped the telephone receiver to the floor and ran rapidly into my husband's home office on the first floor of our home. My hands refused to cooperate with my memory and it required three attempts to open the combination safe.

My husband kept his passport in the office safe, while those of his wife and children were locked inside another safe in his home office.

My fingers riffled through the various documents and papers. Abdullah's passport was missing!

I was then struck with the horrible realization that I could only account for two out of four passports. Looking closely, I saw that Maha's passport had disappeared along with her brother's.

What was going on? How had this happened? No-one, other than Kareem and I, knew the combination of this particular safe.

'No!' I said to myself when I could not find the special papers of permission that Kareem kept signed for the women of his family to travel outside the kingdom without the company of a male member of our family.

I was confused? Had Maha travelled alone? Or, had she and her brother fled the kingdom together?

Kareem's private telephone began to ring in his office.

My husband had tired of waiting for my return to our personal line that I had answered in our bedroom. He shouted, 'Sultana! What is going on?'

I told Kareem of my unsettling discovery.

'And the dollars?'

I had not thought to look for the large amount of dollars that we kept in our safe for the purpose of fleeing the kingdom should a religious revolution ever grip our land. It was money that we hoped we would never be forced to use to bribe safe exit from our country.

I opened the large drawer at the top of the safe. It was as Kareem had expected. The money was no longer there! As our fears of unrest in Arab lands had grown, the money had increased. Abdullah had taken over a million dollars in cash from his parents' safe. Had my son lost all his good sense?

'The dollars have disappeared,' I glumly reported.

'Go, see if Maha is at school. I'm on my way to the airport.'

I cried out, 'Hurry!' I knew that my son was on his way to Lebanon. But, how was Maha mixed up in this? Surely, Abdullah was not taking his sister with him to that dangerous land. I was giddy with fear and confusion.

'I'll try to call you from the car. Now. Do as I say. Find Maha!'

I fetched a simple dress and hastily pulled it over my head. Reaching for my *abaaya*, veil, and *shayla*, I threw on my outer garments as I ran through my home, calling out for my sister, Sara, to accompany me to Maha's school. I yelled at Cora to find Mousa, the youngest of our Egyptian drivers, a man who, I knew from past experience, could be urged to break the city speed limit.

Maha's school was fifteen minutes by car from our palace, but we arrived in ten minutes. Along the route, I told Sara what little I knew of the situation.

The seventeen girls in Maha's history class were taking notes while listening to a male instructor who was featured in the centre of the room on a large television screen. The lesson was being given via video, since it is forbidden in Saudi Arabia for a male professor to come into personal contact with female students.

Maha's face turned crimson red as I burst into her classroom, calling her name. Seeking the face of my child, I hovered over her desk, and said, 'Maha! You're here!'

Maha pushed my arms from her neck, exclaiming, 'Where did you think I was?'

I told the headmistress that I needed my daughter to return home. Without a hint of curiosity over my excited behaviour, the supervisor calmly instructed Maha to gather her books. She asked if Maha would be away for longer than a week. Since I did not know, I said that she would. The supervisor said that she would have Maha's instructors save my daughter's lessons for her return.

'Mother! What is going on?' Maha wanted to know as we settled ourselves in the car.

'I feared that you were with Abdullah.'

'Abdullah?'

My son was supposed to be at his school, at a different location, which was an institution that girls did not attend.

Maha looked at me in astonishment. 'Mother, you're behaving like a mad woman.' She looked at Sara for confirmation. 'Auntie, what's wrong?'

Sara explained the mystery of the passports, saying that we could not fathom why Abdullah had taken his sister's passport.

My sister's eyes met mine across the head of my daughter. Sara's thoughts matched mine perfectly.

'Fayza!' We uttered her name in unison.

I told the driver to take us to Fouad and Samia's home. 'Quickly!'

Abdullah's plans ran clear through my mind. My son had taken Maha's passport for Jafer's wife, Fayza! Abdullah had plotted her rescue. It was Fayza who was travelling on Maha's passport. Fayza was going to Lebanon with my son, not Maha! With veiled faces, it is quite possible for Saudi women to travel abroad using someone else's passport.

When Maha understood the significance of her brother's deed, she pleaded with me for us to return to our home.

'Mother! Let them go!'

It was a difficult moment. If I made no move to notify Fayza's parents, then I was an accomplice in my son's unwelcome intrusion into another man's private affairs by restoring his daughter to the arms of her husband. If I was the cause of Fayza's continued separation from a man whom she had loved enough to wed, then I could never again claim to battle for the rights of women in my land.

Sara and I stared at each other for many moments. Sara's eyes were clear and penetrating, and I knew that my sister was reliving the horrible sexual abuse that she had endured in her first marriage. Had our mother not revolted against our father, risking a divorce and possible permanent separation from her own precious children, Sara would have remained in sexual bondage to a man whom she hated, never knowing the wonderful love that she shared with Asad.

My decision was the result of the intolerance and severe restraints upon women in my country. I thought to myself, women in my country had endured man's harsh abuse through too many centuries.

Wanting to live up to the best, and not the worst in my ancestry, I instructed Mousa, 'Take us home.'

Maha burst into laughter, and kissed me time and again, crushing me against the seat of the car.

Sara's eyes grew luminous. My sister smiled, and squeezed my hand, saying, 'Sultana, don't worry, you've made the correct decision.'

With muscular exaggeration, Mousa's eyes grew wide, and his mouth opened and closed, reminding me of a bird which was suffering from the desert sun. His face grew darker in colour, and I could see that he violently disagreed with the turn of events.

I spoke in French, a language he did not understand. 'Look at the driver's face,' I told my sister and my child. 'He doesn't approve.'

'What man in this country would approve a

woman's right to choose her husband?' Maha wanted to know. 'Tell me one! And . . . and . . . I'll wed him!'

I looked back upon the day and felt a rush of recognition. My heavy spirit at last achieved tranquillity, for I understood that my daughter shared the blood of one who was enlightened, yet had no knowledge of his liberation.

'Abdullah.' I answered quietly. 'Your brother. My son. Abdullah is such a man.'

In happy silence, I stared at my daughter's face, but was imprisoned in my past. I saw the form of my firstborn as he had lain in his mother's arms. The emotions that I had lived on the day of his birth came to me in a flash, such a rush of joy that by its nature must be brief. I had wondered then if my newborn son would uphold and thereby harden the harsh system towards females in my land. I had prayed that it would not be the case, but that he would influence our country's history to my liking and help to bring change to the rigid social customs of Saudi Arabia.

It was difficult to judge Abdullah's actions calmly, but in an honest appraisal of his activity, I knew that my deepest desire had been realized. A male child born of my womb *would* remodel the land of my birth.

How brave my bold son was!

No longer caring about Mousa's reaction, I spoke in Arabic, reminding Sara and Maha that the men of Kareem's generation had once displayed a voice of reason when it came to their women, but that voice had been stilled and silenced by the clash of militant men of religion. Grieving over the timid men of our age, I no longer looked to them for relief.

But hope was not lost, so long as we women of Arabia gave birth to men such as Abdullah.

I told Maha and Sara what I knew to be the truth, that my beloved son was a prince who would one day use all of his power and influence to enhance the status of Saudi women.

Renewed by my son's brave act, I talked of nothing else the remainder of the trip home, scandalizing Mousa with my frank discussion of complete freedom for all women, even for his own wife, a woman whom he forced to live with his parents in a small village in Egypt, while he worked in Saudi Arabia.

Kareem was impatiently awaiting my return. He did not seem surprised that I expressed great happiness, and I imagined that my husband judged incorrectly that my improved mood was linked to the safe recovery of our daughter. Never did he know that my happiness was attached to our son and the fact that Abdullah had turned his back upon injustice, and his face towards a free life for all people.

Maha was a bit frightened by the intensity of her father's blazing eyes, and she mentioned some small task that required her time.

Sara gathered her children and went home to Asad, whispering in my ear that I should call her as soon as possible.

I could hear Amani's voice in the background, rising and falling with the sounds of her deeply felt communication with God.

Finally, I was alone with my husband.

I thought that Kareem's face was hardened by the oppressive weight of his discovery, and I was unprepared for his ruthless accusations.

He declared his feelings without questioning his wife. 'Sultana, there's a whiff of you in Fayza's flight.'

For a short moment, I was silenced by his insinuation. As one who runs to extremes in anger, I appeared at my worst when I struck out at Kareem's arm with my fist.

Well acquainted with my passions, Kareem was prepared. He sidestepped, avoiding the blow.

Over the years, Kareem had disciplined his reactions so that he appeared moderate, always making me appear the worse in our conflicts. Today was no exception. 'Sultana. This is no time to fight. Our son and Fayza have fled the kingdom.' My husband grabbed me. 'You *must* tell me their travel plans.'

All my denials were futile in convincing Kareem that while our son might have inherited my talent for conducting brilliant deception, I had no hand in his action to reunite Jafer with his wife.

Like the town thief who is not believed when a loaf of bread is stolen, my past reached into the present and a frightening avalanche of opinions flamed out against an innocent woman.

I was paying a dear price for my militant past.

I thought that Kareem's conduct as a husband might have been more loyal, and I told him so.

Kareem asked how he could believe me. He said that he had married a woman who was half angel and half devil, and the devil in me often ruled the angel, and when it came to issues that concerned women's lives, that I could not speak without lying and could not act without treachery!

Angrier than I have ever been, for what human endures false censure with grace, I spat at Kareem's feet and left the room, promising never again to enter a conversation with the man whom I had wed.

Kareem thought it best to bury his doubts, for he was concerned that, without my assistance, he might not succeed in finding his son, or in returning Fouad's daughter. Kareem said that he apologized if he were in the wrong and that I must save our son from committing an offence that would further entangle Abdullah in another man's personal affairs.

Suspecting his true motives, I refused to answer his request for forgiveness, squeezing my eyes shut so I did not have to view his face and motioning with my hand for him to go away.

As soon as the door slammed, my pleasure at revenge faded at once.

Where was my son? Was he safe?

For five days there was no peace in our home, for Kareem and I had no peaceful communication. Amani prayed and wept, while Maha sang love songs and celebrated Fayza's escape.

Is anything in life sweeter than success?

With a singleness of purpose, Fayza avoided all the traps that had been set to ensnare her and was reunited with the man she loved.

I could have never anticipated Fouad's and Samia's reaction to Fayza's desperate flight to her husband. Prepared for Kareem to be forced to use his position of prince for protection of our only son, I was pleasantly surprised by Fouad's meek acceptance of his daughter's elopement.

On the fifth day after their disappearance, Abdullah called us from Cyprus. Abdullah had no fear of our reaction and declared firmly to our protests that he had administered justice, not vengeance, in bringing Jafer and Fayza together.

My breath left my body when Abdullah confided that Fayza had telephoned her parents an hour before, and that Fouad and Samia had left their anger behind them and wanted nothing more than a second opportunity to welcome Jafer as their son. Fouad told his child that if she and Jafer would not turn their backs on her family, he promised he would not 'step in the same raging river twice'.

How true it is that humanity refuses compromise during prosperity, and reaches out for arbitration when weak. Swayed by great fear of never seeing their beautiful daughter again, Fouad and Samia had come to the conclusion that they would accept her marriage to someone beneath them in wealth and status.

Being of a suspicious nature, I thought perhaps it was a trick to ensnare Jafer in a land where he had no rights. Once in Saudi Arabia, he could be imprisoned on the slightest pretence, if that were Fouad's wish.

Fayza's parents did not confirm my pessimism.

That day, Fouad and his family flew to Greece and met Jafer and Fayza in a golden land where men had been civilized from an early age. Thoughts more bitter than death were put to rest, and Jafer and Fayza at last found happiness in the family unit that had once challenged the legitimacy of their marriage.

Special permission was obtained for Fayza to wed a Muslim from another land, and a second, more festive wedding was held in a hotel in Cairo, Egypt.

Kareem and I travelled there with our two daughters to join our son for the occasion.

Jafer and Fayza insisted that the male and female guests come together for a reception at the Mena House Hotel. Their great love even made a dour Kareem smile, even though he was a prince ashamed that his son had interfered in his friend's life at home. Kareem's tension was released when Fouad confessed that there could have been no other ending, for long before Abdullah had rescued Fayza, his daughter's extreme misery had led Fouad and his wife to the knowledge that Fayza must be reunited with Jafer. Their daughter's grief could not be ignored. Fouad assured my embarrassed husband that they, themselves, had been on the brink of parental surrender the day that Fayza had fled.

Kareem and I watched as Fouad grasped Jafer and Fayza as if they were one. From the look on Jafer's shining face as he watched his wife, it was clear to see that he loved Fayza more madly than before.

How pleased I was! A Saudi woman was happily wed to one forbidden.

I whispered in Kareem's ear, 'See, every straight line can be forced into a curve!'

A family tragedy was transformed into a scene of great harmony.

Later that evening from the courtyard at our

Cairo villa, Kareem and I watched the loveliness of the Egyptian sky.

My husband surprised me with a heartfelt apology. Hovering nebulously between shame and love, Kareem promised that he would not prejudge me again, that he had been told by Abdullah that I was not privy to his plot to free Fayza.

As though it were an afterthought, Kareem reached into his pocket and brought out the largest diamond that I had ever seen. The stone was set in a gold chain. My husband tenderly fastened the necklace around my neck, and I felt his lips as they brushed my shoulder.

A few years ago, I had hated the bitter emptiness of my married life. Just the month before I had hungrily sought the meaning of life. The moment was a breeding ground for all sorts of emotions – affection, regret, and most of all, confusion. Was Kareem that rare phenomenon, a Saudi husband who was gentle, virile, practical and intelligent? Had I been wrong in my assessment of his character?

How could a Saudi man be the answer to my happiness, for I had fought against Saudi men for all my life long?

I had once heard that a miser is never satisfied with his money, nor a wise man with his knowledge. Was I a woman who would never know fulfilment? That possibility was frightening.

Another thought came to my mind, an Arab proverb, 'If your husband is made of honey, do not consume him.'

I looked at Kareem in a new light. Remembering the numerous insults that I had inflicted upon my husband, I prayed that God would shorten my tongue and increase my powers of reason.

I smiled at my husband. Suddenly, I felt many wounds heal – injuries suffered from my husband's earlier conduct in our marriage.

For some reason, my scars could scarcely be detected.

Chapter Ten

FATMA

Something was dead in each of us
And what was dead was Hope.
Oscar Wilde

The following afternoon, Kareem and I were sitting together with our children on the verandah at our villa in Cairo. An immaculate flower garden encircled the large covered porch, and the sweet scent of roses and honeysuckle permeated the air, reminding one of the wealthy British presence that had once infiltrated an unenthusiastic Cairo. My husband and I were savouring the coolness of the spacious shady area, for there was not a hint of an afternoon breeze, and the concrete structures of the overcrowded city had retained the oppressive heat of the day, dulling the senses of Cairo's eight million occupants.

Our three children whispered among themselves, claiming that we had once again been forgotten by 'Forgetful Fatma', as they often called our Egyptian housekeeper when she was out of earshot.

I warned my children not to make fun, that Fatma was no longer young and her feet had difficulty moving her abundant body. Still, I stifled a smile, thinking that the children were probably right in their assessment of the circumstances, that Fatma had more than likely begun some new chore, entirely forgetting her employers as they waited impatiently for a cool drink. Fatma *was* absent-minded and she did have a consistent inability to remember why she left one room to go into another. Many times Kareem had complained, saying that Fatma should be let go and a younger, more energetic woman hired in her stead, but I resisted his urgings since the woman was dependable and had always displayed a genuine love for my three children.

Kareem accused me of being unable to part with Fatma since the woman delighted me with lively tales of Cairo scandals. But that was not the case.

Fatma had been employed as our permanent, live-in housekeeper since we had purchased the villa many years before. Abdullah had been only two years old at the time Fatma came into our lives, and our girls were not yet born, so Fatma was a constant in their young lives.

Just as I pushed myself from my chair to go and remind Fatma of our earlier request, I heard the familiar scraping of her loose sandals as they struck the marble floor of the interior hallway leading to the veranda.

I looked at Kareem, and he gave an irritated shake of his head. My husband had no understanding of why he should be inconvenienced by the aging of a servant.

Feeling mischievous, I said, 'My husband, do not forget that God is watching you.'

Kareem tartly replied, 'Sultana, do not concern yourself regarding my relationship with God.'

The children thought that we might slip into an argument and ruin the afternoon, so Amani wrapped her arms around her father's neck, while Maha began to rub my shoulders and begged me not to lose my temper.

I felt too good to fight and said so. About that time, my attention was drawn to Fatma. Recalling the graceful and slim Fatma of years past, my eyes affectionately followed the woman's heavy figure as she painstakingly opened the double glass doors that led from the villa onto the veranda. Fatma was enormous and had great difficulty balancing the tray stacked with crystal glasses and a matching crystal decanter filled with freshly squeezed lemonade.

Like many Egyptian women, Fatma had struggled with a weight problem from the moment she bore her first child. With each new addition to her family, she had grown larger and larger, until a childish Abdullah had fearfully questioned me, asking me how Fatma's skin could continue to hold her figure together.

Slowed by her weight, Fatma took many moments to walk the few steps from the doorway to the table of white painted rattan.

Abdullah jumped to his feet and took the tray from a reluctant Fatma, insisting that he would serve the family.

Kareem and I exchanged glances, and I saw that my husband bit the inside of his lip to keep from protesting. Ever since he was young, Abdullah was easily affected by the suffering that comes so often undeserved to mankind. I felt proud of Abdullah's sensitivity, but I knew that his father had no desire for his son to do the work of servants.

To distract Kareem, I asked our son to tell us more of his experiences in Lebanon, for since we had met Abdullah in Cairo, we had enjoyed little private time to hear of his adventure. I remembered that in Kareem's youth, he had spent many happy moments in the beautiful city of Beirut, for large numbers of the Saudi royal family had travelled to Lebanon for rest and relaxation before the days of the mad and senseless war that had destroyed that once lovely land.

Abdullah saw hope where Kareem said there was none. Abdullah said that he had been impressed by the Lebanese spirit, marvelling that the Lebanese people had not only survived, but had endured a most vicious civil war with their optimisim intact, refusing to acknowledge that they could not surpass their brilliant past. Abdullah thought that given half the chance, the Lebanese would once again rise to claim an exalted place in the Arab world.

Abdullah paused and looked at his father. He wondered if Kareem might be interested in investing money in that country.

Kareem rewarded Abdullah with an approving smile. My husband is a man who seeks economic opportunity at every chance, and our son's previous lack of interest in such matters had always been a weight on his mind. Kareem's smile quickly vanished when Abdullah added that the infrastructure of Lebanon was almost completely in ruins and that there were many good causes to which Kareem could donate funds.

I almost dissolved into laughter when I saw Kareem's palid face. Kareem sat up straight and tried to show some interest, but my husband had difficulty in concealing his desperation; he looked at his son as if he were seeing him for the first time.

I knew that my husband had not yet recovered from Abdullah's proud announcement that he had donated the bulk of the one million dollars that he had taken from our safe to the hospital that housed Jafer's older brother. My husband had no heart to reprimand his son for a good deed and had gazed at Abdullah with sad affection, in spite of his agony at losing one million dollars.

Kareem had confessed to me later that in his mind, money donated to Lebanon was equivalent to tossing good money after bad, for who knew when the guns of destruction would once again flame across the Lebanese sky. Let the Lebanese show that they are serious about peace, and Kareem would look into the possibility of assisting those fellow Arabs.

Abdullah had been stricken by the lack of facilities at the institution where Jafer's brother had been, and now he spoke again of that place. He said that he could not forget the wretched condition of the war wounded who lived in the hospital. Abdullah's eyes welled with tears as he told of men and women without limbs, confined to small rooms, for there were no prosthetics or wheelchairs. Abdullah discovered men tied to wooden tables, men who had no movement in their bodies, men stoically accepting the idea of a life devoid of a single pleasure.

Abdullah said that he had learned a tragic truth, that a large number of the Lebanese wounded had no surviving family members to provide funds for their care.

In anguish, Abdullah asked, 'Does the world neither know nor care of the damage done to that country?'

I reminded Abdullah of a happy thought. That Jafer's brother had been luckier than most, since Jafer had routinely sent money for his medical expenses, but even his situation was bleak when compared to the most advanced health care facilities that our oil wealth guaranteed the inhabitants of our land. Jafer's brother would now enjoy the latest treatment available, for Fouad had insisted upon taking his son-in-law's brother from Lebanon to Saudi Arabia to live as one of his family.

Now our son wanted his father to distribute more of his personal wealth for the needy of Lebanon. Abdullah thought that a new hospital supplied with the latest equipment would be an auspicious beginning.

I leaned forward with keen interest to hear my husband's reply, for I knew that it was painful for Kareem to refuse any wish of his beloved son.

Kareem closed his eyes in concentration and began to rub his forehead with his hand, when without warning our family gathering was intruded upon by the most pathetic howling.

Baffled, we looked at each other and then realized that the strange noise was coming from inside of our villa and the sound was made by Fatma!

A look of relief flashed across Kareem's face, for his son's interest was diverted. Abdullah was the first to move inside the villa, and my daughters and I followed Abdullah inside, leaving Kareem on the veranda.

My first thought was that Fatma had burned some part of her body, for she was standing over the kitchen stove, frying beef and onions for our dinner. I quickly saw that her weeping had not interrupted her cooking task, for she continued to stir the ingredients in the pan and seemed not to realize that her wails had penetrated the stone wall of the villa.

'Fatma! What is the problem?' Abdullah asked.

Like the voice of doom, Fatma replied, 'Oh, Abdullah! The female most blessed is she that has never been born! Next to her in happiness is the female who dies in infancy!'

Bereaved to madness, Fatma began to thump her chest.

Maha grabbed the wooden stirring spoon from Fatma's hand, while Amani began to console the poor woman with soothing sounds and comforting words.

Abdullah gave me a questioning look with his brown eyes.

I shrugged, as confused as he. I had no thought other than Fatma's husband might have divorced her and taken a younger wife, though they had seemed a well-satisfied couple in the past.

Fatma's husband, Abdul, doubled as our gardener and family chauffeur, and the couple had often said that they considered themselves fortunate to work for wealthy people who paid a good wage and who were rarely in the country. They were guaranteed plenty of free time to spend with their children, who lived in an apartment in Cairo with Abdul's mother. Yet, I knew that by law Egyptian men, like Saudi men, have full power over their women, and it was not unusual for an old man to take a second wife, or even to divorce his first wife and take a younger, more attractive woman into his home.

My own experiences have taught me that men are generally the root cause of female grief. Thinking of Fatma's bitter words of female misfortune, I imagined a man as their cause, for nothing is more demoralizing to a woman of Fatma's age than to be abandoned by a husband of many years.

Abdullah, Amani and I led Fatma to a large chair in the sitting-room, while Maha tended to Fatma's unfinished tasks.

Fatma moaned as she walked, holding her hand on the top of her head, like someone trying to stop the pain.

Wanting to get to the cause of her grief, I waved my children from the room, and asked her point blank, 'Fatma, has Abdul divorced you?'

Fatma raised her head and looked at me, her languid eyes blinking at my question. She repeated my words, 'Abdul? Divorce *me*?' She then smiled, but only with her lips. 'That old man? Let him try! I'll crack his bald head open like an egg and fry his brains on the pavement.'

I had to struggle to keep from laughing aloud, for in the past, Kareem had often commented that, in his opinion, Abdul lived in fear of his wife, and there was at least one married woman in the Arab world who had no need of feminine advice from me.

Abdul was half Fatma's size, and once Kareem had come upon the couple and had seen with his own eyes Fatma strike her husband on the back with a large board.

I asked, 'Then, if it's not Abdul, what's the problem?'

Fatma's heavily wrinkled face fell, and she became lost in her own morose thoughts. She sighed so heavily that I knew her sadness had a heartfelt source, and I asked myself with dismay what could be behind her mental anguish.

'Fatma?' I reminded her of my presence.

Sudddenly, her face turned ominous, and Fatma's despair burst forth.

'It's my granddaughter, Alhaan! Her father is an evil being, a donkey of a man, that Nasser! I would kill him with my bare hands if my daughter would allow it! But no! She says, she and her family must live their lives as they see fit!'

Fatma's eyes flashed with anger, and her huge bosom heaved with indignation. 'My own daughter demands that I stay out of her family matters!' She looked at me aghast and asked, 'Can you imagine that? To have no say in my own granddaughter's life?'

Feeling utterly bewildered, I asked, 'What has Nasser done to his child? To your granddaughter?'

Surely, I thought to myself, if the mother of the child had no objections, the harm to the child must not exist.

'That Nasser! He's from a small village. What does he know?'

I drew back in surprise as Fatma spat upon our newly carpeted floor.

Fatma was talking in every direction, cursing

Nasser, crying out for her daughter, and begging God to help her grandchild.

I lost my patience, and raising my voice, I demanded to know. 'Fatma! Tell me, now! What's happened to your granddaughter?'

Disconsolate and at a loss, Fatma tightly squeezed my hand and said, 'Tonight. Tonight they'll make Alhaan into a woman. They have an appointment with the barber at nine o'clock. This ritual I do not believe is necessary. None of my daughters were so treated. It's that Nasser! Can you help me, Mistress, please . . .'

The past surged up in my mind. How well I remembered the horrible story told to me by my oldest sister, Nura, when she too had been made into a woman.

Kareem and I had not yet wed, and I was young, only sixteen years old. My mother had recently died, and Nura, as the eldest daughter, was instructed to answer my questions regarding female circumcision. I had not known until that time that Nura and our two sisters closest to her in age had endured the horrific rite, and as a result had been subjected to life-long pain and suffering.

In Saudi Arabia's not so distant past, circumcision of women had not been infrequent, with each tribe following a different custom. Just this past year, I had read a book that my son had purchased while in London. The book was titled *The Empty Quarter* by St John Philby, a respected British desert explorer. With assistance from my grandfather, Abdul Aziz Al Sa'ud, the founder and first king of Saudi Arabia, John Philby had carried out extensive exploration in Arabia in the 1930s.

I had taken the book from my son's room and had derived great pleasure reading the man's history of Arab tribes that make up the population of Saudi Arabia, until I came across a section of the book that told of the Englishman's findings on female circumcision. Knowing what I know, I had imagined the brutalization of my own sisters and had cringed and cried out when reading a conversation John Philby had documented with the Arab men of the desert:

But his strong subject was sex, and he loved to poke fun at Salih by dilating on Manasir practice in the matter of female circumcision. Take it from me, he said, they let their women come to puberty with clitoris intact and, when a girl is to be married, they make a feast for her circumcision a month or two before the wedding. It is only then that they circumcise them and not at birth as do the other tribes – Qahtan and Murra, Bani Hajir, ay, and 'Ajman. Thus their women grow up more lustful than others, and fine women they are too and that hot! But then they remove everything, making them as smooth as smooth, to cool their ardour without reducing their desire . . . the girls are dealt with in their tents by women who know their business, and get a dollar or so for the job. They are expert with the scissors, the razor and the needle, which are all used for the operation.

The idea that such brutalization would make a woman lustful! I wondered at the information provided to the Englishman and came to the conclusion it was nothing more than brash male talk, for I had been told that the procedure made a woman chaste, rather than passionate.

My grandfather, Abdul Aziz Al Sa'ud, was a man who was ahead of his time, and he looked for better ways in all matters. Coming from the Najd, he did not believe in the circumcision of women, or in the flaying circumcision of men, which was as terrifying as female circumcision.

In the flaying circumcision of men, the skin is removed from the navel down to the inside of a man's legs. On witnessing such brutality, our first king forbade the practice. In spite of my grandfather's decree, the old ways died slowly, and people were willing to risk punishment to carry on with what they had been taught by those who came before them.

My own mother paid no heed to the new ruling, and three of her daughters were subjected to the cruel practice of female circumcision.

While some tribes forbade circumcision of their women altogether, others excised the hood of the clitoris only. The cutting of the hood of the clitoris is the least common method, and is the only procedure that is analogous to male circumcision.

Then, there were those poor women who belonged to tribes in Arabia who removed the whole clitoris, along with the labia minora. This is the most common method of female circumcision and is comparable to removing the head of a man's penis. Three of my sisters had suffered this cruel procedure. The remainder of the women in our family had been spared the rite of circumcision, due to the intervention of a Western physician and my father's insistence to my mother that circumcision of females was nothing more than a pagan practice that must be halted.

There is another, more atrocious and dangerous method of female circumcision, named the pharaonic circumcision. I could scarce imagine the pain experienced by the women who received the pharaonic circumcision. This process is the most extreme, and after the rite is completed, a girl is left without a clitoris, labia minora, or labia majora. If such a procedure were done on a male, it would involve amputation of the penis, and the scrotum around the testicles.

How barbarous were these old customs that still lingered in our present day! In Saudi Arabia, much had been accomplished to eradicate the tradition, and most women in my country no longer experience the terrible custom. The men of my own family had forbidden the pagan tradition, but still some families of African descent who lived in Arabia were prepared to risk punishment rather than forgo the rite, swearing that nothing other than the reduction of female pleasure would preserve female chastity.

I had known that the practice of female circumcision was thought to have begun along the Nile valley, and I had speculated in my mind that the barbaric ritual might end where it had begun. Yet, many women in Egypt and thoughout the continent of Africa were still subjected to this most inhumane ritual.

Over the years, when my own family no longer practised this rite, I had been successful in pushing the thought of female mutilation from my mind.

Fatma tugged on my arm. Her imploring gesture

brought me back into the present. With great sadness, I recalled the face of the young girl Alhaan, for she had visited her grandmother in our villa on many occasions. She was a pretty child and had seemed bright and happy. I imagined an indelible image of the girl being led to the barber, undressed by her mother, with small legs spread before the man with a sharp razor.

I recoiled in horror. In disbelief, I wondered how the mother of that child could condone such evil inflicted on her beautiful daughter? Yet, I knew that many mothers were allowing such intolerable practices, for it is estimated by world health organizations that female genital mutilation affects between 80 and 100 million women worldwide. So much pain inflicted on little girls!

With hope in her voice, Fatma examined my face carefully and asked, 'Mistress, can you save my granddaughter?'

I moved my head slowly and heavily. 'What can I do, Fatma, that you cannot. I'm not of your family. My interference would be resented.'

'You're a princess. My daughter would respect someone who's a princess.'

I had learned long ago that those who have no wealth believe that money has provided wisdom along with economic freedom, but this was a matter of deeply ingrained culture. Instinctively, I knew that Fatma's daughter would not welcome my intrusion.

I waved my arms helplessly. 'What can I do, Fatma? Since I reached the age of understanding, I've wanted female freedom from such practices.' My voice fell low, along with my spirits. 'Now, it seems that the world is becoming darker and darker for those of our sex.'

Fatma remained silent, and a sorrowful look came into her black eyes.

I assured her. 'If I could, I would help your granddaughter. I've no authority to voice my opinion.'

Fatma looked disappointed but spoke words devoid of reproach. 'I understand, Mistress.' She stared at me from half-closed lids. 'But, I beg you to come with me. To try?'

Surprised at Fatma's stubbornness, I felt my resolve soften. I felt a shiver run through my body and asked in a weak voice, 'Where does your daughter live?'

Fatma's thick lips exploded with her excited reply, 'Very close, not more than a short ride in a car. If we leave now, we can get there before Nasser comes home from work.'

I summoned all my courage and stood to my feet. I told myself that, in spite of anticipated failure, I must make an effort. I knew that I would be forced to lie to my husband, or he would forbid me to go. 'Fatma, go and get your things. And say not a word to anyone of this matter.'

'Yes, Mistress! I knew that it was God's will that you would help me!'

I watched her as she hurried away, moving faster than I could ever remember. Despite our vastly different worlds, the two of us had become comrades fighting for the same cause.

By the time I combed out my hair, applied lipstick, and located my handbag, I had decided to tell Kareem that Fatma had just that morning learned that her daughter was ill with a rare female disorder, but she refused treatment, saying that if it was God's will that she die, then she would not reverse his decision by accepting treatment from any man. Fatma had pleaded with me to go and convince her daughter that she must fight to live for the sake of her own children. To be more convincing, I would complain that I did not want to go, but how could I forgive myself if the woman died and I had made no effort. It was a weak scenario, but Kareem shied away from female problems and would more than likely grumble but make no move to stop me from going.

As it turned out, I was not forced to tell such a wild tale, for Abdullah said that his father had received a telephone call while I was talking to Fatma. Kareem left a message for me with Abdullah that he was going to join one of his royal cousins in a Cairo casino and that he would not be home until later that evening. I knew that my husband wanted to put time and distance between himself and his son's earlier request to donate millions of dollars to a failing Lebanese economy, and I had a sense that his excuse to leave our home was as dishonest as the lie I had been prepared to tell. Kareem shares a common trait with most Arabs. My husband cannot say no, but would rather tell a small lie and disappear from the sight of the person who requires an answer.

'Good!' I muttered under my breath. Kareem's discomfort at being in his son's company had come at an opportune time.

After advising me of his father's message, Abdullah turned his attention back to the television set, and I saw that he was mesmerized, watching an Egyptian soap opera that was greatly favoured by

Arabs from many lands. I noticed that Amani's lips had formed a disapproving pout. My daughter was not pleased at her brother's selection: that particular show was not allowed in Saudi Arabia, since there were many scenes that hinted at sexual impropriety.

'Abdullah, I need you to drive me to Fatma's daughter's home. Can you come?'

My son looked for any opportunity to drive the new white Mercedes that Kareem had purchased and shipped into the country for our Cairo home. I knew from past experience that Kareem would have taken the older Mercedes into the busy district of downtown Cairo, since he greatly feared the driving practices of the taxi drivers in that teeming city.

Abdullah flicked the remote control button, turning off the set. He gallantly leapt to his feet. 'I'll get the car.'

The Cairo streets were crowded with vehicles of every description, and the traffic was almost at a standstill. Pedestrians threaded in and out of the traffic. People hung onto the sides of buses already packed with humanity; they clung precariously to the doorways or windows as if it were the most natural method in the world to travel.

As our car inched through the city streets, I gazed in amazement at the mass of people who had descended on the city of the Pharaohs, and shuddered as if I had seen some terrifying sight, for it was easy to see that Cairo could not continue to exist as it was.

Abdullah interrupted my thoughts, asking me the point of our errand.

I swore him to secrecy. When I told him of Fatma's source of sorrow, a flash of anger swept over his face.

Abdullah said that he had heard of such things but had thought such tales were exaggerated. 'Is it really true?' he asked. 'Are such things done to young girls?'

I thought to tell him about his Auntie Nura but reconsidered, for it was such a private matter, and I knew that my sister would be keenly ashamed if my son knew of her mutilation. Instead, I told him the history of female circumcision.

While my son was pleased that the custom was ending in our own land, he felt sickened that so many women worldwide suffered unnecessary pain.

We were silent for the rest of the trip, each of us swamped by our own thoughts of the evening's business.

Fatma's daughter lived in a small alley branching off from a main shopping road in the city. Abdullah paid a shop owner for the privilege of parking our car on the pavement in front of his clothes shop and promised the happy man a generous bonus if he would ensure that no damage occurred while we were away.

Abdullah guided us, hands on our backs as we weaved through the pedestrian traffic and entered the alleyway that led to our destination. The alley was too small for cars, so we walked down the middle of the stone-paved street. Strong cooking odours drifted into the street, as we passed a number of cafés specializing in Arab dishes.

Abdullah and I exchanged many glances, for we had never visited the poorer sections of Cairo, and the close living quarters and poverty of the inhabitants was a shock to us both.

Fatma's daughter lived in a three-storey building

at the centre of the alleyway. The building faced the local mosque, which looked worn and was in urgent need of repair. The bottom floor of the building was a bakery, while the two top floors were rented out as apartments. Fatma pointed up and said that her daughter, Elham, lived on the top floor. Incredibly, Elham must have been looking down at the crowd from the flat-roofed building, for she recognized her mother, and began to yell Fatma's name, which we could barely hear over the loud noise of city life.

Abdullah, not knowing this particular family's custom that women may meet men not of their family, for in Egypt the custom varies from family to family, told me that he would wait for me in a small café we had passed that served shawarma sandwiches, which are thin slices of lamb that has been turned and cooked on a spit and placed into a piece of Arab bread, with tomato, mint and onion as added taste. Shawarma sandwiches were a big favourite of all my children. Abdullah said he was becoming hungry.

I agreed with my son and watched his tall slim figure as he walked jauntily through the crowd.

Elham and three of her four daughters met us on the stairwell, all four speaking at once, demanding to know if there had been some illness or tragedy in the family.

My first thought was that Elham looked identical to Fatma when she was young.

Elham gazed at me in fascination when Fatma introduced me as a princess from Saudi Arabia, her employer, for I had never met this particular child of Fatma's, even though I had met most of Fatma's children and grandchildren. I grew very conscious of my showy jewellery, for in my haste, I had not remembered to remove my large diamond earrings or my opulent wedding ring, which I realized was more than conspicuous in such poor surroundings. Elham's youngest daughter, a girl of only six, was slapped by her mother as she rubbed her small fingers across the stone in my ring.

At Elham's insistence, we were led into her small sitting-room, and she left us for a short time to go and boil water for tea. Fatma had two grand-daughters in her lap and a third at her feet. Alhaan was nowhere to be seen.

I examined my surroundings and could see that Elham lived a simple life. I tried not to stare at the threadbare floor coverings and torn loose covers, for I did not want my attention to be misunder-stood. There was an open brazier in the middle of the room, and a square table pushed against the wall was piled with religious books. A small gas lamp hung down from the ceiling, and I wondered if the apartment was not supplied with electricity. I noticed that Elham's house was spotless, and it was evident that she was a proud woman who went to great measures to keep the dust and bugs out of her simple home.

Elham soon returned, serving sweet tea and small almond cookies that she said she had baked herself for the family celebration that they were having that evening. She mentioned to her mother that Alhaan was excited over the event and was on the rooftop, reading the Koran and quietly preparing herself for the most important day in her life.

The atmosphere remained cheerful until that moment, as Fatma brought up the topic on our minds, pleading with her daughter to cancel the planned evening ritual, to spare her child great pain and suffering.

Fatma talked in a rush and seeing that she was making no dent in her daughter's determination, pointed to me and said that if Elham would not listen to her own mother, then she should pay heed to a woman who had been educated by bright minds, a woman who had learned from respected physicians that the mutilation of girls was not encouraged by our religion and was nothing more than a custom that had no basis or meaning in modern life.

The tension built, and though Elham was polite and listened to my thoughts on the matter, I could see the lines of her face were set and her eyes glassed over with stubborn determination. Knowing from Fatma's confidences that the family was notably religious, I shared my knowledge of religious thought, saying that nothing in the Koran spoke of such matters, and if God considered it a necessity for women to be circumcised, then surely he would have given that message to Prophet Mohammed when he revealed his wisdom to his messenger.

Elham admitted that while excision or infibulation of girls is not mentioned in the Koran, the practice was founded upon the customs of the Prophet so that it became *Sunna*, or tradition for all Muslims. She reminded me of a well-known *hadith*, or tradition addressed but not recorded in the Koran. This *hadith* says that Prophet Mohammed one day told Um Attiya, a matron who was excising a girl, 'Reduce but do not destroy.'

It was this tradition that Elham and her husband

were going to follow regarding female circumcision, and nothing I could say would alter their decision.

We discussed the issue until I could see the light begin to leave the room. Sundown was approaching. I knew that Nasser would return to his home soon, and I had no desire to confront the man of the house over such a delicate matter. I made some small mention that it was time for me to return to my children.

Fatma, sensing failure, began to wail and slap at her cheeks until her face was completely reddened.

A look of distress flickered in Elham's eyes at her mother's grief, but she said that the decision had been reached by her husband and that she agreed with his thinking. All four of her daughters would undergo the rite of circumcision at the proper age.

I could see that Elham wished me to leave. Understanding that I could do nothing to halt the frightening shadow cast over the lives of the female children of this home, I stood and said my farewells.

With quiet self-assurance, Elham's eyes met mine, and she politely bade me goodbye. 'You have honoured my home with your presence, Princess Sultana. Please, come again another day for a longer visit.'

Against her daughter's wishes, Fatma insisted upon staying for the ceremony, saying that if the evil deed was going to be done, that she wanted to supervise the barber's work to make sure he cut nothing more than the tip of her granddaughter's clitoris.

I submitted to the inevitable, leaving Elham's home without accomplishing my goal. My feet felt leaden as I walked down the long staircase. In an effort to give myself time to calm my nerves, I stood motionless on the steps and recited aloud a verse from the Koran, 'You cannot lead aright whomever you wish, it is God who leads whomever he wishes.'

My son was waiting, sitting at a small table in the front of the café. His questioning gaze followed me as I made my way to his side.

He peered at me with expectation. 'So?' he asked.

I shook my head, 'No. There is nothing to be done.'

Abdullah's face clouded as I admitted my failure.

'Come,' I said. 'Let's go home.'

I glanced over my shoulder as we left the small alley, gazing into the night. Elham's home had melted into the darkness as though it had never existed.

When my son began to talk, I urged silence pressing my hand against his lips.

I was unable to control my weeping.

Without speaking, my son drove his sobbing mother home.

As soon as I arrived back at our villa, I called out for my astonished daughters to abandon their current activities and pack their belongings: our family would leave Cairo as soon as their father returned from the casino.

I whispered to Abdullah that the city that I had loved since I was a child was in danger of losing my affection, though I hoped that our evening's experience would not result in my vigorous dislike of everything Egyptian.

Abdullah's eyes flashed with understanding, and I was gratified to see that my son appreciated the reasoning behind my words.

Kareem soon arrived with the odour of alcohol spread about him, which brought on a sudden and prolonged prayer from Amani for God to look past her father's sinful acts and restore Kareem to the status of heaven's most favoured. In the context of her plea, Amani began to describe the burning agony of hell that awaited members of her family.

Already in a foul mood, I quickly wearied of Amani's enthusiastic fanaticism. I was incensed that she would take it to the point where she spoke critically of her family. Face to face, I told her in no uncertain terms that I had not yet received notification that God had appointed my daughter to the sacred role of frightening mankind into decency.

I reached across to pinch the skin on her face, but Kareem grabbed my hand and held it tight to his chest, ordering Amani to leave our presence, suggesting that she complete her prayers in the privacy of her room.

Kareem then became noisy in the irritating manner of a drunkard, saying that he had often observed my inability to control my destructive temper, and he thought that the time had come to teach me a useful lesson.

We looked at each other for a time. Kareem stood still, waiting for my response. His lips were curled in contempt, and it was easy to see that Kareem was in a rare mood to fight.

I quickly scanned the room for a weapon with which to bang my husband's head, for I am a woman who meets threats with violence, but Kareem knows me well and placed himself in a position between me and the brass pot which I had decided to use against my husband.

The will to fight left my body in a rush, for there are times when I can think reasonably, and Kareem is twice my size. Without a weapon, I am at a notable disadvantage and once disarmed can be quickly overcome. Besides, it was best that I decided not to escalate our disagreement into a brawl, for my past had taught me the impossibility of winning an argument with Kareem when he was drunk. But I was filled with scorn, and had difficulty remembering why I had ever loved Kareem in the first place.

Wishing to avoid a confrontation that could provide me with no benefit, I knew that I must recapture the favoured position.

I laughed, and said to Kareem, 'Look at you! You look like an elephant threatening an ant!' I then smiled at my husband and said that I was more than pleased that he had returned early, that I yearned for his companionship at a time of great sorrow.

Kareem was not at his prime mentally, and was easily bested. Bewildered for a short moment at my change in tactic, he fell easily into my trap and became very remorseful for his unthinking words, patting my shoulder, offering apologies, and wondering why his dear wife was distressed.

I looked at my watch and saw that it was nearly nine o'clock. Half insane with the consciousness that the innocent child, Alhaan, would soon undergo female mutilation, I instantly forgot thoughts of self, and with tremendous sadness I told my husband that there is no loveliness in life for women and that in my mind it would be advantageous for all females to die.

Kareem could not fathom the reasoning behind my dark ideas. He asked, was my life not perfect?

Was there anything that I desired that my husband did not provide?

Knowing that my main source of inner conflict rested with the social injustices directed towards women, he reminded me that together we had ensured that in our home, our daughters felt little of the prejudice that exists against females in our land. What more could one man do, he wondered, than to protect those whom he loved.

Kareem smiled sweetly and tenderly brushed my lips with his fingers.

I had a quick thought that Kareem *was* endowed with a winsome charm that atoned for his less admirable traits.

Unsure how to address the ambiguous issue of my general dissatisfaction with female status, Kareem announced that it was my inescapable destiny to be born in Saudi Arabia, and in the end women must accept the limits imposed by our culture. My husband reminded me that God knew all things, and his purpose in planting my feet in Saudi soil had not been made known to those bound on earth.

My emotions in a whirl, I once again felt dislike for Kareem, regretting that all men could not be turned into women and live in our limited and often cruel world for sufficient time to attain understanding. I wanted to rage at my husband's distance from my knowledge of the pain that women endure.

How can woman bind man to the grief that walks the earth and settles at the feet of each woman by turn? Sensing the futility of longing for men to suffer women's position in society, while women enjoy the status of male rank, I told myself that I was too keyed up to be capable of a normal conversation and suggested to my husband that we go to sleep early, and then rise refreshed to a day of new thoughts.

Because he follows a set pattern of fighting, and then sleep after drinking alcohol, Kareem agreed and willingly prepared himself for bed, while I located the children and gave instructions for them to eat their evening meal without us and be available with packed bags to leave Cairo in the morning.

By the time I returned to our quarters, my husband had begun to breathe deeply and peacefully as one already at rest.

With my mind in conflict between my own rebellious thoughts and Elham's traditional beliefs, I considered what Kareem had said, that I was a woman at odds with my fate. Yet, in spite of my second-class status, I knew that I could never yield to meek acceptance of female circumcision.

Before falling into a troubled and unsatisfying sleep, I vowed to myself that my fury over the fate of girls such as Alhaan would outlive the barbaric custom that had aroused it.

Chapter Eleven

MONTE CARLO

*To call women the weaker sex is a libel; it is man's
injustice to women. You will guard your wife's
honour and be not her master, but her true friend.
Let not either of you regard another as the
object of his or her lust.*
Mahatma Gandhi

Fatma's face was contorted in an effort to appear
cheery as she bid us good morning. She had
been hard at work in the kitchen when the family
awakened and seemed distraught at our abrupt
announcement that we were leaving Cairo and
travelling to Monte Carlo that very morning. There,
on the French Riviera, we would join three of my
sisters and their families who were holidaying in the
small principality of Monaco.

I had already imagined in my mind the scene of
her granddaughter's circumcision and knew that the
tragic evening did not lend itself to words. Still, I
manoeuvred a quiet moment away from my family
to enquire about Alhaan's safety.

With clasped hands and a steely glint in her eyes that reflected her lingering anger, Fatma said that the child had not fared well. On her son-in-law's instruction, the barber had removed all of the girl's clitoris, along with her labia minora. Fatma said that special compresses had to be made to stop the flow of blood.

Feeling undeserved guilt that I had had no ability to halt Alhaan's brutalization, I asked in alarm, 'Do you fear further complications?'

Fatma tried to relax her expression when she saw that my eyes were filling with tears and realized that I was becoming distraught.

'Mistress,' she hugged my neck as she spoke. 'The deed is done. Now we must live with it. You did all that you could. I bless you for your love of another who is not of your own blood. Take comfort from my belief that Alhaan will recover.'

I could find no words to speak. Fatma turned me loose and her eyes met mine. Our gazes stayed fixed on one another for a long time. Neither of us looked away or moved, and I felt a great love surging from Fatma to me.

Fatma moistened her lips before she continued. 'Princess Sultana, you entered my dreams last evening, and now I feel that I must convey the message of the dream.'

I held my breath, afraid of what I might be told, thinking that I had never fared well in supernatural predictions.

Fatma gazed at me with sad affection. 'Mistress, you are surrounded with life's possessions, yet you appear empty. This discontent comes from having the heart of a child in the body of a woman. Such a combination will bring great difficulties to one's soul. Neither you, nor any other child of God, can resolve all of mankind's problems. I was told to tell you that it is not shameful to bow to reality and that you should allow the lust for conflict to cool in your veins.'

My mother's face appeared to me as a dark dream of disconnected memories. There was no doubt in my mind that my mother was using the form of the earthbound Fatma to communicate with her youngest child. Fatma's words were just the sort of advice that my mother had often given to me in the days of my childhood. When I was young, her words of wisdom were unclear and seemed to have no connection to me. Now that I was an adult, that was no longer the case.

I had known then, even as a child, that when my mother understood that she was dying that her only regret in passing from earth was that she was leaving my untempered character without a firm guide. Her fears had been that I would react to adult controversy in the same hasty manner with which I had confronted problems when I was a child, when I had no goal but success, embroiling myself in one conflict after another.

My beloved mother was communicating with me!

I felt a warm glow throughout my body and felt calmer than I had in days. My memories were no longer obscure, and I keenly felt my mother's divine presence.

I had no explanation to give for the sudden whimpering that I heard arise from my throat, or for the sobbing and incoherent woman who threw herself into Fatma's strong arms, a woman who still felt as a child, longing with all her heart to have but one short moment with the woman who had given her life.

I cried out to a sympathetic Fatma, 'How blessed are those who still have their mothers!'

When leaving the city of Cairo, I could not help but think of the gloomy fate awaiting many young girls in the country of Egypt. I whispered to my son that such tragic events make Egyptian life less bright and cheerful than is fitting in such a country.

Late that afternoon, our private plane landed at the Nice-Côte International Airport. My three sisters' husbands had rented a large villa in the hills above Monaco, which they had assured Kareem was a short drive from the airport. On short notice, Asad had arranged for three limousines to meet our arrival and transport our family and baggage from the airport to the villa.

Actually, at one time the villa had been a palace belonging to a French aristocrat and had over sixty rooms, so there was more than enough space for our combined families. None of my sisters was married to a man who had taken more than one wife, so our group of eight adults and sixteen children was unusually small for an Arab gathering of four families.

There are three highways which go from Nice to Monaco, but none of us had a desire to travel the coastal road or the Inférieure Corniche, which is generally traffic-packed. The Moyenne Corniche is the middle road, and the Grand Corniche is the high road.

I expressed a desire to take the Moyenne, since I

knew it was the best road of the three and had wonderful views of the coastline.

Kareem disagreed, saying that our daughters should choose the road we would travel.

I pinched the flesh on his leg, indicating that his idea was not sound, but he continued to ask their opinions.

As I knew they would, Maha and Amani began an immediate squabble, with each of them insisting upon a different route.

I whispered to Kareem, 'I told you so.'

Our daughters had never reached agreement on any issue, regardless of the subject, since the time they had learned to speak. I admitted to myself that nothing in our lives had been simple since I had given birth to three children.

The driver settled their argument by saying that a truck loaded with eggs had suffered a mishap, and that the Moyenne was temporarily blocked. Since two of the three roads were congested with traffic, he suggested that we take the Grande.

Like the baby she is, Amani pouted, but Maha and Abdullah were joyful, pointing out various interesting sights that they had not remembered from our last trip to Monaco over three years before. The drive took us along the precipices of the Maritime Alps' southern slopes and the scenery was spectacular.

I couldn't help commenting that, after viewing the uninspired brown and beige shades of desert countries, the lush greenery of Europe was restful to my eyes.

Amani took my comment as a slur upon the home of the Prophet, whereupon Kareem lost his patience and asked his daughter *please* to omit religious interpretations of the simplest social remark.

I thought to myself that my own precious daughter was becoming thoroughly unlikable. My love flowed as strongly as ever, but there were moments when I suffered extreme distaste for Amani's overbearing and 'holier than thou' attitude.

Pleased that my family's confined journey was coming to an end, I was happy to see my sisters Sara, Tahani and Nura, when our car pulled up the circular driveway to the front of the villa. How welcome I felt that the three of them had evidently been eagerly waiting by the door for our arrival.

My pleasure was short-lived.

'Reema has been hospitalized!' Nura announced as soon as we had completed our greetings and my three children had left the area to go and seek out their cousins.

'What?' I responded, while trying to imagine what illness had struck the fifth sister in age in our family.

'She's been injured,' Sara volunteered, while exchanging a meaningful look with Nura.

'Yes?' My voice was so low that the sound barely left my throat. I had a sudden fear of a car accident, for traffic accidents are the main source of death in Saudi Arabia, where many young boys recklessly race their vehicles through the streets.

My sisters and I stood without speaking, awkwardly facing one another. I moved my weight from foot to foot, waiting for someone to enlighten me about my sister's condition.

Kareem and Asad stood to the side of our small gathering, watching but not speaking.

When no-one spoke, my stomach churned. Was my sister dead, and was there no-one in my family with the nerve to tell me.

Finally, I asked weakly, 'Is her injury serious?'

'It seems that it isn't life-threatening,' Nura stated.

The Arab manner of avoiding bad news is maddening! I felt the urge to scream, for someone to tell me all that there was to know, to release me from the agony of attempting to force small bits of information from my reluctant sisters.

'What's happened?' I demanded. 'Anything is easier to accept than this torturing doubt!'

My sisters looked at each other strangely. Surely, Reema was dead!

'Let's go into the villa,' Asad suggested, as he placed a tender hand on Sara's arm. 'I'll have tea prepared.'

I followed Sara into the villa, taking no notice of the rooms as we passed them by. I was thinking of poor Reema. The fifth daughter in our family had always inspired family sympathy. From the date of her birth, Reema had not been blessed with obvious skills or beauty. While my sister was not born with a face scarred or misaligned, there had been nothing in her appearance that brought forth envy from other young mothers.

Nura had once confided that Reema was the only daughter whom our mother had felt no need to protect with the blue stone that was believed to ward off evil spirits, for who would wish the evil eye upon an infant so displeasing in appearance?

In addition, the young girl Reema had been cursed with a heavy figure that brought her cruel taunts from unfeeling children.

Of my nine sisters, Sara is the most beautiful. Of the remainder of our female family members, four sisters are notably pretty, three sisters are appealing, another sister is elegant and graceful, while Reema lacks a single mark of beauty. In a family of ten daughters, Reema was the unattractive sister who failed to excel in school or in games. Her one outstanding accomplishment was her ability to duplicate our mother's cooking skills, improvising delectable Arab and French dishes that did nothing to help her expanding figure.

Living in a country where nothing is more admired than female beauty, Reema was not esteemed.

Once we had settled ourselves in the sitting-room, Kareem and Asad left us to go and arrange tea. As the door was closing, I heard Asad speaking in a low voice to my husband, and knew that Kareem had discovered Reema's fate before her own sister had.

'I must know the truth. Tell me. Is Reema dead?'

'No.' Nura responded. Yet, my sister's gloomy face reflected the seriousness of the situation.

'She was attacked by Saleem,' Tahani finally said.

I felt cold all over. 'Truly?' I asked.

With tremendous emotion, Nura added, 'Our dear sister was viciously attacked by her own husband.'

'Why would Saleem want to hurt Reema?' I wondered. 'Surely, she gave him no motive!'

Like many unattractive people, Reema had always been pleasing in character, striving to make all around her feel delightful and gay, as if her joyful countenance could outwit nature, eliciting admiration from those in her company.

Saleem? My memory of Reema's husband flashed

through my mind. Saleem, like Reema, was not blessed with physical beauty. But he was known to be a most quiet and gentle man. As we often say in the Arab world, 'every pot has its cover'. Saleem was considered a perfect partner for Reema, and their union seemed to suit them. His violent action was completely unexpected and out of character.

I put to Nura the most logical possibility, 'Did Saleem lose his mind? Is that why he assaulted Reema?'

I was not prepared for what I heard.

Approximately a year before Saleem's attack on his wife, Reema had expressed great anxiety to her oldest sister, Nura, that a dark secret was consuming the light in her life. Reema said that her dear husband was undergoing a bizarre personality change that had begun with a strange restlessness and dissatisfaction. Suddenly the formerly contented Saleem had been overcome by the blackest melancholy. Where Saleem had once been well pleased with his home, he was now irritable, finding endless fault with his wife and four children. He no longer expressed an interest in his work, and for many days he would remain in bed until mid-afternoon. Saleem was caught in the tyranny of his own emotions, which prevented the entire family from living a normal life.

While Reema's attachment to Saleem had increased during the years of their married life, Saleem coldly told Reema that he had never loved her, that as a matter of fact he had never known love at all, and had married Reema for no reason other than to gain prestige from her family name.

Reema confronted Saleem's unreasonable hostility

with faithful love and genuine concern. Reema told Nura that she feared that Saleem must have a brain tumour, or at least be suffering from a chemical imbalance. Why else would a man so radically change, when nothing in his life had undergone trauma?

Reema pleaded with her husband to seek medical attention. Instead of looking for professional help for his misery, Saleem dwelled on his unhappiness. Saleem, a man who rarely drank alcohol, began to drink with increasing frequency. When drinking, he would become violent towards Reema and the eldest of their daughters.

Reema told Nura that she feared she would soon be divorced, separated from her two youngest sons, for Saleem had threatened to liberate himself from Reema, insisting that was the only way to free himself from his unhappiness.

Nura was helpless at giving advice, for Saleem was from a family that none of our family could approach without tension, for their family had recently requested that one of Nura's daughters be wed to their youngest son. The engagement did not materialize, since Ahmed and Nura had already arranged a different husband for their child. Saleem's family had held themselves at a distance since that time, taking offence where none was intended.

Nura said that while Saleem slowly pulled himself together so that he began to function at work, his contempt for Reema only grew more intense. Saleem began to take frequent trips to the Far East, and Reema knew from some of the brochures that she found in her husband's belongings that the trips were not of a business nature. Saleem was participating in sexual junkets to Bangkok and Manila.

Just the month before, Reema had come to Nura's home with a bruised face and a horrifying story. Our sister had discovered her husband in bed with one of the Sri Lankan maids. When she protested, Saleem had come at her with his fists and threatened Reema with the loss of her children if she dared open her mouth to anyone in his family. Saleem's family was known to be devout and religious, and they would have expressed great shame at his conduct, though they would have been helpless to change his mood.

While it is true that many Saudi men turn to secret pleasures with women to whom they are not wed, none of the females in our family had married a man so insensitive as to flaunt sexual relations with a servant in his own home.

Reema, perplexed and not sure where to turn, went to an Egyptian female Imam, asking that the woman put in writing the answer to the question: Does Islam permit a man to have sexual intercourse with his maidservant without marrying her? Surely, her husband would heed a religious ruling, if she brought it to him in writing. To go against the teachings of the Koran would be unthinkable in the mind of our pious sister!

Nura said that Reema had confessed that she was going to confront Saleem with the ruling. Nura had cautioned our sister, concerned that Saleem no longer enjoyed total sanity.

I asked if Nura recalled the words of the ruling.

She replied that she had taken a copy for herself and filed it with her other religious material. Who knew what other woman might have a need for the information at a later date?

Nura said that to the best of her memory, 'the Imam's ruling clearly states that Islam does not allow a sexual relationship between a master and a servant'. The idea was outrageous, and only through marriage could a sexual relationship exist in Islam.

The Imam acknowledged that what happens in actual life is not always sanctioned by Islam and that there were many cases in the kingdom which had been brought to her attention involving a master forcing his servant to yield to his wishes, exploiting her weakness in their relationship to get cheap fulfilment of carnal desire.

The Imam had ruled that such a relationship was illicit and led to the three evils expressly forbidden by Islam. The evils of which she spoke were: 'Any relationship which adversely affects the moral fabric of society, or leads to promiscuity, or affects the rights of any individual. In Islam, the only lawful way to have sexual intercourse is through marriage.'

Reema's courage in seeking an outside opinion caused me some surprise, for she was meek in nature.

'Was the ruling the cause of Saleem's attack?' I asked my sisters.

Nura answered in the negative, causing me some surprise.

'Then?'

Sara began to weep and left the room, saying that she could not bear to hear the details again. Tahani rose to follow her, but Asad was standing near the door. I caught a glimpse of him wrapping his arms around his wife as he led her to a private corner.

Tahani returned and sat by my side, and began to pat my hand nervously.

I thought to myself that I was being prepared for some distressing details.

'The physician would not tell us the full details, but Father and Ali went to his office and were told the truth of the matter, for Saleem finally confessed to the physician what exactly had happened to Reema.

'It seems that Saleem had just returned from a short trip to Bangkok and had smuggled in pornographic video tapes. After a night of drinking and viewing the tapes, Saleem thought to have sex with his wife, although he had not displayed affectionate interest in Reema for some time.

'When Saleem awakened Reema in the middle of the night for sex, he was told that she was having her monthly period.'

With half-shut eyes, Nura leaned back on the sofa.

Like all Muslims, I know that the Koran forbids sexual relations during a woman's menstrual cycle. The Koran clearly states: 'They ask, concerning women's courses, respond: they are a hurt and a pollution, keep away from women in their courses, and do not approach them until they are clean, but when they have purified themselves, you may approach them in any manner, time, or place, ordained for you, by God.'

Had Reema fought her husband, only to be raped and beaten during a time when she was forbidden to him?

I could tell that Nura was thinking of what she was going to say and how she was going to say it. I watched Nura's face as it became white with anger. 'Saleem, in a drunken state, became angry at his wife's condition and refusal.' My sister took a deep, ragged breath. 'Sultana, Reema was badly beaten, and then Saleem raped his wife in a region of her body not allowed to her husband. The physician at the private clinic informed Father that Saleem's attack was so violent and brutal that emergency surgery was performed. For the remainder of her life, Reema will be forced to wear a colostomy bag.'

My mouth opened in a soundless howl. Reema? Disabled and encumbered for life? I found myself seething with hostility. Now I understood why Sara had fled the room, for she herself had been subjected to that same type of sexual abuse when wed against her will to her first husband, a man who was sick in his head.

I got to my feet and stamped my foot so hard that a vase tottered and threatened to fall from a tall stand. 'If Saleem were in this room, I would attack him with my hands,' I shouted. In an uncontrolled rage, I asked, 'And Saleem? Has he been gaoled?'

Tahani made a clicking sound with her tongue. 'Gaoled? He's Reema's husband. He's free to do as he likes.'

Nura's face was becoming even paler in her grief and bitterness over the fate of our innocent sister.

I protested, 'But his conduct was forbidden! Surely, we can make a case for a religious investigation!'

Nura looked at me with great love mingled with sadness. 'Sultana, you speak as a child. Who, in our land, will take the side of a woman against her husband? Our own father and brother have directed that this is a personal matter between Reema and Saleem and that no-one in our family is to interfere.'

Tahani confided, 'Father prohibited us from telling you, but we decided that we must, for when you see Reema next, her condition will be obvious.'

I insisted, 'Reema must divorce him! That, at least!'

Nura reminded me of the reality of Reema's situation. 'And lose her children? Both girls have reached puberty, and the boys are now eight and nine. Saleem has the right to take them from their mother. And that he would do. He has already threatened her with their loss. Sultana, Reema would die without the presence of her children.'

When Nura saw that I was still fiercely angry, she asked, 'Tell me, Sultana, could you live if your children were taken from you?'

In my land, in the event of a divorce, the mother has the right to retain her children if they are still suckling. But in most cases, a mother maintains custody of daughters until a girl child reaches puberty. In the case of male children, the boy should be allowed to remain with his mother until he is seven. When he reaches his seventh birthday, he is supposed to have the option to choose between his mother or father. Generally it is accepted that the father will have his sons at age seven. A son *must* go with his father at the age of puberty, regardless of the child's wishes.

Often, in the case of male children, many fathers will not allow the mother to retain custody of a son, no matter what the age of the child. I have personally known women who have lost custody of their children at young ages, never seeing those that they gave birth to again. Unfortunately, if a father seizes the initiative and takes his children, there is no authority to enforce the return of the children to their mother.

I knew that if Saleem refused Reema visits to her children, then my sister would be banned from their presence for ever. There was no court of law that would reverse the husband's final decision about the destiny of his children.

I moaned, thinking of the possibilities we would know if we had male support. If only the men of her family, our father and Ali, would stand behind Reema, then her position in negotiating for her children would strengthen. Since our father and brother thought that a man should be unencumbered to do as he would with the females in his family, they would be of no assistance to Reema.

It was a serious moment.

'Perhaps Saleem will come to his right mind,' Nura hopefully suggested.

'Never try to straighten a dog's tail. In vain you do,' Tahani muttered to no-one in particular.

After further discussion, my sisters and I decided that we were needed in Riyadh. We would leave our husbands in Monte Carlo with our children, and travel back to Saudi Arabia the following day.

Later that evening, Kareem tried to lift my downcast spirits by reminding me that my sister had not died from her injuries and where there was life, change might come. He said that a better day would soon be known, that in his opinion, Saleem was suffering from nothing more than a male crisis that would pass.

Kareem had become concerned when I promised him that Saleem would suffer for his attack on the gentle Reema.

Trying to ease my murderous rage, he had joked, 'Sultana, I don't wish to see you ready for the executioner's sword! You must spare Saleem's life.'

My husband continued to speak, but I listened to his words without hearing, thinking that it was most lamentable that so much ignorance should prevail in a land that is home to a great religion.

Chapter Twelve

HOME

A girl possesses nothing but a veil and a tomb.
Saudi Arabian proverb

Our brother, Ali, met us at the King Khalid International Airport twenty-two miles from Riyadh. He seemed preoccupied and curtly informed us that we would be taken directly to the private clinic to visit our sister, Reema, for she was suffering a particularly bad day and had continually asked for Nura since early morning.

The traffic was heavy, and the drive took more than an hour. Each of us was lost in our thoughts of Reema. At the beginning of the journey, the conversation was strained and sparse, with nothing of any consequence being said.

Ali, tiring of the silence, confided that he, himself, was involved in a family crisis. With a touch of annoyance in his voice, my faithless brother said that Reema's unfortunate injury could not have occurred at a worse time, and that he had been greatly inconvenienced by the necessity of becoming involved in Saleem's private family affair. In all earnestness, Ali wondered aloud what Reema had done to arouse Saleem's hostility.

Ali was blaming Reema for Saleem's unprovoked attack!

Sara and Tahani looked quickly at Ali, and I detected in their evasive glances faint reprimands at his unfeeling comment.

I could not restrain my tongue and said, 'Ali, with each day, your ignorance grows while your intelligence shrinks!'

I felt a keen urge to slap my brother, but not wanting to appear less than admirable in front of Nura and Tahani, consoled myself with silent criticism of Ali. Ali was only a year older than me, but he looked no less than ten years my senior, with lines in his face and pouches under his eyes. In his youth, Ali had been handsome – vain about his looks. In middle age he had grown a bit stout, and his chin had doubled. Ali's affluent, over-indulged lifestyle was clearly evident in his face and form. I was cheered to see his physical appeal decaying.

My eldest sister's face clouded, and in a voice filled with tenderness and concern, asked Ali what crisis there was in his life.

Out of ten sisters, only Nura truly loves Ali. The emotions of the remaining nine sisters for their only brother range from pity, contempt and envy, to open dislike. Nura, understandably, is protected from acute disapproval of her only brother by the division of many years, for Nura is the oldest child among us, and Ali is one year from the youngest. Nura was married with children when Ali was born, and was mercifully spared his overbearing spoiled conduct. In addition, Nura inherited the kindly character of our mother and belonged to that minority who instinctively make apologies for those around them, while accepting the most feeble explanations for inexcusable deeds. Thus, Nura's reaction to Ali's insensitive statement differed from that of his other three sisters.

Ali frowned slightly. He looked out of the car window and then said distantly, 'I have divorced Nada.'

Nura gasped. 'Again?'

Ali looked at Nura and nodded.

'Ali! How could you? You promised Nada that never again would you divorce her!'

Nada was Ali's most beautiful and favoured wife. He had married her seven years before, and together they had had three lovely daughters.

Under Muslim law, a man's freedom to divorce his wife is justified in the Koran. This system of the threat of divorce looming over a woman's security is most unsettling to women in my land. It is intolerable that many men stretch this ruling to the utmost of its flexibility, demanding divorce for the most trivial causes, ending with the continuous social degradation of their women.

Women do not have the same options, since a divorce in a woman's favour is given only after a thorough investigation into her life. More often than not, women will not be allowed to divorce, even when there is just cause. This female lack of freedom so enjoyed by males creates one-sided, often cruel methods of male control and power over their women. The words of divorce slip most easily off the tongue of a man who wishes to punish his wife, 'I divorce thee', or 'I dismiss thee', sending the woman into exile from her married home, often without her children.

Ali, a man rarely in control of his tongue or his temper, often used divorce as a weapon against his wives.

I knew that my brother had divorced each of his wives at least once, and Nada had been divorced twice. More times than not, Ali's anger receded, he would repent the divorce and retain the wife he had divorced the day or night before. Ali had this benefit, for men are not only given the option of divorcing their wives with the greatest of ease but are allowed to take back the divorce and resume their marriage as if nothing out of the ordinary had occurred. Under Muslim law, a man is given this option twice. If a man divorces his wife for a third time, then the procedure becomes more complicated.

In a fit of anger, Ali had divorced Nada for the third time and, according to our law, he could not resume marriage with Nada until she had married another man and had then been divorced by that man. Through his childlike conduct, Ali had finally and truly divorced himself from the only one of his wives for whom he felt true affection.

I tried not to smile as I quoted words from the Koran, doing my best to remember every word.

'You may divorce your wives twice; after that you must either retain them with kindness, or put them away with benefits. If then the husband divorce her a third time, it is not lawful for him to take her again, until she shall have married another husband.'

I stuck my face in my brother's and asked, 'Ali, who is Nada now going to wed?'

Ali glared at me with bulging eyes, and answered coldly. 'La! La! (no, no) Nada has no desire to wed another!'

'Ha! Nada is famous within the female community for her beauty. Once it is known that she is free, many mothers and sisters will send their sons and brothers to ask for Nada. Wait and see!'

Sara intervened, not wanting our lifelong, unending feud to lead to a fierce argument in a confined area. 'Ali. What led to this divorce?'

Ali was clearly embarrassed to say. He said that the matter of the divorce was private, but he did ask Sara and Nura if they would visit Nada, to convince her that the words were spoken in haste, and as such, Ali should be given another opportunity to prove that he had no real desire to divorce Nada. If Nada chose to ignore the situation and did not notify the authorities, then Ali might be able to avoid an order to allow Nada to leave his home, thereby becoming eligible for another man to pursue.

Nura and Sara agreed to talk to Nada.

The car began to slow down, and Ali peered through the dark blue curtains of the limousine and then pointed at the black assortment of veils, *abaayas*, and *shaylas* that were spread over the car seat. 'Hurry. Prepare yourselves. We're there,' he commanded.

It was a struggle for the four of us to cover ourselves in the black garb of decency within the small space of the car. Ali had met our private aeroplane on the tarmac, so we had not bothered with our required outer coverings until the last moment.

We had arrived at the private clinic that Ali said was owned jointly by a Lebanese and a Saudi Arabian. The clinic was one often frequented by royal family members when confidentiality was desired. I was acquainted with three princesses who routinely entered the clinic for treatment of drug and alcohol abuse.

Our family was escorted inside the building through a little-used door; we were met there by one of Reema's physicians. The man informed us that he was an internist, a specialist from Beirut, and had recently been hired by the owners of the clinic to care for members of the royal family. It was easy to see why the man had been selected to treat influential Saudis, for he was a tall, attractive man, deferential, yet with an air of confidence that provided us with a sense of well-being for our sister's safety.

The physician walked between Nura and Ali, and though I made an attempt to lean forward and involve myself in their quiet conversation, I failed to hear the words that he spoke. We passed a group of Asian nurses who were clustered around an elongated nurses' station. Once close, I could tell by their accents that they were Filipinos.

The windows in Reema's room were still closed, but the blinds were slightly open, allowing a small amount of the sun's glow to penetrate and wash the room in a soft light. The room was completely white, and above Reema's head hung a large pearl-white chandelier that looked strangely out of place in a clinical setting.

Reema was resting, but when she heard us she opened her eyes. I could see that my sister suffered a moment of confusion before reality rushed back to her. Her face was of the palest hue, and her eyes were those of a frightened child. My sister was receiving fluids from bottles hanging from metal stands, and I could not count the tubes that had been placed in her arms and nose.

Nura rushed to her side, placing her arms around the form that was Reema. Sara and Tahani held hands, fighting back tears, and I could scarcely see as I flung myself in a white armchair. I bit my lips until I tasted blood, and I pressed my hands into the arm of the chair with such force that I broke three fingernails.

Ali, uncomfortable with our display of grief, whispered to Sara that he would return within the hour to escort us to our homes. Before leaving, he reminded Sara that it was imperative that she see Nada on that very evening.

I was seething with rage at the sight of my wounded sister and thought to myself that I would like to send the hottest fire raging throughout the whole country. Let the evil of my land die with the flesh of those Saudi men who dared to use the holy Koran as a basis to molest those of my sex!

I attempted to calm my thoughts, for there was no purpose in creating chaos and adding to Reema's pain. I remembered the Prophet's promises of punishment to those who so sin, but my religion could not soothe me, even in the knowledge that Saleem would suffer everlasting agonies in hell for what he had done to my sister. I had no patience to wait for divine intervention. Nothing would cool my boiling blood but the sight of Saleem's mutilated remains!

Once comforted by Nura, Reema talked to each of her sisters in turn, pleading with us to treat Saleem with the same courtesy as before, reminding us that one of the duties of good Muslims is to forgive those who do wrong. Seeing the anger in my face, Reema quoted a verse from the Koran. 'Sultana, don't forget the words of the Prophet: forgive, even when angry.'

I could not hold back my words. Remembering the text of the Koran that followed, I replied, 'Let evil be rewarded with evil.'

Sara pinched me on my buttocks, reminding me not to cause further anguish to our sister. I left Reema's side and stared out of the small openings of the window, seeing nothing of what I was looking at.

Reema began to speak once again. I could not believe what I was hearing and was chilled by Reema's words, which were delivered with the impassioned eloquence of a woman whose reason for living was at stake.

I returned to my sister's bedside and stared at her face.

As the intensity of Reema's feelings increased, her brow became furrowed, and her lips grew tight with determination. My sister said that Saleem had repented and had promised that there would be no other violence. She was not going to be divorced, nor would she seek a divorce.

Suddenly I realized what was in Reema's heart. My sister's only fear was to be deprived of her children, and those four children were the inspiration for Reema's ability to forgive Saleem for his heinous attack. She would accept any indignity so long as her relationship with her precious children was not severed.

Reema asked, would we assure her that no-one in our family would seek retribution on her behalf?

It was the most difficult promise ever to pass my lips, and my tongue would scarce obey my mind. But my word was given, and I knew that I had no choice but to abide by my sister's sincere wish.

Once recovered, Reema would return to the home of the man who had an infinite capacity for cruelty, well hidden for many married years. I knew that, once unleashed, Saleem's ugly temperament would not soften. There was nothing else that we could do.

Our frustration only increased when an Egyptian nurse employed at the clinic confided in Nura that Saleem had visited his wife earlier that day. In the presence of that nurse, Saleem had lifted his wife's hospital gown, viewing the hole that had been made in her side for her bodily waste to be expelled, and had expressed shocking disgust at the sight.

The nurse said that Saleem had then made a most callous remark, telling his wife that while he would not divorce her, that he would never again come to her bed, for he could not bear the sight or smell of one so repugnant.

I marvelled at my ability to control my rage.

My sisters and I had entered the clinic as a united force, swelled with determination to snatch our sister from the grasp of her evil husband. Defeated by Reema's legitimate apprehension of the possible loss of her children, we retreated from the clinic as nothing more than a group of black shrouded and nameless wives, without the ability to force justice upon a single man.

The sting of defeat was unbearable.

Who could deny that the main bulwark of Saudi social order remained male dictatorship?

Since our husbands and children were still in Monte Carlo, my sisters and I decided that we would remain together in Nura's house. From the clinic, we had Ali transport us to her home. Nura and Sara pledged to Ali that they would have one of Nura's drivers take them to visit Nada that evening and said that it was best for him to stay in the home of another wife that night.

Once we had telephoned our husbands in Monte Carlo, advising them of news of Reema, Tahani pleaded exhaustion and retired early to bed. I insisted on accompanying Sara and Nura to Nada's palace. I was forced to make a second promise, guaranteeing that I would make no suggestions to Nada for her to quit Ali while she had the opportunity.

My sisters know me well. Admittedly, I had already made a plan in my mind to try and convince Nada that she must quickly move to marry another. My brother had treated women with contempt all of his life and in my opinion it was time for him to learn not to use divorce as a weapon. Perhaps if he lost the only wife for whom he felt affection, then he would temper his bullying tactics.

Now, I had a second difficult promise to keep.

It was nearly nine o'clock in the evening when we arrived. Ali's compound seemed more peaceful than we had ever seen. We saw none of his wives, concubines or children as our car drove through the wide circular drive that wound around the four palaces belonging to our brother. Nada's palace was the third building within the compound walls.

Nada's Egyptian housekeeper informed us that her mistress was having a bath but was expecting us and had instructed the housekeeper to bring us to her living quarters.

We followed the woman to the interior of Ali's home.

Nothing about my brother is modest. The influence of Saudi oil wealth was evident at every turn. Conspicuous consumption met my eye as I entered the front hallway laid with white marble that was the width of an airport terminal. The towering staircase gleamed with the glow of silver, and I remembered Ali's proud announcement that the columns bracing the structure were coated with real silver. Fifteen foot high doors with solid silver doorknobs led into Nada's private living quarters.

I tried not to gloat, recalling that my brother had taken a serious financial loss with the worldwide run on the silver market in the 1980s. In his greed, Ali must have purchased more of that precious metal than we had realized, only to see his fortunes tumble. Now, Ali's financial loss was the gain of a silver enhanced palace!

I had never visited Nada's bedroom, though I had once received an invitation to view the bedstead. I had been told by a shocked and saddened Sara that the bed was carved in solid ivory, and now I saw that the description was true. Ali had once bragged about the number of elephants that had died to support his bulky frame, but now I could not recall the figure that he had quoted.

Looking around my brother's opulent home, I had a vision of justified Al Sa'ud exile from the Kingdom of Saudi Arabia, for such inherent corruption of wealth deserved no other fate. Would we one day share royal displacement with the likes of King Farouk of Egypt, the Shah of Shahs of Iran, or King Idris of Libya? There was one certainty in my mind, that if the working class of Saudi Arabia ever viewed the private living quarters of Prince Ali Al Sa'ud, revolution was inescapable.

This terrifying idea numbed my body.

At that moment, Nada swept into the room, her hair fashionably coiffured; she had a haughty expression, and her opulent bosom was crammed into a blinding gold lamé dress. It required little imagination to understand how our brother was ensnared by his infatuation for his most beautiful wife. Nada had achieved fame in our family through her daring fashions and her will to do battle with a man who had met little resistance from women throughout his life. In spite of Nada's ability to torture Ali, I had always thought the expression in her eyes looked subtly malicious and had never veered from my opinion that Nada's itch for gain had been her only purpose in marrying Ali. I did remember Sara's words that it was Nada's insecurity in her marriage that made her appear what she was not, for she had no idea when Ali might dispense with her, as he had other women. Such a position creates the need to accumulate future economic security. But I still had my lingering doubts about her true nature. I did admit to myself that Nada had paid dearly for the softer luxuries, for married life with Ali surely must be grim.

Nada said, 'Ali sent you, didn't he?'

I watched Nada's face, thinking that she was pouting and mourning, as if our visit were all a mistake. I alternated between like and dislike, and as Nura and Sara gathered around our sister-in-law, I excused myself, saying that I was going to the bar to fetch myself a drink.

The house was completely quiet and there was no-one about. After preparing myself a gin and tonic, I felt no desire to rejoin my sisters, and I wandered through my brother's palace, finding myself in his private study located on the lowest level of his home.

I was overcome by childlike curiosity, and displayed the traits of a voyeur, sifting through my brother's personal belongings and making a discovery that first puzzled me and then brought great amusement.

I opened a small packet on the top of his writing desk, and read with vague curiosity about a set of undergarments that my brother had obviously purchased during a recent trip to Hong Kong.

A flimsy sheet of instructions accompanied the underpants, and I read the sheet with interest.

Wonder Garment: Congratulations on the purchase of your new Wonder Garment! The garment that you have purchased should be worn daily. This garment is guaranteed to improve the wearer's sexual performance.

The secret of these miracle underpants lies in the 'strategic' pouch which maintains the sexual organs at the correct temperature and under optimum conditions.

The Wonder Garment is recommended for all men, but most especially for those who maintain an active sexual life and for those who sit down at their work.

I began to giggle, and an evil spirit came over me. I stuffed the slim plastic bag containing the undergarment and instruction sheet under my long dress. I had no thought of what I was going to do with the item but felt an urge to share the secret with Kareem. Feeling as I had in the days of my childhood rivalry with Ali, I gleefully imagined how my brother would frantically search through his home for the magical pants.

I met my sisters on the staircase and could see from their eyes that they had had no success with Ali's wife.

Nada was leaving Ali.

Unlike poor Reema, Nada was not worried that her children would be taken, for Ali had little love for his female offspring and had made no secret to his wife that their three daughters were of no value to him, and that they would be allowed to live with their mother.

I left without saying goodbye. I cradled my gin and tonic in the car. My theft of Ali's personal possessions had brought forth childish emotions, and I felt quite daring as a princess in the House of Al Sa'ud riding through the streets of Riyadh, enjoying an alcoholic drink.

I asked Sara why Nada was leaving the tempting life of an Al Sa'ud, for in spite of my brother's distasteful character, Nada had a dubious family background, and it would be difficult for her to duplicate the wealth enjoyed as a wife of Ali. It had been Nada's great beauty, and not her family connections, that had won her a husband of immense riches.

Nura said that from what she could gather it seemed that Nada and Ali's divorce had come about over an evening of love.

Nada had tearfully confessed to my sisters that she had been divorced on three occasions over the issue of sex, saying that Ali insisted she accommodate him at odd hours in the night, often waking her from a heavy sleep. The week before, Nada had refused her husband sex, and Ali had insisted, saying that when a man calls his wife to intercourse, she must not resist him even though she might be on a camel! When Nada still refused, Ali had divorced her.

Sara then told me that Nada had made a surprising second declaration, saying that while she had some affection for Ali's other wives, she had grown increasingly weary of the bastards that sprang from Ali's infidelities, for our brother was the father of seventeen legitimate children and twenty-three illegitimate offspring. The compound that Nada called home was overrun with her husband's concubines and their children.

At the mention of all that sexual activity which produced endless offspring, I could not avoid thoughts of Ali's Wonder Garment and laughed until tears streamed down my face, refusing to divulge the source of my uncontrolled merriment to my two sisters, who feared that the day's events now threatened their youngest sister's sanity.

Epilogue

*O God, make the end of my life the best of my life,
And the best of my deeds, their conclusion, And the
best of my days, the day on which I shall meet Thee.
O God, make death the best of those things we
choose not, But which we await; And the grave the
best dwelling in which we shall dwell, And, then
death, make best which follows death.*
A Pilgrim's Prayer

It had been a week since we left our families in
Monaco. In two days our husbands and children
would return to Saudi Arabia.

On this night, each of the ten female children of
my mother had gathered in Nura's home. We were
blessed that Reema was among us, for that morning
Reema had been dismissed from the clinic and had
come to stay in the home of her oldest sister until
her health was further improved.

The occasion was bittersweet, for we had come
together on the twentieth anniversary of our dear
mother's death. This was an annual ritual that we
had never failed to commemorate, for our mother
was sorely missed, even after twenty years. On past

occasions we had celebrated our mother's memory by calling to mind our favourite childhood stories of her – telling of the wonderful influence she had had on our lives. Tonight, due to our sadness over Reema's recent tragedy, our mood was subdued, and our woeful spirits led us to themes more sorrowful than in the past.

'Twenty years?' Sara mused. 'It cannot be so long since I looked upon my mother's face.'

Each of us agreed that the years had moved more rapidly than we liked.

I had a sudden realization that of ten daughters, eight were now older than our mother had been at her death. Sara and I were the two exceptions. When I gave voice to this thought, there were many moans and frowns.

Nura demanded, 'Sultana! Say no more! Please!'

Nura now had grandchildren, and our eldest sister's age had become a topic forbidden in the past few years.

Reema asked us to hush, saying that she had a small story about our mother that she had never shared, for she had thought that I might take offence.

My eyes flashed with interest and surprise, and I agreed that nothing Reema could say would create controversy.

'You must promise, Sultana! And, keep your word, no matter what your emotions!'

I laughed and agreed, my curiosity aroused.

When I was only eight years of age, Reema had been called into our mother's bedroom, and Mother had asked Reema to give her a solemn promise. Shy Reema had been awed at the thought of a special secret that she, alone, would share with our mother. In great anticipation, she had given her word that no-one would know of their conversation.

Mother told her that she had made a disturbing discovery about Sultana. Mother told Reema that 'Sultana is a thief!'

My eyes popped in surprise, while my sisters burst into loud laughter.

Reema held her hand in the air, asking for silence so that she could complete her story.

Mother had caught her youngest child stealing from personal belongings of others in our home. Mother said that I had been discovered stealing toys, books, candy, cookies, and even items for which I had no use, such as Ali's record collection. Mother told Reema that she had tried every tactic and punishment and nothing succeeded, that I was a child who could not be shamed into obeying her mother. Now, Mother needed Reema's assistance in saving my soul.

Mother made Reema swear that each time she prayed, for the rest of her days on earth, Reema would never cease to ask God to protect Sultana, guide Sultana, and forgive Sultana.

With teary eyes glistening, Reema looked at me and said, 'Sultana, I have wearied of worrying about your sinful conduct. That promise has been a great burden, for I am a Muslim who not only prays the five obligatory daily prayers, but who prays on many other occasions. A promise made to my dear mother can never be broken, so I know that I must pray for you until I pass from this earth. But, now, I pray that you are no longer a thief and my prayers have been answered!'

The room burst with the sound of eight other voices, for each of my sisters was whooping with laughter, screaming over the sounds of the others. Once calm had returned, we made the discovery that my mother had requested and received the identical promise from each and every sister! Each had been convinced that she was the only sibling privy to the secret that her baby sister was a little thief! For twenty years, none had broken her promise by telling. When the truth of the situation came over us, our wild and hysterical laughter could be heard throughout Nura's palace.

I felt a keen sense of relief. Surely I was protected by many of God's angels, for each of my sisters was devout and said many daily prayers.

In a joking manner, Tahani asked me point blank, 'Sultana, we would like to know if God has answered our prayers. Have you taken anything not belonging to you since the time of your youth?'

I could see that my sisters expected me to reply in the negative, for they could not imagine that I was still a petty thief. I could not keep my face free from a trembling smile and began to fidget, remembering Ali's Wonder Garment that was packed away with my belongings in the room that I was occupying.

Surprised at my hesitant reaction, Nura said, 'Sultana?'

'Wait a moment,' I said, and ran to get the garment that I had stolen from Ali's home.

No-one could believe their eyes or ears when I returned to the room wearing Ali's underpants, and when I read the instruction sheet and placed two bananas into the special 'strategic' pouch, Nura tried to be firm in her disapproval, but hysterical laughter overwhelmed my sisters, and three had to leave the room, while another claimed that she had wet her pants.

We could not control our glee, even after three of Nura's servants came running into the palace, fearful of the tremendous noise that they heard from distant gardens.

After calm had returned, the telephone rang, and our thoughts switched to more serious matters. The caller was Nashwa asking for her mother, Sara. It seemed that Nashwa was telephoning from Monaco to complain to her mother about her cousin, Amani. My daughter had been following her cousin in Monaco and had appointed herself a one-woman 'vice and social corruption committee'.

Nashwa's indignation was running high, for Amani had gone so far as to take her cousin's make-up, nail polish, and sunglasses, saying that for Nashwa to wear such things made her a violator of Islamic mores!

Nashwa told her mother that if someone did not control Amani, she was going to have three French friends follow Amani that evening and strip off her clothes, leaving her clad only in her underwear in an area filled with tourists. That should get the prude's mind on other topics rather than Nashwa's morality.

The evening's conversation shifted away from Ali's underpants, and none of my sisters could shake the ironic thought of Sultana's daughter caught in religious fervour, while Sara's child was happily lounging in discos.

I left the room for a moment to call Kareem, advising him of the tension between our child and our cousin. My husband said that he had already decided to keep Amani by his side until she was safely returned to Riyadh, for our daughter had on that day confronted a manager of a hotel in Monte Carlo, demanding that he provide separate elevators in his establishment for men and women, advising him that members of the same sex that were unrelated had no business confined together in a close area.

I rolled my eyes in disbelief, agreeing when Kareem declared that Amani would be put into counselling when they returned to the kingdom. Maha's successful recovery from her earlier mental imbalance had turned Kareem into a staunch believer of psychiatric counselling.

I lived a short moment of relief, thinking of how Maha had rejoined our family as a responsible girl. My eldest child's thoughts now centred on her education and plans for a normal life.

When I re-entered the room, there was a heated discussion of the threat of militant fundamentalism that was now challenging our family's leadership of Saudi Arabia and my thoughts returned to Amani and her extreme interest in her faith. Each of my sisters stated that their husbands had expressed great fear of the growing gap between the monarchy and the pristine ideological movement now gathering power. The Islamic fundamentalist leaders are known to be young, educated and urbanized. This group preaches an uncompromising return to the Koran and is on a collision course with our regime, which is linked with modernization and westernization of the kingdom.

I said little even though I had done much investigation of the movement, for my own child was part of an extremist group that had indicated opposition to the monarchy. I felt too close to the subject at hand and made myself busy preparing pillows to place behind Reema's head.

I asked myself, what disturbances would I live to see in the land that I called home? Would my own child be a part of the opposition that brought down the legitimate government of Saudi Arabia?

When talk of the Muslim extremists ran dry, Reema said that she had another bit of news that she wished to share.

I hoped that no further sin of mine was going to be made public knowledge, and I tried to make my expression unconcerned.

Reema spoke without emotion, saying that Saleem had made plans to take another wife.

While our mother had been greatly humiliated by our father's taking of four wives Reema was the first of my sisters to undergo such an ordeal.

My chest tightened and my eyes flooded with tears, but Reema asked that none of us cry, that she would happily live her life as an ignored wife. Nothing could shake her resolve to live a life of peace, so long as she was not separated from her children. She declared in a loud voice that she was happy, but Reema's eyes spoke a different truth.

I knew that my sister had loved Saleem with a true and honest love. Reema's reward for being a faithful wife and loving mother had not come to her on earth.

For her sake, Reema's sisters made a pretence of belief and congratulated our sister on her small victory.

Nura announced that Nada had once more become Ali's wife. Our brother had signed a document giving Nada wealth in her own right, along with a trip to Paris to purchase diamonds and rubies fit for the Queen of England.

When Tahani asked how he had overcome the religious edict that forbade him to remarry Nada, I was not surprised to hear that Ali had hired a Saudi cousin to wed Nada without consummating the union. After the marriage, a divorce had taken place. Then Ali and Nada had wed again.

I quoted from memory my Islamic knowledge of such a deed and told my sisters that such was not allowed. The Prophet himself said that God curses men who are parties to such an arrangement, for it is nothing more than a trick against God and is considered a grave matter.

'Who is going to intervene?' Sara asked.

Nura admitted the truth – no-one. 'But, God knows,' she added, and each of us felt great sympathy for Ali, for he had piled yet another sin upon his soul.

The evening was coming to an end when the telephone rang once again. One of Nura's servants came and said that Tahani was wanted on the telephone.

Those of us who had left our loved ones in Monaco thought perhaps another crisis had come about and told Tahani to spare us details of our children's follies.

We heard Tahani cry out, and we rushed to her side. Once she replaced the telephone on the hook, it took us many moments to calm our sister, and our fears were high that a member of our family had met with misfortune.

A grief-stricken Tahani finally spoke. 'Sameera has died.'

No-one could speak, no-one could move.

Could it be true?

I counted on my fingers, trying to calculate the number of years that dear girl had spent locked in the 'Woman's Room', a padded cell in the home of her savage uncle.

'How long?' Sara asked, seeing me struggle with my memories.

'Almost fifteen years,' I told her.

'I have committed a grave sin,' Tahani confessed. 'For many years, I asked God to take her uncle from this earth!'

We had heard that Sameera's uncle was wrinkled and frail, and that knowledge had given us hope that after his death, Sameera would return to us.

I sarcastically commented, 'We should have known that such a one could not be depended upon to die soon enough.'

Sameera was born fortunate, to a mother and father who doted on their only child. When her parents had been killed in a car accident, her father's brother had assumed control over her life. Sameera had fled from him with a young man whom she had loved. Tricked into returning to the kingdom, Sameera had been wed to a man not of her choice. When the discovery had been made that she was no longer a virgin, her uncle's fury had led him to confine his niece to the 'Woman's Room'.

Over the years, many had tried to win Sameera's release, saying that her sin did not merit eternal earthly punishment, but her uncle felt that he alone knew the wishes of God, and his harsh verdict had not been lifted.

Sameera had been brilliant, beautiful and sweet in temperament. What nature had given her, cruel fortune had taken away. This woman whom we had loved had been slowly consumed by the horrors of solitary confinement.

Tahani began to sob, her cries chopping through her words. It took her many moments to reveal that Sameera had been buried on this day. Sameera's auntie had confided that despite her emaciation, Sameera was still beautiful when wrapped in the white linen shroud in which she would appear before God.

How could we bear the pain of her cruel death?

Choking back sobs, I tried to remember a verse from Kahlil Gibran on the question of death. I first whispered it, and as my memory of it returned, I slowly raised my voice, until all could hear me. 'Only when you drink from the river of silence, shall you indeed sing. And, when you have reached the mountain top, then you shall begin to climb. And, when the earth shall claim your limbs, then shall you truly dance.'

My sisters and I joined hands, remembering that we were like a chain – as strong as the strongest link, weak as the weakest link.

As never before, we belonged to a sisterhood more powerful than that of our own blood. Never again would we sit back and wonder at the cruelty of men and the obscene arbitrariness of innocent female death, brought about by men's evil.

I said, 'Let the world know that the women of Saudi Arabia are gaining strength in the knowledge that they are right.'

My sisters looked at me one by one, and for the first time, I knew that each of them understood why I do the things that I do.

At that moment, I promised myself that somehow the moral order of our world would be changed, and right would triumph some day.

The great movement of human rights for women in Saudi Arabia had just begun and it will not be defeated by men of indoctrinated ignorance.

The men of my land will grow to mourn my existence, for I will never cease to challenge the evil precedents that they have allowed to flourish against the women of Saudi Arabia.

A Few Facts about Saudi Arabia

With an area of 864,866 square miles, Saudi Arabia is one-third the size of the United States and the same size as Western Europe. It extends from the Red Sea in the west to the Persian Gulf in the east, and borders Jordan, Iraq and Kuwait in the north, and Yemen and Oman to the south. The United Arab Emirates, Qatar and Bahrain lie to the east. A harsh desert land with no rivers and few permanent streams, Saudi Arabia is home to the Rub Al-Khali (Empty Quarter) which is the largest sand desert in the world. The mountain ranges of Asir Province rise to over 9,000 feet in the south-west.

The nation is composed of tribes who can trace their roots back to the earliest civilizations of the Arabian peninsula. The ancestors of modern-day Saudis lived on ancient and important trade routes and much of their income was realized by raiding parties. Divided into regions and ruled by independent tribal chiefs, the various warring tribes were unified under one religion, Islam, led by the Prophet Mohammed, in the seventh century. Before the Prophet died at the age of sixty-three, most of Arabia had become Muslim.

The ancestors of the present rulers of Saudi Arabia

307

reigned over much of Arabia during the nineteenth century. After losing most of Saudi territory to the Turks, they were driven from Riyadh and sought refuge in Kuwait. King Abdul Aziz Al Sa'ud, father of the present-day king, returned to Riyadh and fought to regain the country. He succeeded and founded modern Saudi Arabia in 1932.

More than one-quarter of the world's known oil reserves lie beneath the sands of Saudi Arabia.

In 1933, Standard Oil Company of California won the rights to prospect for oil in Saudi Arabia. In 1938, oil was discovered at Dammam Oil Well no. 7, which is still producing oil today. The Arabian American Oil Company (ARAMCO) was founded in 1944 and held the rights to continue to search for oil in the kingdom. In 1980, however, the Saudi government assumed ownership of ARAMCO.

The kingdom's oil wealth has ensured that Saudi citizens live an opulent lifestyle enjoyed by few. With free education and interest-free loans most Saudis prosper. All Saudi citizens, as well as Muslim pilgrims, receive free health care. Government programmes provide support for Saudi Arabians in the case of disability, death or retirement. The entire country is an impressive socialist state. Economically, Saudi Arabia has developed into a modern, technologically advanced nation.

Saudi Arabia is an Islamic state and the law is based on the *Shari'a*, the Islamic code of law taken from the pages of the Koran and the *Sunna*, which are the traditions addressed by the Prophet Mohammed. The Koran is the constitution of the country and provides guidance for legal judgments.

Executive and legislative authority is exercised by the King and the Council of Ministers. Their decision are based on *Shari'a* law. All ministries and government agencies are responsible to King Fahd Ibn Abdul Aziz Al Sa'ud (officially known as 'The Custodian of the Two Mosques').

Today Saudi Arabia has a population of approximately 24 million, of which 6 million are expatriate workers and 18 million are Saudi. 95 per cent belong to the Sunni branch of the Muslim faith while five per cent belong to the Shiite branch. The Shiite population suffers much discrimination and injustice from the Sunni government, since there is great distrust and dislike between the Sunni and Shiite sects.

As the heartland of Islam, Saudi Arabia occupies a special place in the Muslim world. Each year, millions of Muslim pilgrims journey there to Makkah to pay homage to God. For this reason, Saudi Arabia is one of the most traditional Muslim countries and its citizens adhere to a strict interpretation of the Koran.

A Muslim has five obligations, called the Five Pillars of Islam. These obligations are: (1) Profession of faith: 'There is no god but God; Mohammed is the messenger of God.' (2) A Muslim should pray five times a day, facing the city of Makkah. (3) A Muslim must pay a fixed proportion of his income, called *zakat*, to the poor. (4) During the ninth month of the Islamic calendar, a Muslim must fast. During this time, called Ramadan, Muslims must abstain from food and drink from dawn to sunset. (5) A Muslim must perform the *Haj*, or pilgrimage, at least once during his lifetime (if he has the economic means).

Saudi Arabia uses the Islamic (hegira) calendar based on a lunar year rather than the Gregorian calendar which is based on a solar year. A lunar month is the time between two successive new moons. The lunar year contains 12 months, but is 11 days shorter than the solar year. For this reason, holy days gradually shift from one season to another. Lunar year dates are derived from AD 622, the year of the Prophet's emigration, or *Higra*, from Makkah to Madinah. The Islamic holy day is Friday. The work week in Saudi Arabia begins on Saturday and ends on Thursday.

The Saudi *riyal* is the basic monetary unit in Saudi Arabia. The *riyal* consists of 100 *halalahs* and is issued in notes and coins of various denominations. There are 3.75 *riyals* to the American dollar.

The recent history for the women of Saudi Arabia starts in 1963, when, despite religious protests, the first school for girls opened in the kingdom of Saudi Arabia. Saudi Arabia's third king, Faisal, and his wife Iffat, were the driving force behind women's rights in the kingdom. At the assassination of King Faisal on 25 March 1975, the movement to further women's position in Saudi Arabia came to a halt. In 1977, King Khalid, the fourth King of Saudi Arabia, issued two decrees: one that forbade a woman to travel outside her home unless escorted by a male member of her immediate family, and another that decreed a Saudi woman would no longer be allowed to travel abroad to study unless she was accompanied by a male member of her immediate family. Women have never been granted the right to drive or to study or work in the presence of men.

During the 1991 Gulf War, a new atmosphere of freedom reigned briefly for women in Saudi Arabia, because of the presence of Allied troops and Western journalists. With the withdrawal of the troops and news reporters came further harsh restrictions on the female population by the religious authorities. In addition, a law was passed in the kingdom forbidding women to drive. Prior to the driving demonstration of Saudi women during the Gulf War, the ban on female driving had been one of social restriction rather than legal law.

Human rights groups have recently sprung up to protest violations of all human rights, including that of women, but the government has been actively disbanding these groups, even arresting and imprisoning some of their members.

While large numbers of Saudi women are becoming educated and their power is growing within their homes, their personal freedoms have lessened outside their walled villas.

Glossary

Abaaya	A black, full-length outer garment worn by Saudi women
Abu	Father
Al Ras	School for girls in Saudi Arabia
Al Sa'ud	Ruling family of Saudi Arabia
Assiut	Village in Southern Egypt
Bedouin	A nomadic desert people, the original Arabs
bin (or ibn)	Follows a man's given name and precedes a father's, grandfather's or great grandfather's name which means 'son of'
Dhu al-Hijah	The twelfth month of the *hejira* calendar
Dhu al-Qida	The eleventh month of the *hejira* calendar
Gamaa Al Islamiya	Islamic extremist group formed in Egypt in the early 1980s
Green Book	Qaddafi's Green Book: Philosophy of Colonel Qaddafi of Libya
Hadiths	Sayings and traditions of Prophet Mohammed which help to formulate Islamic law

Haj	Annual pilgrimage to Makkah made by those of the Islamic faith
Hajii	Pilgrim who makes the pilgrimage to Makkah (a title that denotes honour)
Hijira	Islamic calendar which started on the date that Prophet Mohammed fled Makkah and escaped to Madinah (622)
Ihram	Special time during *Haj* that all Muslims refrain from normal life and dwell on nothing but religious matters
Imam	Person who leads communal prayers and/or delivers the sermon on Fridays
Jeddah	Saudi Arabian city located on the Red Sea
Kaaba	Islam's holiest shrine, a sacred sanctuary for all Muslims. The Kaaba is a small building in the Holy Mosque of Makkah, nearly cubic in shape, built to enclose the Black Stone, which is the most venerated Muslim object
Kohl	A black powder used by Saudi Arabian women that goes on the eyelid to enhance the beauty of a woman
Koran	The Holy Book of all Muslims that contains the words of God as they were given to Prophet Mohammed
La	Arabic word meaning 'no'

Madinah	Second holiest city of Islam. The burial place of Prophet Mohammed
Mahram	Male to whom a woman cannot be married, such as her father, brother or uncle, who is allowed to be a woman's escort when travelling. Must be a close relative
Makkah	Holiest city of Islam (also known as Mecca). Each year, millions of Muslims travel to Makkah to perform the annual pilgrimage
Morals police	Religious authorities in Saudi Arabia who have the power to arrest those they believe commit moral wrongs or crimes against Islam or go against the teachings of Islam
Muezzin	The crier who calls the faithful to pray five times a day
Mut'a	Temporary marriage allowed to those of the Islamic faith
Mutawwa	The religious police, also known as the morals police. Men who seek out, arrest, and punish those who do not abide by Saudi religious law
Najd	The traditional name for central Arabia. The inhabitants of this area are known for their conservative behaviour. The ruling family of Saudi Arabia are Najdis
Purdah	A practice of confining women to their homes. This total seclusion of females can occur in some Muslim countries

Purification	The ritual of cleansing prior to offering prayers to God practised by Muslims
Riyadh	The capital city of Saudi Arabia which is located in the desert
Riyal	Saudia Arabian currency
Rub Al Khali	An enormous desert wilderness which occupies the south-east portion of Arabia. It is often referred to as the 'Empty Quarter'
Sana'a	The capital city of Yemen
Shawarma	Popular sandwich sold in Saudi Arabia and other Arab countries made of lamb, beef or chicken wrapped in pita bread, mixed with sauces and tomatoes and peppers
Shayla	Black gauzy scarf worn by women of the Muslim faith in Saudi Arabia
Shiite	The branch of Islam that split from the Sunni majority over the issue of Prophet Mohammed's successor. One of two main sects
Sunna	Traditions of the Islamic faith as addressed by Prophet Mohammed
Sunni	The majority orthodox branch of Islam, Saudi Arabia is 95 per cent populated by those of the Sunni sect. The word means 'traditionalists'. One of two main sects
Taif	Mountain resort city in Saudi Arabia which is located close to Makkah
Thobe	A long shirtlike dress which is worn by Saudi men. It is usually made of

	white cotton, but can be i[...]heavier, darker-coloured fabr[...]the winter months
Umm al Qurrah	'Mother of Cities' or 'The Blesse[...]City' which is Makkah
Umrah	A short pilgrimage (to Makkah) undertaken by those of the Muslim faith which can be made any time of the year
Veil	Black fabric which is used to cover Saudi Arabian Muslim woman's face. The material can be sheer or thick
Woman's Room	Room in a man's house used to confine Saudi Arabian women who go against the wishes of their husbands, fathers or brothers. The punishment can be for a short period or a life sentence
Zakah	Obligatory alms giving required of all Muslims which is the third pillar of Islam

PRINCESS
by Jean P. Sasson

'Unforgettable . . . fascinating . . . a book to
move you to tears'
Fay Weldon

Think of Saudi Arabia and what do you see? Terrorists
spreading fear? Religious zealots? A corrupt government
and a fabulously wealthy Royal family living lives of
unbelievable luxury?

Jean Sasson captures the flavour and reality of life in a
country full of extremes and contradictions. Princess
'Sultana', a real Saudi princess closely related to the King,
lives those contradictions, with priceless jewels, many
servants, unlimited funds at her disposal, but no freedom.
A prisoner in a gilded cage with no vote, no control, no
value but as a mother of sons, she is totally at the
mercy of the men in her life . . . her father,
her brother, her husband.

For the first time, a royal Saudi woman opens the door to
give readers an unvarnished look inside a closed society.
'Sultana' lifts the veil on the shocking world of forced
marriages, sex slavery, honour killings and other outrages
against women, both royal and common.

Princess is a testimony to a woman of indomitable spirit
and great courage. By speaking out, 'Sultana' risks the
wrath of the Saudi establishment and for this reason, she
has told her story anonymously through the bestselling
author Jean Sasson. This is a real-life story you
will never forget.

'It had to come from a native woman to be believable'
Betty Mahmoody, bestselling author of
Not Without My Daughter

0 553 81695 0

BANTAM BOOKS

DESERT ROYAL
by Jean Sasson

In *Princess*, readers were shocked by Sultana's revelations about life in Saudi Arabia's royal family. Royal women live as virtual prisoners, surrounded by unimaginable wealth and luxury, privileged beyond belief, and yet subject to every whim of their husbands, fathers, and even their sons. *Daughters of Arabia* featured Sultana's teenage daughters, determined to rebel but in very different ways.

And now, in *Desert Royal*, Sultana's fight for women's rights in a repressive, fundamentalist Islamic society, has an extra sense of urgency. The threat of world terrorism, the gathering strength of religious leaders and the discontent of impoverished Saudis are threatening to topple the comfortable world Sultana has known. But an extended family 'camping' trip in the desert brings Sultana and her relatives face to face with their nomadic roots, and nourishes her will to carry on the fight of women's rights in all Muslim countries.

This updated edition contains an all-new chapter as well as a letter from Sultana herself, encouraging all women to take up the struggle for freedom for their abused sisters throughout the world.

0 553 81694 2

BANTAM BOOKS

MAYADA: DAUGHTER OF IRAQ
One Woman's Survival in
Saddam Hussein's Torture Jail
by Jean Sasson

Mayada Al-Askari was born into a powerful Iraqi family. When Saddam Hussein and his Ba'ath party seized power, Mayada little imagined the devastation that it would wreak upon her life. But soon she found herself alone in Baghdad, a divorced mother of two, earning a meagre living printing brochures – until the morning in 1999 when she was arrested by Saddam's secret police and dragged to the notorious Baladiyat Prison, accused of producing anti-government propaganda.

There she was thrown into a cell already housing seventeen other 'shadow women'. These women came from different backgrounds, but all shared the same fate: imprisonment and torture without trial, and the threat of execution. To block out the screams of other prisoners, like latter-day Scheherazades the shadow women told each other their stories. Mayada's tales of her privileged former life were a source of particular fascination, including her own encounters with Saddam himself.

'Captivating'
Daily Express

'An astonishing read'
Woman's Own

0 553 81640 3

BANTAM BOOKS